AN
EMPIRE
IF YOU CAN KEEP IT

D0916115

AN
EMPIRE
IF YOU CAN KEEP IT

Power and Principle in American Foreign Policy

THOMAS M. MAGSTADT

CQ PRESS

A Division of Congressional Quarterly Inc.
Washington, D.C.

CQ Press
1255 22nd Street, N.W., Suite 400
Washington, D.C. 20037

Phone, 202-729-1900
Toll-free, 1-866-4CQ-PRESS (1-866-427-7737)

www.cqpress.com

⊛ The paper used in this publication exceeds the requirements of the American National Standard for Information Sciences—Permanence of Paper for Printed Library Materials, ANSI Z39.48-1992.

Cover design: Circle Graphics

Printed and bound in the United States of America

08 07 06 05 04   5 4 3 2 1

The Library of Congress Cataloging-in-Publication Data are available under 2004000410.

To unsung heroes, wherever you are

Contents

1

America's Foreign Policy:
Product, Process, and Purpose   1

2

Ideals and Self Interest:
The American Way   35

3

Hegemony and Insolvency:

The Burdens of a Great Power   60

4

Between Wars:

Collective Security and Delusions of Peace   85

5

The Cold War:

Containment and Deterrence   103

6

7

8

9

Power, Principles, and War:

Preface

The title of this book is a play on a famous comment attributed to the redoubtable Dr. Benjamin Franklin in 1787 after the adjournment of the Constitutional Convention. When a woman asked Franklin what the convention had bequeathed the country, he replied, "A republic, madam, if you can keep it." Franklin had done as much as any other living American, including heroic figures like George Washington, Thomas Jefferson, and John Adams, to gain independence from the British. America thus made its debut in the world as a republic, one that owed its existence to a heroic struggle against an empire. History is replete with ironies great and small, but few with more far-reaching consequences than this: the infant republic, despite its anti-imperialistic origins, grew up to be an empire. It can be argued that America's relentless territorial expansion in the nineteenth century is what has made the nation great, that America was destined to become a great power, and that events conspired to draw America out of its isolationist shell in the twentieth century. What cannot be disputed is that today America is a very different country from the one Franklin helped to create. Now the question for the nation and the world is whether America can keep its empire, and if so, at what cost to the republic that even Franklin did not expect to endure.

An Empire If You Can Keep It is an effort to bring a new perspective to American foreign policy. It was conceived and written after September 11, 2001. As a result, I have had a distinct vantage. Books on U.S. foreign policy written before the September 11 attacks can be revised, new material can be inserted, or a new final chapter tacked on. But a book on politics is bound to be a product of its time, and the resulting perspective, for better or worse, places an indelible stamp on the whole.

In modern history, only the attack on Pearl Harbor compared in scale and impact on American society, government, and public policy. Previously, observers could not view the panorama of U.S. foreign policy from the vantage point of a new crusade—a "war on terrorism"—with a new set of rules, including preemptive military action. This perspective belongs exclusively to the post–September 11 period.

The best and only way to solve any political puzzle is to put "the problem," whatever it might be, into perspective. The importance of perspective in the analysis of foreign policy can be gauged from the everyday experience of trying to read a map without knowing where north is or trying to guess how high a mountain might be by flying over it at 35,000 feet.

An Empire If You Can Keep It is also an exploration of the meaning of power in the modern world. Power is placed in perspective—that is, power is not viewed as one-dimensional (equating it, for example, with military force) but as multidimensional (including psychological and moral components). "Soft power" (the ability to get others to want what we want) is seen as vital to the effectiveness of American foreign policy despite the fact that the United States has unparalleled military and economic might.

Finally, this book treats moral principles as elements of power. Moral character, as well as the size of its armed forces, determines the strength and longevity of a nation. From George Washington to George W. Bush, America's leaders have couched the country's external relations in language reflecting the consciousness of a people given to believe that democracy is destined to triumph in the world and that America is a nation of destiny. The means have varied greatly, from reliance on words and the power of example in Washington's time, to reliance on weapons of war and the power to induce "shock and awe" today.

From the start, a sense of mission, often accompanied by righteous indignation at the shortcomings of other governments, has distinguished America's foreign policy. In the final analysis, Americans have always equated democracy with virtue and, with the one notable exception of the Vietnam War era, never doubted the virtue of America.

Anyone who has studied international politics recognizes the role of power in state behavior; anyone who has studied American foreign policy cannot fail to notice the idealism and oft-repeated reference to principles. Realists point out correctly that the logic of international politics points to the paramount importance of power. But the science of human behavior tells a somewhat different story. It observes not one but two kinds of behavior—rational and emotional. If the rational dimension focuses on power, the emotional one focuses on principle.

Reason dictates that states in an anarchic system behave in ways designed to maximize power. Anything that gets in the way of this goal is inconvenient and unhelpful, if not fatal. But decision makers are human, and human beings are not "men without chests," in the memorable phrase of C. S. Lewis in *The Abolition of Man*. Decision makers have an emotional side just like the rest of us. Behavioral studies and everyday observation both point to the conclusion that emotions such as patriotism and values such as honor and duty are powerful motivators.

Human beings attach emotions to ideas and principles and act on the basis of these emotional attachments. America has always shown an uncommon tendency to talk about principles and to downplay power in its public discourse about politics and policy. Foreigners often notice this idealistic streak in American politics and find it curious if not downright annoying. In the eyes of the world, Americans are obsessed with matters of principle.

This is not to say that America always *acts* on its principles. In fact, the country rarely if ever bases its actions abroad on pure principle. But America tells itself that it is morally superior, and for the most part Americans act as if they believe it. I argue that this belief is the key to America's success. It may appear false and hypocritical, but it has sustained the nation through two centuries of extraordinary expansion and prosperity. Success does not in itself justify everything America has done unless one believes that "might makes right," but it makes the continued assertion of moral superiority appear to have greater validity than it deserves.

ORGANIZATION AND A LOOK AHEAD

Chapter 1, "America's Foreign Policy: Product, Process, and Purposes," deals with why foreign policy is important. The discussion implicitly lays out the argument for an ongoing process of analysis and reevaluation. By first addressing U.S. foreign policy as a product—the strategies, leadership, doctrines, and role in the world as a soft power force—and then as a process balanced among the president, the bureaucracy, Congress, and other domestic sources, I set the stage for the central role both power and principles, realism and morality play in America's influence abroad.

This book, as readers will know by its compact size, is not a history or survey of American foreign policy from "A to Z." Nonetheless, it is a study of necessity grounded in history. I say "of necessity" because the raw material of all political inquiry is found in the record of human behavior. Readers can rest assured that history is not neglected in the pages that follow, but they will need to look elsewhere for a comprehensive history. Although it draws extensively on both American and world history, the narrative is driven by logic and analysis rather than the other way around. For students of politics and public policy, history is the raw material, not the finished product. Explaining history is the task of science and scholarship.

The importance of history and tradition in understanding America's foreign policy is an important theme of Chapter 2, "Ideals and Self-Interest:

The American Way," which covers the period from the nation's inception to the Spanish-American War. For example, the tradition of "isolationism," like all tradition, came to be regarded with a kind of reverence normally reserved for religious beliefs. In fact, it was a pragmatic response to the reality of America's early extreme vulnerability and later to its relative invulnerability.

The roots of American insular thinking can easily be traced to the words and deeds of legendary figures in American history—George Washington, Thomas Jefferson, and James Monroe. Invoking tradition gives the invoker an automatic advantage in any political argument or policy struggle, which is to say that it becomes an independent variable, possibly equivalent to such "realities" as the actual power distribution in the world or the relative weight of one's own national economy.

The impact on American diplomacy of changes in the physical shape and size of the United States and the balance of power in Europe is examined in Chapter 3, "Hegemony and Insolvency: The Burdens of a Great Power." Moving from the Spanish-American War through World War I, I trace the origins of American extroversion and elucidate how and why the United States extended the American sphere of interest beyond the Western Hemisphere at the end of the nineteenth century. Chapter 4, "Between Wars: Collective Security and Delusions of Peace," includes a look at the resurgence of isolationist sentiment after World War I and the fateful decision not to join the League of Nations. The story is told of what can happen when Congress, a deliberative and often fractious body, ties the hands of a president who, as commander in chief, has primary responsibility for matters pertaining to peace and war (the essence of foreign policy).

During much of America's history, there was a notable congruence between America's image of itself and the world's image of America. As explained in Chapter 5, "The Cold War: Containment and Deterrence," after World War II the world looked to America for leadership, and Europe looked to America (its progeny) for salvation. Tragically, the Vietnam War tarnished America's self-image and its image abroad, as the reader will discover in Chapter 6, "Intervention against Communism: From Kennedy to Reagan." President Ronald Reagan restored the nation's self-confidence, but it was the tearing down of the Berlin Wall at the end of 1989 that finally left bitter memories of Vietnam buried in the rubble. Communism's failure was democracy's success.

For almost a decade, America basked in the sunshine of the new world order, an era free of superpower confrontations and the nuclear arms race, a major theme in Chapter 7, "Democracy and Anarchy: America in the New World Order," which deals with the period from George H. W. Bush's tenure through Bill Clinton's first term. The end of the cold war also brought the end of a Soviet-imposed order in the Slavic zone of Europe and the breakup of Yugoslavia. The world looked on in horror as "ethnic cleansing" reared its ugly head and terrorism continued to tear at the fabric of security in many places.

Nonetheless, the 1990s saw a resurgence of American economic vitality and a renewed optimism reflected in a buoyant stock market, which rose to what many observers called a "bubble" economy (based on inflated expectations rather than real growth). But America's bubble burst on September 11, 2001, when teams of hijackers turned commercial airliners into lethal terrorist weapons. The attacks were carried out in full view of a nationwide television audience. President Bush's reaction mirrored that of the American people: first dazed, then defiant. The result was a resolute, fist-in-the-face foreign policy, the unfurling of the Stars and Stripes across a nation angry, energized, and ready to take on the world if necessary. The new foreign policy embodied in the so-called Bush Doctrine, and the move it represents from Clinton's interventionist policies, is the focus of Chapter 8, "From Intervention to Preemption: America's New Crusade."

Chapter 9, "Power, Principles, and War: The Limits of Foreign Policy," is reflective. It returns to some of the main themes in Chapter 1, and the question is raised of the wisdom of distilling the complex process of policy formulation into "doctrines" that frequently come back to haunt future decision makers. Also asked is whether there are any basic principles compatible with the fundamental need for pragmatism and flexibility in meeting the challenges of an ever-changing world that never fails to surprise even the most clear-eyed policy analysts, and if so, what sort of principles they might be.

An Empire If You Can Keep It is an attempt to interpret, explain, analyze, and elucidate contemporary American foreign policy. It is not the first, of course, nor will it be the last. The authors of many other books try to do the same thing, and many succeed admirably. In fact, whatever merit the present book may have owes a large debt of gratitude to the scholars who have blazed the trails I have followed, explored, and sought to map here.

As these words are written, America's moral leadership in the world is being put to the test, and called into question, as never before in the nation's history. Seen in this perspective, the challenge facing the United States is not only to bring about a more peaceful and stable world; the challenge for future generations is to restore America's role as a beacon pointing the way to a more hopeful future for all—one in which principles guide the exercise of power in both theory and practice.

The capture of Saddam Hussein in mid-December 2003 occasioned celebration in both Baghdad and Washington. It was widely and justifiably hailed as a victory for the Bush administration and for the Iraqi people. Tragically, it came much too late for countless victims of Saddam's brutal rule. Did it justify the invasion of Iraq? The answer will depend in no small measure on what happens in the aftermath of this startling turn. The supreme irony of the situation, apparently lost on the media, was that having failed to find weapons of mass destruction in Iraq, American military forces found a tyrant hiding in a hole in the ground—a more dangerous weapon of mass destruction is hard to imagine.

This moment of triumph, however, was fraught with political danger, not only for President Bush and the United States, but also for the Iraqi people and the Arab world. If the insurgency continued despite Saddam's capture, the effect on public opinion in the United States and on the morale of the Iraqi people might be reversed in the weeks and months to follow. If American security forces in Iraq were compelled to go to extremes in the fight against terrorism or to prolong the occupation or to delay handing over sovereignty to an Iraqi government, all sorts of baleful consequences for American foreign policy, as well as Middle East "peace and stability," might ensue. The strange ambivalence of Arabs in the street toward the captured Saddam—aversion to his deeds mixed with embarrassment at seeing him "humiliated" in the eyes of the world—was emblematic of the emotional radioactivity that continues to poison Arab politics. For the Bush administration, Saddam's capture was a major milestone, but one that could yet turn out to be a millstone, instead.

ACKNOWLEDGMENTS

The writing of this book has been an uncommon pleasure from start to finish. Going back and rereading volumes that I had not, in some cases, looked at since my days in graduate school; engaging friends and colleagues in discussions about history, philosophy, world affairs, and foreign policy; refining my own ideas in the process, and then reducing them to words on paper that others might profit from reading—I expected this intellectual odyssey to be stimulating and challenging but not necessarily a lot of fun. In fact, it was all three, thanks mainly to the people behind the scenes who have worked so closely with me to make this book as good as it can be given the fallibility of its author. I begin with my family, friends, and colleagues. Above all, thank you, Becky, for the unfailing encouragement and the loving companionship that have sustained me in this and other endeavors. I owe a large debt of gratitude to the people at CQ Press, who have treated me at every turn with the utmost courtesy and civility, exhibited the highest standards of professionalism, and deserve high praise for creating a culture in which there is ample room for both rigor and goodwill. I am especially grateful to Brenda Carter and Charisse Kiino for believing in this book at an early stage and following through on that belief. As to the actual editing, Michael Kerns did the heavy lifting. His substantive insights, suggestions, and stylistic improvements represent the kind of contribution that humbles an author by making him (in this case) look considerably better than he is. Joanne S. Ainsworth did an extremely careful job of copyediting the manuscript, a process that is tedious and demanding but critically important to the quality and accuracy of the final product. I also want to thank Daphne Levitas, the production editor, for making everything come together at the end and making it look easy, which it most certainly is not. In addition, several academic reviewers read and commented on the manuscript and offered constructive criticisms that proved most helpful. They were Manochehr Dorraj, Texas Christian University; Colin Dueck, University of Colorado; Donald Goldstein, University of Pittsburgh; Robert Kennedy, Georgia Institute of Technology; Harry Targ, Purdue University; and a sixth, anonymous reviewer. To anybody who had a hidden hand in seeing this project through to completion, thank you sincerely. For any errors of fact or analysis, I can only ask that my readers be forgiving.

North America circa 1800

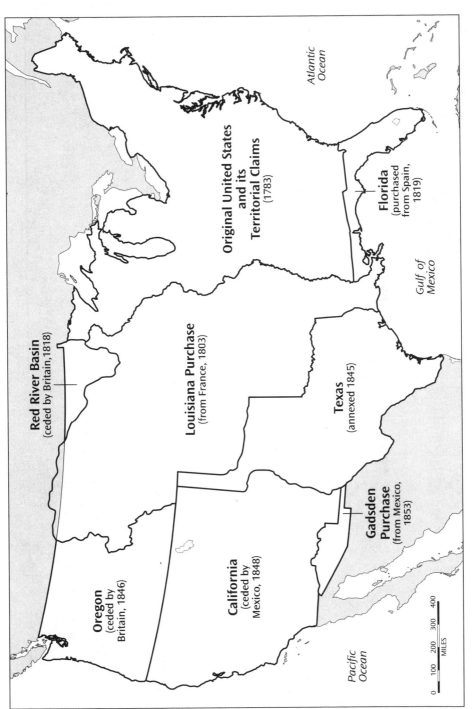

Red River Basin
(ceded by Britain, 1818)

Oregon
(ceded by
Britain, 1846)

Louisiana Purchase
(from France, 1803)

California
(ceded by
Mexico, 1848)

Gadsden
Purchase
(from Mexico,
1853)

Texas
(annexed 1845)

Original United States
and its
Territorial Claims
(1783)

Florida
(purchased
from Spain,
1819)

Atlantic
Ocean

Gulf of
Mexico

Pacific
Ocean

0   100   200   300   400
MILES

Westward Expansion of the United States, 1800–1853

AN
EMPIRE
IF YOU CAN KEEP IT

America's Foreign Policy
Product, Process, and Purpose

OVERVIEW

In this book I discuss American foreign policy within the framework of the tension between power and principles. First I look at foreign policy as a product, paying particular attention to what foreign policy is and to the important aspects of American foreign policy. Next I survey the benefits and burdens of world leadership. The many meanings of "America" in the eyes of the world are examined, as is the question of why it matters how the rest of the world sees the United States. A discussion of the foreign policy process focuses especially on the primacy of the president and the watchdog role of Congress. I note the inherent tension between power and principle in international politics and argue that the proper role of policymakers is to strike the optimal balance between self-interest and idealism, between vigilance and virtue, and between force and justice. I then examine political realism as a concept that seeks to solve this policy puzzle, stressing that no state, not even a superpower, can ever afford to make unlimited commitments or overextend itself. The chapter closes with a brief look at how American foreign policy, and the approaches to this balance, changed after September 11, 2001.

Since the founding of the Republic, a tension between power and principles, self-interest and ideals, has characterized American foreign policy. To say that there is "tension" between power and principles is not to deny that power can often be exercised within the realm of one's principles but, rather, to point out that interstate rivalry and national ambition create temptations, opportunities, and threat perceptions that militate against the strict observance of moral principles or legal constraints. The argument in this book draws on the theoretical insights of political realism, which views international politics as an arena of anarchy and conflict. The tension between power and principle thus arises from the dangers inherent in a world order that comprises competing states, as well as from domestic political pressures to act in ways that are at odds with the nation's core values or true interests. As the United States grew in territory and power, this tension also grew, as did the political controversy it generated. To understand America's role in the world today, it is necessary to understand how and why the relationship between the nation's principles and its interests has changed over time.

In the 1790s the United States, a vulnerable and untested federation of thirteen former colonies huddled along the

Atlantic seaboard, was a small power separated from the world of the great powers by a vast body of water and a political system directly at odds with the monarchies that prevailed in Europe, including France, Great Britain, the Hapsburg Empire (Austria-Hungary), Prussia, Russia, and Spain. Within the European balance-of-power system, the great powers competed for wealth, territory, and prestige—in a word, for power.[1] Significantly, Europe's rivalries extended to the Western Hemisphere: the British, the French, and the Spanish had major holdings in the Americas at the end of the eighteenth century. In addition, Russia laid claim to territory along the Pacific Coast from present-day Alaska to California.

The United States and the entire Western Hemisphere at first played virtually no role in this competition except as a potential pawn. The very weakness of the United States left the nation's early leaders with little or no choice but to assert the importance of certain moral principles in politics and diplomacy. When power is not immediately attainable, nations, like individuals, naturally fall back on principle. The United States at the time of its founding is an excellent example of this behavior.

Today, the United States finds its role in the world reversed. Instead of being one of the weakest powers it is the strongest, despite the fact that the international system now encompasses the entire globe rather than a single region or continent. Power in its starkest form—namely, military power—is a major ingredient in American foreign policy. Indeed, critics charge that it has become the primary ingredient, that force has replaced diplomacy in the conduct of American foreign policy, and that power has eclipsed principle.

That the question of principle has not disappeared from domestic debates about foreign policy in the United States attests to the strength and endurance of America's liberal-democratic political culture. And that the United States can now intervene almost at will in the world attests to the success of the experiment undertaken at Philadelphia in 1787.[2]

---

1. Three classic "realist" theories of international politics emphasizing the balance-of-power concept that have greatly influenced my understanding of foreign policy are Edward Hallett Carr, *The Twenty Years' Crisis, 1919–1939: An Introduction to the Study of International Relations,* 2nd ed. (New York: Harper Torchbooks, 1964); Hans J. Morgenthau, *Politics among Nations: The Struggle for Power and Peace,* 5th ed. (New York: Knopf, 1973); and Kenneth Walz, *Theory of International Politics* (Reading, Mass.: Addison-Wesley, 1979). A fourth "realist" book, which may in time become a classic, is John J. Mearsheimer, *The Tragedy of Great Power Politics* (New York: Norton, 2001). In addition, any short list of "must read" books on the balance of power would include Inis Claude Jr., *Power and International Relations* (New York: Random House, 1962), and F. H. Hinsley, *Power and the Pursuit of Peace: Theory and Practice in the History of Relations between States* (Cambridge: Cambridge University Press, 1967).

2. The historian Catherine Drinker Bowen called the constitutional convention at Philadelphia a "miracle"; there is little doubt that many Americans would agree. Catherine Drinker Bowen, *Miracle at Philadelphia: The Story of the Constitutional Convention May to September 1787* (Boston: Atlantic Monthly Press / Little, Brown, 1966).

Two competing and contradictory tendencies have shaped American foreign policy since the nation's founding—isolationism and internationalism. Both
were present at the creation and continue to influence the way Americans see the
world, but the relative importance of these two tendencies has been reversed.
Whereas isolationism was the main tendency then, internationalism triumphed
after World War II. In the second half of the twentieth century, American internationalism became closely identified with an assertive use of military force, commonly known as "interventionism."

As we will discover in the chapters to follow, there have been at least seven
distinct eras in American diplomatic history. During the first, from 1789 to
1848–1849, the United States combined isolationism with a commitment to the
status quo in the New World (formalized in the Monroe Doctrine). In the second, from 1850 to 1898, westward expansion under the guise of "manifest destiny" replaced the previous status quo policy, but America remained isolationist
vis-a-vis the Old World. During the third, between 1898 (the Spanish-American
War) and 1914 (the outbreak of World War I), this isolationist tradition broke
down as the United States ventured beyond the Western Hemisphere for the first
time. After World War I, President Woodrow Wilson preached internationalism
and led the drive to create a new League of Nations and ensure world peace
through collective security.

In the fourth era, between 1918 and 1941, the United States reverted to its
isolationist ways rather than join the League, but the seeds of internationalism
sown in different ways by three presidents (William McKinley, Theodore
Roosevelt, and Wilson) after 1898 would germinate in the hothouse of World
War II. In the fifth era, during the cold war (1947–1989), the United States enthusiastically embraced internationalism but soon abandoned President Franklin
Delano Roosevelt's dream of collective security (symbolized by the United
Nations) in favor of a policy of containment through "collective self-defense"
(symbolized by the North American Treaty Organization, or NATO, and various
other made-in-America military alliances).

During the sixth era, after 1989, the era of containment rapidly gave way
to a "unipolar moment." Unrivaled in power and prestige, the United States
teetered between interventionism and a tendency to turn inward.[3] As we will
see, President William J. Clinton's administration did not shrink from the unilateral use of force but avoided large-scale military actions. President Clinton

3. Steven W. Hook and John Spanier, *American Foreign Policy Since World War II*, 16th
ed. (Washington, D.C.: CQ Press, 2004), pp. 246–251. For a neoisolationist argument by a
respected American scholar, see Eric A. Nordlinger, *Isolationism Reconfigured: American Foreign
Policy for a New Century* (Princeton: Princeton University Press, 1995). For a view by a pundit
and would-be president, see Patrick J. Buchanan, "America First—and Second and Third,"
National Interest, Spring 1990, pp. 77–82.

was careful to justify U.S. intervention in Bosnia and Kosovo on "humanitarian" grounds and to seek the approval of the United Nations and the international community.[4]

Finally, all this changed after September 11, 2001, when the administration of George W. Bush embarked on a course of action that reflected the two contradictory tendencies of interventionism and isolationism in American foreign policy. The former assumed the form of preemptive military action; the latter appeared in the guise of "homeland security."

The reader will find this skeletal treatment of American diplomacy fleshed out in greater detail in subsequent chapters. This chapter has two main purposes: namely, to provide a brief introduction to the subject matter of the book and to tantalize the reader with some thought-provoking questions. The purpose of the rest of the book is to help the reader find the answers.

Two elements—power and principle—provide the framework for this book as well as the keys to its main line of analysis. Power is the ultimate commodity in international politics, and more is better than less. When power is scarce and more is unattainable, as often happens when a new state is born, the country naturally falls back on moral defense because it cannot resort to military offense and can only hope that potential adversaries will refrain from doing so at its expense. In this manner, principles become embedded in the country's core values—a part of its political culture—and cannot be discarded once greater power is achieved without simultaneously discarding vital elements of the political culture that also support the nation's basic political institutions. For example, American presidents cannot declare that they are indifferent to political repression in other countries (including strategic partners such as Egypt, Pakistan, or Saudi Arabia) without raising serious questions about America's commitment to freedom and democracy. However, when domestic pressures or personal presidential preferences are given priority over strategic national interests the results are almost always disappointing and sometimes disastrous (for example, the Bay of Pigs).

Thus, power and principle are often rivals in the policy arena, and it is always necessary to find the best balance between the two when that happens. The difficulty of finding that balance—and gaining a national consensus around it—largely explains why foreign policy criticism has long been a hallmark of American democracy. It is significant that the critics of America's foreign policy both here and abroad often evoke principle and argue that the United States relies too heavily on military power while giving only lip service to moral considerations. Today,

---

4. Nonetheless, President Clinton did commit combat troops to the Balkans, where, as of late 2003, they remain.

economic and military power defines America in the eyes of the world, but principle remains integral to America's political culture.

In the following section I define "foreign policy" and identify what is and is
not unique about the American approach, the way America relates to the rest of
the world and defines its role in the world. Next, I weigh the consequences of
being a dominant, or hegemonic, power with global responsibilities. I then consider the meaning of "America," noting that it means different things to different
people, and ask why it matters how others see us. Following that discussion is a
look at foreign policy as a process and an examination of how the role of the president and Congress has evolved, what it means, and whether it might be necessary to adjust the balance of power within the existing matrix of branches,
departments, and agencies that formulate and implement foreign policy. The rest
of the chapter is devoted to a discussion of political realism in the post–cold war
era. I ask whether the American penchant for foreign policy "doctrines" is a good
thing or not. I also consider the limits of American power in a world that is not
"unipolar" despite the popularity of this misconception. Finally, I look at some of
history's lessons and try to assess whether, or to what extent, contemporary
American foreign policy reflects the kind of wisdom that comes from learning
from past mistakes.

FOREIGN POLICY AS PRODUCT: A U.S. APPROACH

Before getting started with the main themes of this foundation-building chapter,
I must first define what I mean by "foreign policy." Foreign policy can be defined
as a set of ideas, assumptions, and strategies aimed at promoting the national
interests of sovereign states in an environment of anarchy. (The term "anarchy"
is commonly used in this context to emphasize the absence of world government.) The word "policy" is similar in meaning to "strategy," and whereas the latter often refers to military matters the former typically refers to politics and
economics. In fact, the two words are used interchangeably: hence, we frequently
talk about "defense policy" and "negotiating strategy," although "defense" is primarily a military term and "negotiation" is primarily political. Foreign policy is
closely related to diplomacy, and these two terms are often used synonymously.
Strictly speaking, they are not identical because "diplomacy" refers to the political conduct of foreign policy, rather than to the content of policy itself.

As for American foreign policy, it bears the same stamp of self-interest no
less than the foreign policy of other sovereign states, but it also exhibits several dis-
tinctive characteristics. This book is about what sets American foreign policy apart,
as well as about what the United States has in common with other great powers,
past and present. My thesis is that the United States has always struggled with the
tension between power and principle; that the oscillations and contradictions that

characterize American foreign policy can best be explained by reference to this struggle; and that the search for the proper balance between realism and idealism, between the demands of survival in a dangerous world so vividly portrayed by Thomas Hobbes (1588–1679) and the desire for something better and more ennobling represented in the writings of John Locke (1632–1704), took on a new urgency after September 11, 2001.[5]

This struggle between the proponents of "power politics" and the advocates of a high-minded morality was clearly discernible in the debates at Philadelphia. It is also evident in the constitution the Founders drafted and in the *Federalist Papers,* which so lucidly explained the theory behind those remarkable documents.[6]

As a makeshift nation the United States is a kind of artifice created by reason and conscious design rather than by a natural process of political evolution. The contrasting experience of the United Kingdom (the "parent") and the United States (the "offspring") illustrates this point: the British parliamentary system is organic, the result of a long historical process; the American presidential system is mechanistic, the result of a constitutional convention that met in a certain place at a certain time. What happened in the United Kingdom is akin to horticulture; what happened in Philadelphia in 1787 was all about architecture.

The structural integrity of the "edifice" found in that blueprint depends on the balance—and the dynamic tension—between the idealism and realism of its authors. The same attempt to find a balance between idealism and realism is evident in American foreign policy, and has been since the nation's inception. In a real sense, the attempt to reconcile this quest for a more principled world order with the realities of power and the imperatives of security in an anarchic system is the essence of American foreign policy. This struggle has surfaced time and again for more than two centuries. More recently, it has been at the center of a policy debate within the George W. Bush administration and, more broadly, in the Washington policy community, as we will see later.

The necessity for foreign policy is glaringly apparent in today's world, but it was not always so. The United States always needed a foreign policy even during the first century and a half of its existence, when the isolationist impulse called

---

5. For a synopsis of the contrasting views of Hobbes, Locke, and Jean-Jacques Rousseau on human nature and the causes of conflict, see Thomas Magstadt, *Understanding Politics: Ideas, Institutions, and Issues,* 6th ed. (Belmont, Calif.: Wadsworth, 2003), esp. pp. 473–485; on Locke, see also pp. 369–370 and 428–429. Hobbes and Locke were both Englishmen. The American founders were particularly influenced by the ideas of John Locke, but there is a great deal of Hobbes to be found in the letter and spirit of the *Federalist Papers,* as well. See Douglass Adair, *Fame and the Founding Fathers* (New York: Norton, 1974), p. 90.

6. Written by Alexander Hamilton, James Madison, and John Jay, the papers explain the theory behind the U.S. Constitution. They stand out as the most important and original work of political theory in American history. They were first published in 1787–1788 to influence public opinion and thus boost the chances of ratification.

this truism into serious question. Since World War II the fate of the world, not only one nation, has to an unprecedented degree rested on the foreign policy of a single state, known everywhere as simply "America."

The word "America" is universal and carries heavy freight in most every language. It has many meanings, both good and bad, and has different connotations depending on the cultural, linguistic, and ideological context in which it is used. All this adds up to a powerful case for the importance of America's foreign policy. The United States needs a sound foreign policy because it is the preeminent state actor on the world stage. Above all, it needs a smart foreign policy because other great powers are always looking for a chance to gain more power at the expense of potential rivals.[7] At present, because of its global reach and pervasive presence, the United States is a potential rival of every other great power (including such allies as France, Germany, and Japan).

Burdens and Benefits of Leadership

The power vacuums that existed in Europe and Asia after World War II cast the United States in a historic leadership role. In many ways, President Harry S. Truman was an ideal chief executive at that moment in the nation's history. According to one distinguished presidential scholar, he was a decisive and self-assured "active-positive" personality type of strong moral character.[8] President Truman had a sign on his desk declaring, "The buck stops here." By his own testimony, Truman never lost a night's sleep while in the White House, not even when he made the controversial decision to drop two atomic bombs on Japanese cities (that is, on civilian targets). He carried the burdens of leadership remarkably well, but can a president who is not troubled by an act of mass annihilation directed at civilians be a good leader? Is the use of military power without moral constraint consistent with the principles of American democracy?

Since 1945 America's leaders and citizens have carried a heavy burden. Until the collapse of the Soviet Union in 1991, the U.S. president was not only the leader of the nation but also of the "free world"—a vague term encompassing all democracies and elastic enough to include all non-Communist countries. The cost to American taxpayers of defending America's allies in Europe and Asia during the

---

7. Mearsheimer, *Tragedy of Great Power Politics,* pp. 29–40.

8. James David Barber, *The Presidential Character,* 3rd ed. (Englewood Cliffs, N.J.: Prentice Hall, 1985). Barber identifies four presidential character types: active-positive, passive-positive, active-negative, and passive-negative. Barber places Franklin Roosevelt, Harry Truman, and John Kennedy in the active-positive category. A president of this type is energetic, self-confident, enjoys his work, tends to be productive, adjusts readily to new situations, and generally feels good about himself. See also George C. Edwards III and Stephen J. Wayne, *Presidential Leadership: Politics and Policy Making,* 2nd ed. (New York: St. Martin's, 1990), esp. pp. 217–247.

cold war is difficult to calculate, but the reader can get a sense of the sums involved from a widely publicized estimate of U.S. expenditures on nuclear and other weapons between 1945 and 1996—$8 trillion.[9]

In the language of politics, America was not only the hegemonic power in the Western Hemisphere (meaning that it had no serious challengers in the region) but also the paramount military power in the North Atlantic, Western Europe, and the Pacific Rim. As such, the United States bore the burden of deterring a Soviet attack on the European democracies and of preparing to defend these countries (America's NATO allies) in the event that such an attack occurred. In addition, the United States fought two major wars in Asia during this period (in Korea and Vietnam); both these wars came at enormous human, economic, and psychological costs and ended without victory (see Chapters 5 and 6).

Most Americans like being Number One and would not want it any other way, which implies that on balance the benefits of leadership outweigh the burdens. The price of world leadership can be very high, especially when Americans are fighting and dying on foreign soil. The Korean War (1950–1953) and the Vietnam War (1961–1975) were by far the bloodiest, but there have been numerous other conflicts in which American soldiers have fought: the first Gulf War (1990–1991), the "war against terrorism" involving the U.S.-led invasion of Afghanistan (2001–2002), and the second Gulf War (2003) are three well-known recent examples. In addition, the United States has sent military forces into many other countries in the past half century, including Lebanon (1958), the Dominican Republic (1965), Cambodia (1970), Grenada (1983), Panama (1989), Somalia (1992–1994), Haiti (1994), Bosnia (1995), and Serbia (1999). There have been other costly moments of decision when presidents have asked Congress and American taxpayers to expend huge sums for foreign aid (for example, the Marshall Plan in 1948) or national defense (for example, under John F. Kennedy, 1961–1963; Ronald Reagan, 1981–1988; and George W. Bush, after September 11, 2001). Significantly, in all of these historical examples, both the quest for power and the pursuit of principle can be discerned—the question raised throughout this book is whether or not these two elements were kept in balance during these "moments of decision."

The fact that the United States alone emerged economically unscathed from World War II put America in a position of economic and military superiority unprecedented in history. Far from being destroyed by the war, the American economy rose by 70 percent between 1941 and 1945. It was the point in time when America was at the very peak of its power in international relations. In 1947 the United States accounted for fully half of all the goods and services produced

---

9. Jeremy Isaacs and Taylor Downing, *Cold War: An Illustrated History*. This is the companion book to the *COLD WAR—cold war* series aired by CNN. The excerpt from which this figure was obtained can be read at http://www.cnn.com/SPECIALS/cold.war/episodes/24/epilogue/

in the whole world.[10] America was the world's preeminent factory, farm, and exporter. At the same time, it also enjoyed the prestige and military prowess that accompanied its (short-lived) status as the world's only nuclear power. As that fleeting moment illustrates, nothing lasts forever.

Doctrines and Foreign Policy

To a large extent, the immediate period after World War II shaped America's self-image in the years that followed. Fear of a new totalitarian threat to freedom and democracy—the very principles on which America was founded—personified by the Soviet dictator Joseph Stalin, was a major motivating factor; hubris, bravado, and a sense of invincibility, understandable in light of the American-led victory over the Axis powers (Germany, Italy, and Japan) in the world war just ended, were also major factors. Finally, a belief in the moral role of America as the defender of freedom and democracy, the world's best (and only) hope of stopping the march of "godless Communism" through a vigilant policy of containment, gave Americans a vibrant sense of purpose.

When the United States belatedly entered World War I in 1917, President Woodrow Wilson cloaked our involvement in the noblest of purposes: it was not to restore the discredited balance of power in Europe, but rather "to make the world safe for democracy." Similarly, when the United States embarked on the cold war with the Soviet Union after World War II, our new "containment" policy was, again, couched in lofty moral terms. We were not simply adopting a long-term strategy to defend America's national (and international) interests, but rather our aim was to make the world safe from tyranny. When Greece was threatened with a Communist insurgency in 1947, President Truman asked Congress for $400 million in arms and economic aid for the beleaguered governments of Greece and Turkey. In his historic address to Congress, he declared, "it must be the policy of the United States to support free peoples who are resisting attempted subjugation by armed minorities or by outside pressures."[11] Here was not merely a policy aimed at dealing with a specific problem; here for the first time in more than a century was a *doctrine* designed to serve as a universal principle.

---

10. Paul Kennedy, *The Rise and Fall of the Great Powers* (New York: Vintage Books, 1989), p. 432. Kennedy presents a lot of statistical evidence showing that the U.S. share of world gross domestic product (GDP) declined sharply between 1945 and 1980, when it was barely more than 21 percent. In the 1990s the U.S. share rose again (to nearly 30 percent of world GDP by the end of the decade), but it has never approached the high-water mark it hit at the end of World War II. Also, Europe's combined GDP is now roughly equal to America's.

11. See, for example, Thomas M. Bailey, *A Diplomatic History of the American People,* 7th ed. (New York: Appleton-Century-Crofts, 1964), pp. 796–799.

The Truman Doctrine was only the first in a series of doctrines that have defined and framed American foreign policy. This foreign policy by formula—what one professional diplomat and critic has called "the diplomacy of doctrine"—became a substitute for a far more subtle, flexible, and pragmatic diplomacy—what the same critic calls "the diplomacy of reason."[12]

Not surprisingly, America's allies and adversaries alike often see American foreign policy as crude, doctrinaire, and overly dependent on military force. In the eyes of the world America the beautiful now looks more like America the bully.

When the Soviet Union collapsed in 1991, so did the edifice of American foreign policy. The end of the cold war led many people at home and abroad to question America's purpose in the world. That, in turn, raised a deeper question: What is America?

The Many Meanings of America

Ask middle-class Americans to associate a single word with the idea of America and many will reflexively focus on America's virtues, such as democracy, liberty, and justice.[13] Ask members of minority groups and lower economic classes, however, and the word associations will often be far less flattering. Whether American democracy has been—or is now—a vehicle of freedom or repression depends very much on who you are and where and when you lived. The simple and undeniable truth of this observation is less likely to persuade than to offend a wide swath of American society, especially in times of fear-tinged patriotic fervor. Yet particular groups, irrespective of social or economic class—Native Americans, African Americans, Asian Americans, Mexican Americans, and Arab Americans—are far more ambivalent about the meaning of American history and the benevolence of American democracy than European Americans. Japanese Americans, for example, have not forgotten the humiliating policy that incarcerated them *as a group* in concentration camps during World War II.

By the same token, most people(s) in the world beyond our borders view America with a mixture of admiration, envy, fear, and anger. The ambivalence of the outside world toward the United States is the result, on the one hand, of America's unrivaled position as the world's oldest, richest, and most powerful constitutional democracy and, on the other, of America's heavy military, economic,

---

12. Monteagle Stearns, *Talking to Strangers: Improving American Diplomacy at Home and Abroad* (Princeton: Princeton University Press, 1996), esp. pp. 20–54.

13. See, for example, "Night Fell on a Different World," *Economist*, Special Report, Sept. 7, 2002, p. 22. Opinion polls show that 80 percent of Americans say "yes" when asked, "Do you think your country is better than any other?" Ninety percent say "yes" when asked, "Would you rather be a citizen of your country than any other?" Similarly, 96 percent of respondents say they are "very proud" to be Americans.

and political footprint in literally every region (and virtually every country) of the globe in the past half century. The deadly terrorist attacks of September 11, 2001, on two of the most prominent symbols of American power and prowess—the World Trade Center towers and the Pentagon—were a stark reminder that America's presence in many parts of the world is perceived as hostile and malevolent rather than helpful and benevolent.

Americans ought not to be surprised at this perception but often are; we ought to be alarmed but are not. Why? That Americans remain deeply insular in their mentality despite the presence of American military bases and corporations in every corner of the world, are ignorant of world history and geography despite universal and compulsory education, and display little interest or proficiency in foreign languages despite the fact that the United States has spearheaded the march toward globalization begs an explanation.

How "They" See "Us": World Opinion and Soft Power

Europeans tend to see Americans as naive, shallow, and materialistic with a peculiar bent for navel-gazing; nowhere is this view more prevalent than in western Europe—that is, in the very countries with which the United States is most closely allied. This perception is no doubt due in part to simple prejudice, for Europeans are not immune from the jealousy and resentment that America's postwar success has sparked elsewhere in the world. But many Europeans also see America as bullying and hypocritical, a country that talks incessantly about morality (principles) but relies first and foremost on its military establishment (power) to get its way. America is all about hard power, in this view, whereas soft power is generally preferable and often more effective. The open clash between the United States and several of its NATO allies (including France and Germany) over the timing of the invasion of Iraq in 2003 is a prime example of this policy divergence.

There is another America, as well, that Europeans know. It is the only America most foreigners ever see; namely, the America depicted in Hollywood movies (*Marathon Man, Pulp Fiction, Terminator,* or *The Silence of the Lambs*), TV series (for example, reruns of *Miami Vice, Hunter* and *NYPD Blue*), and video games (*Grand Theft Auto; Vice City; Mortal Kombat; Doom*). The America they come to know in this way is a violent place where crime is rampant, everybody has a gun, good cops are thwarted by bad politicians, and crooked lawyers keep criminals out of jail. American pop music, which has an even greater impact abroad than American movies, often conveys similarly negative images. From heavy metal to "gangsta rap" this music creates the impression that growing up in America is all about self-indulgence, defiance, drug abuse, and promiscuity. The commercial side of American pop culture also has a big impact abroad. The "golden arches" are now ubiquitous. Not only McDonald's, but many other American fast-food chains dot the urban landscapes of virtually every major city in the world. The first (and only) taste of America that foreigners often get is at Dunkin' Donuts or Pizza Hut, seen by many natives as a threat to local commerce, customs, and cuisine—or simply in bad taste.

The image of the "ugly American" is largely false, but the impression Americans working or traveling abroad often create without realizing it is almost as bad. As Americans, we almost always rely on the ability of the natives to speak English. Indeed, many Americans *expect* waiters, cab drivers, and shopkeepers in the countries they visit to speak our language. As a result, people in the host country get the impression that Americans are rich but unsophisticated. Anyone who has lived abroad for any length of time knows that this stereotype is commonplace.

Americans on the whole have access to more information but often know less about the outside world than educated people in other developed countries, despite the fact that virtually anybody can enroll in a public university in the United States. Thanks to the information superhighway the sheer volume of published material on politics and foreign policy is enough to overwhelm the most avid speed-reader. Books by the dozens, foreign policy journals and newsmagazines, the op-ed pages of daily newspapers, the nightly news on network and cable television, provide a steady flow—indeed, a barrage—of information. Yet poll after poll drearily demonstrates that most Americans are poorly informed and apathetic. Only the gathering of war clouds in crisis situations is likely to rivet public attention on any piece of real estate or problem outside of the United States and then only for the duration of the crisis.

As a result, Americans typically do not know much about the world even though "America" is a pervasive presence in every part of it. Yet despite the bad impression Americans often make as a result of this glaring deficiency, most people in most foreign countries do not hate Americans. In the eyes of the world what is wrong with America is most often not its ideals or its people but its leaders and the policies of its government.

In one sense, it does not matter whether this view is fair or unfair because it is a reality that policymakers must deal with one way or the other. It can be ignored but only at America's peril. In the long run this problem left unattended will almost certainly foster other problems and make the solutions more difficult. The reason has to do with the importance of "soft power" as opposed to the kind of coercive (or hard) power we commonly associate with military capabilities or economic sanctions. This kind of power is discussed at greater length later in the chapter in the section "The Limits of American Power." The point here is that asking "Why do they hate us so much?" as many Americans did after September 11, 2001, begs the question: Who or what do "they" hate?

What the rest of the world finds to hate or love about America is not personal, it is political—it is American foreign policy in all its facets, including trade policy, arms sales, military interventions, peace initiatives, and the like. It is not only what America does that can cause problems but also what America chooses not to do—for example, not intervening in civil wars or not imposing economic sanctions against dictators who are friendly to the United States. In much the same way as Americans expect people around the world to speak English, the rest of the world expects America, more than any other country, to be true to its ideals.

This is a tall order. Indeed, it is impossible. Why? Because America's principles are so high—too high to be upheld 100 percent all the time. The fact that the world holds America to higher standards than it holds other countries (or the world itself) is a kind of tribute as well as a challenge. It is a tribute in the sense that America stands for goodness, hope, and decency in the minds of people everywhere—it has been the most powerful people magnet in the history of the world since the nineteenth century. It is a challenge because it requires the United States to play "by the rules" even when others do not.

FOREIGN POLICY AS PROCESS: GETTING ORGANIZED

The U.S. Constitution is an "invitation to struggle" involving the executive and legislative branches of government.[14] In this policy struggle, both Congress and the president use principles as "weapons" because it is a struggle played out in the public arena under the glare of stage lights with the voters as spectators, many of whom become active participants at election time. But it is also a struggle for power within the government, as the authors of the Constitution intended it to be. Thus, the twin themes of power and principle are illustrated in the tug-of-war over foreign policy—the very essence of the foreign policy process—that often occurs between the White House and Capitol Hill, especially when the same political party does not control both branches (or both houses of Congress).

Focusing on the relationship between process and product can be both fascinating and frustrating for students of foreign policy. Describing foreign policy requires little attention to the political process involved in its formulation. Analyzing foreign policy, however, is a different matter. It is no more possible to explain the content and quality of various policies without reference to organizational issues than it would be to explain the quality of modern automobiles without reference to assembly lines, robotics, working conditions, design teams, training programs, crash tests, and the like. Simply put, any product is the result of a process. If the product falls short of expectations, it stands to reason that the process it embodies could be one of the causes, whether or not the keen interest

---

14. The phrase "invitation to struggle" is the title of a classic book on this subject. See Cecil V. Crabb Jr. and Pat M. Holt, *Invitation to Struggle: Congress, the President, and Foreign Policy* (Washington, D.C.: Congressional Quarterly, 1980).

in "process" is always justified. Today, when a major policy fails the first question often asked is, "Why did the policy fail?" The second question is, "How can the problem that led to the failure be fixed?" These questions, rightly or wrongly, often lead directly to an inquiry into the policy process, the role of the various agencies and actors, and the like. Often this quest for answers takes the form of a search for "intelligence" failures or some flaw in the way the federal government is organized to deal with specific problems such as illegal immigration or drug trafficking or international terrorism.

The foreign policy process changed after World War II as a result of a dramatic change in the foreign policy machinery in 1947 (see below). The reader might question how organization affects the policy process and whether it makes any difference if, say, a new agency is created and given a place in the cabinet. (The cabinet comprises the appointed members of the president's "team" who serve as secretaries of departments and agencies.) In fact, it does matter, for reasons that are spelled out in the next few pages.

Throughout this book I will periodically point to extragovernmental domestic influences (including political parties, interest groups, and public opinion) as they relate to various policy questions. In general, domestic factors are important, but factors relating to the international system usually take precedence when these two sources of influence diverge. I will reiterate from time to time that when domestic political factors are given greater weight than systemic or strategic considerations, the results are often regrettable. I will also be careful to note when and how domestic pressures bring questions of principle into "great debates" over foreign policy.

The "Imperial" Presidency and the Foreign Policy Bureaucracy

In the center of the "inner circle" sits the president. Under the Constitution, the president is commander in chief of the armed forces but shares responsibility for the nation's defense with Congress, which alone has the power under Article I "to raise and support Armies" and "to provide and maintain a Navy." The Framers also left it to Congress "to make Rules for the Government and Regulation of land and naval Forces" and, of course, to declare war. But the Constitution allows chief executives great latitude in the conduct of foreign policy, and the commander in chief has frequently asserted presidential prerogatives not found in the Constitution in matters of war and peace.[15] Indeed, the

---

15. See Amos A. Jordan, William J. Taylor Jr., and Lawrence J. Korb, *American National Security: Policy and Processes,* 3rd ed. (Baltimore: Johns Hopkins University Press, 1989), pp. 84–85. The authors note, "In 1793, George Washington asserted the prerogative of the president to act unilaterally in time of foreign crisis by issuing, without congressional consultation, a neutrality proclamation in the renewed Franco-British war."

president did not bother to seek a declaration of war in Korea or Vietnam, and presidents have frequently ordered military interventions without first seeking formal approval by Congress. "Time and again the law of national self-preservation was seen to justify placing extravagant power in the hands of the President."[16]

The machinery of American foreign policy was radically overhauled in the late 1940s, giving institutional expression to the broad sweep of presidential powers and prerogatives in the realm of "national security."[17] Prior to this time, the distinction between war and peace was clearly reflected in the way the foreign policy "furniture" of the executive branch was arranged. Responsibility for defense was lodged in the War and Navy Departments, whereas responsibility for diplomacy was the province of the State Department. There was no central foreign-intelligence-gathering unit. The National Security Act of 1947 formalized what some critics have called the imperial presidency and others less provocatively label the institutional presidency.[18]

This act created four new entities of major importance: the Department of Defense (DOD), the Joint Chiefs of Staff (JCS), the Central Intelligence Agency (CIA), and the National Security Council (NSC). Today, the NSC has four statutory members—the president, vice president, secretary of state, and secretary of defense—and two statutory advisers—the director of the CIA and the chairman of the joint chiefs. In addition, the assistant to the president for national security affairs, the secretary of the treasury, the chief of staff to the president, the assistant to the president for economic policy, the U.S. representative to the United Nations, and the director of homeland security have been regular (nonstatutory) attendees in recent years. (The exact lineup changes somewhat from administration to administration, however.) This council as originally constituted balanced the need for a strong defense and intelligence presence at the highest decision-making level with the desire to uphold the principle of civilian control over the military. With "bipartisan" approval in Congress, President Truman established a separate NSC staff *within* the White House, thus making it crystal clear where "the buck stops" in the formulation and execution of foreign policy.

16. Richard Haas, "Congressional Power: Implications for American Security Policy," Adelphi Papers, no. 153 (International Institute for Strategic Studies, London, summer 1979), p. 3.

17. The term "national security" came into vogue at this time and became a common substitute for terms such as "foreign policy" and "diplomacy" in the official vernacular that frames virtually all concepts and daily communications inside the Washington bureaucracy.

18. See, for example, Arthur M. Schlesinger Jr., *The Imperial Presidency* (Boston: Houghton Mifflin, 1973). Schlesinger, a Pulitzer Prize–winning historian and member of President John F. Kennedy's White House inner circle, argues, "Time and again, the law of national self-preservation was seen to justify placing extravagant power in the hands of the President" (p. 291). See also Jordan, Taylor, and Korb, *American National Security*, pp. 87–104.

In retrospect, this period was a watershed in American diplomatic history. Truman's decision to create a national security adviser and staff in the executive office, thus placing it beyond the "advise and consent" reach of Congress, set the stage for an assertive foreign policy, including undeclared wars (Korea, Vietnam, the Persian Gulf), frequent military interventions (Cuba, Grenada, Panama, Lebanon, Somalia, and Afghanistan, among others), and various covert actions and special operations (Iran, Guatemala, Cuba, Laos, the Congo, and Chile, to mention but a few known cases). For a time, assassination plots also played a limited role in this secret foreign policy.[19] The last time Congress itself declared war was after the Japanese attack on Pearl Harbor in 1941.

In addition to strengthening the president's hand in dealing with Congress, the postwar reorganization also greatly changed the policy process *within* the executive branch. Prior to World War II, the State Department was the president's single most important source of advice and information on foreign policy issues of the day. Not only was the State Department the proprietor of the Foreign Service and the conduit through which all embassy reports from around the world were filtered, but the secretary of state faced no rival in foreign affairs within the federal bureaucracy. As a result, presidents relied heavily on foreign embassies to provide a window on the world, and the secretary of state enjoyed the second-most prestigious position in the federal government (next to the president, of course).

The only other member of the cabinet with an important role in international affairs was the secretary of war, but the importance of that post was diminished by the fact that the United States was at peace during most of the nineteenth century—except for the Civil War, armed conflicts were rare and short (the War of 1812, the Mexican War in 1848, and the Spanish-American War in 1898). The "winning of the West" during the nineteenth century was

---

19. John Stockwell, *In Search of Enemies* (New York: Norton, 1978), p. 236: "In late November 1975 more dramatic details of CIA assassination programs were leaked to the press by the Senate investigators. The CIA had been directly involved with the killers of Rafael Trujillo of the Dominican Republic, Ngo Diem of South Vietnam, and General René Schneider of Chile. It had plotted the deaths of Fidel Castro and Patrice Lumumba." (Stockwell is a former Marine and was the chief of the CIA's Angola task force in the 1970s. After twelve years as a CIA officer, he resigned in 1977.) Evidence of a "rogue elephant" CIA was unearthed in the mid-1970s by the Senate Intelligence Committee and the Rockefeller Commission created by President Gerald Ford at that time to investigate charges of CIA misconduct. In 1976 President Ford issued Executive Order 11905 forbidding U.S. involvement in political assassinations, but not before the controversy and public revelations badly damaged the CIA's reputation at home and complicated (as well as compromised) its activities abroad. On the background to Executive Order 11905, see Jordan, Taylor, and Korb, *American National Security Policy*, pp. 130–155, esp. pp. 148–149.

bloody, but contrary to popular myth it was accomplished without a major military call-up or any other extraordinary measures.[20] So even the secretary of war was no match for the secretary of state in the competition for the president's ear.

Indeed, the whole idea of "competition" in the foreign policy bureaucracy does not become an issue until after World War II. Today, as everybody who has worked in Washington's sprawling foreign policy bureaucracy knows, it is a major factor. There have been many attempts by policy analysts and academicians to make flow charts showing precisely how foreign policy decisions are made in theory. These diagrams all emphasize the "flow" of information, foreign intelligence, and analysis through the "system," usually with lots of arrows that show how it all pours into a great funnel located in the White House. That "funnel" is the NSC, which functions as both a funnel and a filter.

In fact, by the time information gets to the president, it has been filtered many times on many levels. This filtering process serves a useful purpose, but it is routinely taken to extremes in large bureaucracies. For thousands of operatives and analysts at the "working level" within the government, this filtration system is so extensive that they often see no relationship between the "inputs" they make and the "outputs" (actual policy). In fact, "worker bees" in the bureaucracy grumble a lot (to each other) about White House declarations and decisions that ignore policy papers they painstakingly draft and guide through the "system"—often over a period of many months. How often that happens depends on factors entirely beyond the control of people on the working level.

Clearly, the policy process is cumbersome and complicated. No model can capture how it works in practice, because there are too many human variables and because, in the final analysis, the president can short-circuit or ignore "the process" as he sees fit. Every president since World War II has brought his own decision-making style and foreign policy team with him upon taking office. The permanent bureaucracy is always at the mercy of the short-timers, who may be gone in four years.

For this reason, if for no other, presidents and presidential advisers often regard the permanent bureaucracy—the professionals—with disdain and distrust. There is no law that says they must pay attention to the professionals. Furthermore, when problems arise presidents often have to act (or react)

---

20. On this point, see Mearsheimer, *Tragedy of Great Power Politics,* pp. 77–78. Mearsheimer notes, "The American military remained much smaller than its European counterparts during the latter half of the nineteenth century because it could dominate the hemisphere on the cheap. Local rivals such as the various Native American tribes and Mexico were outgunned by even a small U.S. army, and the European great powers were unable to confront the United States in a serious way."

quickly. Bureaucracies do not move quickly. So the real policy process is often much more restricted in practice than it appears to be on paper; in practice, it is not that different from the decision-making process. Under most presidents since World War II, this process has been exclusive, not inclusive: it usually comes down to a very few high officials in the government.

However, the existence of this exclusive decision-making "club" or cabal by no means implies unanimity or the absence of competition. One famous theory of presidential decision making called "groupthink" does, in fact, stress the consensus-seeking behavior of the president's inner circle and sees this tendency as one of the causes of past foreign policy failures.[21] As compelling as this study was when it first appeared (and still is), it fails to take into account the strong evidence of competition and friction within the president's inner circle.

The reported clash of views between Secretary of State Colin Powell and Secretary of Defense Donald Rumsfeld over the war in Iraq and other matters is a contemporary case in point. Similarly, President Jimmy Carter's national security adviser, Zbigniew Brzezinski, and his secretary of state, Cyrus Vance, often gave him conflicting views on policy questions. President Richard Nixon deliberately chose a weak secretary of state (William Rogers) who brought nothing to the table. Nixon used NSC adviser Henry Kissinger almost exclusively, in effect acting as his own secretary of state and marginalizing Foggy Bottom (a synonym for the State Department) in the process.

At various times, the CIA director has also played a key role in the policy process. For example, William Casey was President Reagan's close friend and confidant when he ran the agency in the 1980s, as Allen Dulles (the brother of Secretary of State John Foster Dulles) was President Dwight Eisenhower's in the 1950s. In contrast, Stansfield Turner, the CIA director under Carter, wanted a kinder, gentler foreign intelligence service and in the process weakened the competitive position of the agency he headed.

In most cases, the secretaries of state and defense, the CIA director, and the NSC adviser are in the best position to compete for "access" in the realm of foreign policy—and most often they do compete. In Washington, access to the president is everything. A secretary or director with easy access to the president is likely to get respect from the professionals within the part of the bureaucracy he or she heads. The competition (or conflict) within the president's foreign policy team is rarely acknowledged openly even when it may be widely reported in the press. If it becomes an obstruction or embarrassment to the president, however, he can always replace one of the disputants by quietly asking one or the other to resign. In the final analysis, presidents consult whomever they please and make foreign policy by whatever process they chose.

---

21. Irving L. Janis, *Groupthink,* 2nd ed. (Boston: Houghton Mifflin, 1982).

The Watchdog Role of Congress

One of the main functions of Congress in the realm of foreign policy is to act as a check on the president. This role places Congress at odds with the president at times. When the president seeks to assert powers not granted by the Constitution, for example by waging an undeclared war, Congress has the prerogative, if not the solemn duty, to stand in the way. Such confrontations, although infrequent, have occurred at crucial times in American history and always revolve around questions of constitutional and moral principle. This clash of principles, however, cannot disguise the fact that an institutional power struggle is taking place at the same time. Such power struggles in turn typically involve a contest between the two major political parties.

The idea of a bipartisan foreign policy is not found in the Constitution. Indeed, the Constitution makes no mention of political parties at all. Nor is bipartisanship in foreign policy a long-standing tradition in the United States. Instead, it was the product of a unique set of circumstances arising after World War II. The fear of Soviet totalitarianism at that time gave rise to the new spirit of bipartisanship in Congress. The perceived danger to the nation meant that politics, it was said, had to stop at the water's edge. The fact that politics had greatly impeded presidents in the realm of foreign policy (including President Roosevelt) prior to World War II reinforced the tendency of Congress to defer to the president during the cold war, especially in times of crisis.

The Constitution gives Congress the power of the purse, as well as the power to declare war and to regulate interstate and foreign commerce. It also gives the Senate the power to approve or reject treaties. Both houses can and do hold hearings to investigate the government's policies, programs, and practices. Of these powers, none is more vital than control over "ways and means"—the purse strings of government. Every year the White House must ask Congress for money to carry out its programs at home and abroad. The budget process is thus a vital part of the foreign policy process, and one that necessarily involves Congress in the details of diplomacy and national defense.

Congress thus has the potential to impede or even block executive action by moving or threatening to withhold funding. For the first 150 years, this power meant that Congress could and did assert itself in the foreign policy process.

Power and Policy: A Question of Balance

We noted at the outset that American foreign policy is uniquely driven by a creative tension between ideals and self-interest. Americans often seem surprised to learn that the United States "plays rough" in its foreign dealings. That is less because Americans are naive or idealistic than because our leaders have always made a point of couching official policy in moral platitudes. No one can seriously dispute the right of a state to use force in self-defense, but what about military intervention, covert action, political assassination, and preemptive strikes? In a perfect world, it would not be necessary ever to resort to such measures. Unfortunately, we do not live in a perfect world.[22] Violence is a fact of life. But it is most effective when it is used sparingly, in a judicious and fair way, especially by a democracy that prides itself on liberty and bases its claim to world leadership on moral rather than military grounds.

Balancing liberty and justice is never easy, even in domestic politics. In international politics it is far harder. The essence of sound foreign policy is a different kind of balance, namely, bringing means and ends into alignment: "[A] foreign policy consists in bringing into balance, with a comfortable surplus of power in reserve, the nation's commitments and the nation's power. The constant preoccupation of the true statesman is to achieve and maintain this balance."[23] If balance is the end, diplomacy is the means.

Balancing power and commitments requires skillful diplomacy. It is a job for professionals, not amateurs or political appointees (which often amounts to the same thing). It is up to the president as commander in chief to make the right decisions, but sound decision making depends on good information, expert analysis, and sound advice. Under the current set of institutional arrangements dating back to the early years of the cold war, the National Security Council has eclipsed the State Department as the primary source of foreign policy support to the president. If a secretary of state wants to talk to the president about a diplomatic problem, he or she has to get into a line that includes the national security adviser, the secretary of defense, and the director of central intelligence, among others. The president thus has a personal "foreign policy cabinet" complete with an in-house foreign policy staff supervised by the NSC director. Under this system, the Department of State could be abolished were it not for that fact that our foreign embassies would then become institutional orphans, lost in the wilderness of the Washington bureaucracy.[24]

---

22. For example, who can say that the world would not have been far better off if Hitler had been assassinated in 1936 after his intentions were known but before he started mass-murdering Jews and invading neighboring countries?

23. Walter Lippmann, *U.S. Foreign Policy: Shield of the Republic* (Boston: Little, Brown, 1943), p. 9. Walter Lippmann (1889–1974) was a famous syndicated columnist and the author of many books on politics and foreign policy.

24. The State Department, like other parts of the executive branch, was not established in the Constitution but rather by an act of Congress; it *could*, therefore, be abolished in the same manner, although no one has seriously suggested doing so.

Under the current system, nothing gets to the president without going through the White House filtration system. If the secretary of state is forced to compete with other cabinet-level officials for the president's attention, ambassadors are often cut off from the White House altogether.[25] Moreover, the reports written by professional political and economic officers pouring in on a daily basis from embassies around the world are seldom read by the political appointees who are most likely to have the president's ear (or the ear of someone high up who is rumored to have it). Finally, these reports must compete with foreign intelligence that is gathered in mass quantities and that gives the foreign policy establishment a chronic case of indigestion.

This system made more sense in 1947 than it did two decades later as events in Vietnam spiraled out of control. It made even less sense two decades after that when Col. Oliver North, an obscure NSC staffer, was busy running a covert arms-for-hostages operation, involving Iran (a country the Reagan administration called the leading sponsor of international terrorism and the current Bush administration considers part of the "axis of evil") and Nicaragua (where the United States was backing an insurgency against the Marxist government of Daniel Ortega). It makes even less sense today when the specific danger the current system was designed to counter, namely the Soviet threat, has ceased to exist.

With the collapse of Soviet communism, the policy of containment, which was based on the assumption of a bipolar distribution of power and which subordinated all other global issues to the East-West conflict, became irrelevant. The idea of Pax Americana (American hegemony) was not a viable alternative for a nation with liberal-democratic traditions and principles.[26]

A study of the way the more venerable practitioners of American statecraft conducted foreign policy prior to the nuclear age points to one conclusion of the greatest significance: in a multipolar world there is no formula, framework, protocol, or theory to be found, no "doctrine" that can substitute for good old-fashioned reason and pragmatism in foreign policy. However unsatisfying or frustrating it may be to some, there is no substitute for a knowledge-based foreign policy that is as resistant to political rhetoric and ideological zeal as

25. Stearns, *Talking to Strangers*, pp. 148–178.
26. For a cogent argument against the notion that America's superpower dominance is a permanent fixture of international politics, see Charles Kupchan, *The End of the American Era: U.S. Foreign Policy after the Cold War* (New York: Knopf, 2002). The author argues that the rise of Europe as an economic and political force in the world and the decline in the American public's willingness to bear the heavy burdens of an internationalist foreign policy foreshadows the end of "unipolarity" and a return to the sort of great-power rivalry associated with the pre–cold war period.

possible.[27] In a democratic society, providing public education in world history, geography, and foreign languages is an essential and indispensable safeguard.

REALISM AND IDEALISM IN AMERICAN FOREIGN POLICY

The United States has never gone to war solely for idealistic or moral reasons, nor has American foreign policy ever been placed wholly in the service of ethical principles. That is not the American way any more than it is the British, Chinese, Egyptian, French, Israeli, or Russian way; governments, whether democracies or dictatorships, do not act out of altruistic motives but, rather, out of calculations rooted in a conscious (though not necessarily correct) set of notions about the national interest. In the words of the late Hans J. Morgenthau, perhaps the most influential political realist of the twentieth century: "International politics, like all politics, is a struggle for power. Whatever the ultimate aims of international politics, power is always the immediate aim."[28] This dictum is also interesting for what it does not say. It says nothing about ends ("ultimate aims") or means. If power is "always the immediate aim," diplomacy, as I pointed out earlier, is the means except, of course, in the extraordinary event of war.

America's revolutionary beginnings and unique geography have given rise to a popular misconception that the United States was (and is) qualitatively different from other states, a "city on a hill."[29] In part, this idea that America is

27. Sporadic, event-driven outbursts of patriotic emotion are a domestic political factor that elected officials cannot afford to ignore. In a country increasingly susceptible to anti-American "blowback" (which includes but is by no means confined to international terrorism), such outbursts are an ever-present possibility. (The term "blowback" was actually invented by officials at the CIA and intended only for the agency's internal use, according to Chalmers Johnson: "It refers to the unintended consequences of policies that were kept secret from the American people. What the daily press reports as the malign acts of 'terrorists' or 'drug lords' or 'rogue states' or 'illegal arms merchants' often turn out to be blowback from earlier American operations" [Johnson, *Blowback: The Costs and Consequences of American Empire* (New York: Holt, 2000), p. 8]). In this context, reported anti-Arab incidents in the United States following the attacks on the World Trade Center and the Pentagon caused alarm in some quarters but were surprisingly limited in scope given the scale of the destruction involved. President Bush embraced Arabs and Muslims immediately after the 9/11 tragedy in an effort to counteract retaliatory acts by an outraged and aroused citizenry against innocent bystanders.

28. Morgenthau, *Politics among Nations,* p. 31. For a clear and concise discussion of realism and how it differs from idealism, see Mearsheimer, *Tragedy of Great Power Politics,* pp. 14–27.

29. For example, the distinguished Seymour Martin Lipset (author of the well-regarded *American Exceptionalism* [New York: Norton, 1996]) argues that Americans "exhibit a greater sense of patriotism, and of belief that their system is superior to all others . . . than the citizens of other industrialized democracies." Cited in "Night Fell on a Different World," *Economist,* Special Report, Sept. 7, 2002, p. 22. The "city on a hill" was a phrase originated by John Winthrop (1588–1649), the first governor of the Massachusetts Bay colony.

exceptional can be traced to the rhetoric of George Washington, Woodrow Wilson, and others. We will return to this theme in the next chapter, but for now suffice it to say that the belief in American "exceptionalism" can affect the way we think about foreign affairs—and obscure reality.

A realistic approach to foreign policy is necessary because what is at stake in international politics is survival. What is realism? "Realism," according to the late E. H. Carr, a well-known British realist, "tends to emphasize the irresistible strength of existing forces and inevitable character of existing tendencies, and to insist that the highest wisdom lies in accepting, and adapting oneself to these forces and these tendencies."[30] Realists make three basic assumptions about international politics. First, sovereign states are the main actors, and the Great Powers are the ones that shape world history. Second, the behavior of Great Powers is dictated by the external environment, not by internal characteristics (such as regime type, race, culture, nationality, or ideology). Realists often see little difference in the external behavior of democracies and dictatorships because the logic of survival in an anarchic world is essentially the same for all states.[31]

Third, realists stress that the struggle for survival forces states to compete for power and that this competition frequently involves war. In the words of Carl von Clausewitz, the famous nineteenth-century military strategist, "War is a continuation of politics by other means." Political realists, therefore, see war as a normal phenomenon in world politics, not as an aberration.[32] Political realists emphasize the primacy of power in politics, coining the term "power politics." The first priority of every state is to maximize power.

Thus, the world is a dangerous place, self-interest is the driving force, and trust is notable for its absence. The natural state of international politics is disorder; without a central governing authority the only hope for order is the balance of power. Acting rationally, states will seek to maintain a balance. When a hegemon (dominant power) challenges the status quo (and thus the survival of existing states) the defenders of existing order must make common cause against the challenger. To hardcore political realists, this basic logic is a universal law.

Political realism stresses that morality has a different meaning in public and private life. The standards of personal or private moral conduct cannot be mechanically applied to policymaking. Morality has a place in public life, but it must not be allowed to impede the clear-eyed, dispassionate pursuit of national interests. The same goes for idealism. In politics, however, idealists who let hopes

---

30. Carr, *Twenty Years' Crisis*, p. 10.

31. Mearsheimer, *Tragedy of Great Power Politics*, pp. 17–18.

32. Ibid. The famous dictum that "War is a continuation of politics by other means" is found in Carl von Clausewitz, *On War*, trans. and ed. Michael Howard and Peter Paret (Princeton: Princeton University Press, 1976).

and dreams guide policy choices inevitably fail. In the process, they may do more harm than good.

But realism requires us to see ourselves as others see us. It also requires us to hold ourselves to standards that are the same as (or higher than) those to which we hold others—or face the consequences—because failure to do so opens America to the charge of hypocrisy and erodes the trust on which diplomacy thrives. This is where America's principles and ideals come into play. There is more than a grain of truth in the notion that our principles *are* our interests—that is to say, America's ideals are what appeals most to "them" (the global community or world opinion) about "us." Because the United States is the world's preeminent economic and military power, American foreign policy is on exhibit everywhere and is felt the world over. As Americans, no matter where we go, the people we encounter have experienced "America" in various ways. Often that experience has involved U.S. military or intelligence operatives. Some of these encounters have happy endings for the indigenous peoples, but many do not. In these cases the fallout is likely to "blow back" on us in one form or another.[33]

It is not "idealistic" to question the use of military force as a first rather than last resort—quite the opposite. Realism, above all, requires the balancing of power and commitments.[34] No country has unlimited resources and capabilities because no country has a monopoly of power—not even the United States. In the absence of such a monopoly, it is necessary to use military force prudently (the political dimension) and parsimoniously (the economic dimension).

Idealism is the main alternative to political realism, and it has a time-honored place in American foreign policy. Idealism is rooted in European political thought during the seventeenth and eighteenth centuries, especially in the Enlightenment, which immediately preceded (and some historians would argue culminated in) the French and American Revolutions.[35] During the period of the Enlightenment intellectuals and political leaders celebrated the role of reason in human affairs and embraced the idea that "man is the measure of all things."[36] Idealists tend to be considerably more optimistic about the possibility of peace and harmony in the world. They also tend to believe that human beings are basically good but are often led astray by bad institutions, ideas, and individuals.[37] Realists, not surprisingly,

---

33. See Johnson, *Blowback.*

34. Lippmann, *U.S. Foreign Policy,* pp. 9–10.

35. Mearsheimer, *Tragedy of Great Power Politics,* p. 15.

36. Kenneth Clark underscores this point in his famous documentary, *Civilization.* See also F. H. Hinsley, *Power and the Pursuit of Peace,* part 1, and Torbjorn L. Knutsen, *A History of International Relations Theory: An Introduction* (New York: Manchester University Press, 1992), chap. 5.

37. For a discussion of the differences between liberals and conservatives, see Magstadt, *Understanding Politics,* chap. 12, esp. pp. 369–373.

tend to dismiss idealists as naive. The success of realist thought can be roughly gauged by the fact that nowadays calling somebody an "idealist" is often a form of rebuke or an easy way to dismiss that person's opinions.

Intellectual heirs of Wilson believe in the basic goodness of human beings and tend to see conflict, war, and disorder as aberrations caused by some defect or other that can be found and fixed. If war occurs it is because something that could have been done to prevent it was not. The proper response to war, then, is to figure out why it happened and take steps to correct the problem. If only the governments of the world would get together, decide what to do, and then do it, war could be eradicated (or greatly reduced in frequency and scale). So, too, could poverty, hunger, and disease. The balance of power was not a success if peace is the criterion. On the contrary, it was a "war system"—that is, war was the main mechanism for keeping order (peace). The paradox of an unstable "balance" was a recurrent theme in the Old World order (prior to the two world wars of the twentieth century).

This idealistic brand of internationalism favors world organization and collective security over unilateral action, military alliances, and the balance of power. Today, Wilsonian idealists typically do not see American values as superior to all other value systems in the world and would not try to impose our institutions or ideas where they are not wanted. They generally abhor imperialism in all its manifestations and cannot stand to see America act like a bully or throw its weight around.

Of course, not all idealists would agree that war can ever be abolished or that poverty, hunger, and disease will ever vanish from the earth, but the tendency to think that the world could be a much better place is common to this school of thought, as is the tendency to distrust power (and power politics). In this view, morality is a better guide to action than self-interest in public as well as private life. Indeed, morality is not the enemy of power but its best ally. In the world according to Wilson's heirs, morality multiplies power, especially "soft power"—the ability to get others to want what we want.

Realism and idealism are both present in American foreign policy. Often, individuals who consciously reject the latter are nonetheless inclined to embrace at least some of its assumptions. To make matters even more confusing, the terms "liberal" and "conservative" are used in different ways. In foreign policy debates, liberals often lean toward idealism and conservatives pose as tough-minded realists. Liberals tend to believe that there is a close relationship between the internal makeup of states and the external behavior they exhibit. To be more specific, liberals tend to believe that democracies are less war-prone than dictatorships.[38] Despite the success of realism as reflected in America's huge postwar

---

38. Mearsheimer, *Tragedy of Great Power Politics,* pp. 15–17.

investment in "national security," this belief has informed the foreign policy of virtually every administration since World War II and it has survived the end of the cold war.

Liberals also place less emphasis on power as a motive in international politics. They often assume that there are good states and bad states. Good states will not do bad things even if they have the means and opportunity. Bad states will try to acquire the means and will not pass up any opportunity to grab more power. In recent times, the Taliban regime in Afghanistan and the dictatorship of Saddam Hussein in Iraq are prime examples of how this idea plays into American foreign policy. The practice of linking Soviet-style communism with war and revolution before 1989 is another good example of this same tendency.

In practice, it is not so easy to identify realists and idealists, or "conservatives" and "liberals." More often than not, these two tendencies compete, not only within society or the two major parties, but also within individuals. In March 1991, the first President Bush told a joint session of Congress, "We can see a new world coming into view, a world in which there is the very real prospect of a new world order, a world where the United Nations—freed from cold war stalemate—is poised to fulfill the historic vision of its founders; a world in which freedom and respect for human rights find a home among all nations."[39] Woodrow Wilson could not have said it better. In this speech, George H. W. Bush sounded a lot like a disciple of Jimmy Carter, the "liberal internationalist" he had campaigned against in 1980. Ironically, as we will see later in the book, Carter himself had largely given up on "world order politics" by the end of his term.[40]

Similarly, President George W. Bush, a staunch conservative, expressed a liberal belief when he called for "regime change" in Afghanistan and Iraq. In other respects, however, the foreign policy of the second Bush administration appears to be steeped in realist assumptions about international politics, particularly the need to maximize power.

The Clinton administration's foreign policy appeared to be more consistently liberal-idealistic in its assumptions. One astute observer has summarized President Clinton's worldview as follows: (1) "prosperous and economically interdependent states are unlikely to fight each other"; (2) "democracies do not fight each other"; and (3) "international institutions enable states to avoid war

39. Quoted in Stanley R. Sloan, "The U.S. Role in a New World Order: Prospects for George Bush's Global Vision," Congressional Research Service Report to Congress, March 28, 1991, p. 19.

40. Jeral A. Rosati, *The Carter Administration's Quest for Global Community* (Columbia: University of South Carolina Press, 1987), pp. 142–149.

and concentrate instead on building cooperative relationships."[41] But his strong support for market-based economic policies and his unilateral use of force in ordering air strikes against Sudan and Afghanistan suggest that, deep down, Clinton was a realist.

Thus, the radical distinction between realism and idealism is misleading and more often confounds than clarifies debate over foreign policy. The fact is that self-proclaimed realists seldom if ever agree on what is the best course of action in a given set of circumstances. The charge of "idealism" is often used to discredit or dismiss views some realists find objectionable.

President Woodrow Wilson is the most celebrated example of a leader who has been categorized (and criticized) by academicians and others as a starry-eyed idealist. In fact, however, there is ample evidence of "realism" in Wilson's words and deeds.[42] President John F. Kennedy described himself as an "idealist without illusions." Despite obvious differences in personality and presidential style, Wilson and Kennedy were cut from the same cloth. Together, these two presidents personify a uniquely American approach to world politics, one that combines realism and idealism.

THE LIMITS OF AMERICAN POWER

Just how new is the new world order? On one side of the debate, conservatives argue that some things (for example, the primal force of nationalism and power-maximizing behavior of tyrannical states) never change, and they tend to minimize the importance of that which clearly has: above all, the collapse of the Soviet Union. On the other side, liberals counter that the end of the cold war transformed the international system and argue that, although nationalism is not

---

41. Ibid., p. 9. On the theoretical link between economic interdependence and peace, see Norman Angell, *The Great Illusion: A Study of the Relation of Military Power . . . to . . . Economic and Social Advantage* (New York: Putnam's, 1912); Thomas L. Friedman, *The Lexus and the Olive Tree: Understanding Globalization,* rev. ed. (New York: Farrar, Straus, and Giroux, 2000); and Edward D. Mansfield, *Power, Trade, and War* (Princeton: Princeton University Press, 1994). Among the many works on democracy and peace, two of the more recent works are James L. Ray, *Democracy and International Conflict: An Evaluation of the Democratic Peace Proposition* (Columbia: University of South Carolina Press, 1995), and Bruce Russett, *Grasping the Democratic Peace: Principles for a Post–Cold War World* (Princeton: Princeton University Press, 1993). On the theoretical link between international organizations and peace, see Robert O. Keohane, *After Hegemony: Cooperation and Discord in the World Political Economy* (Princeton: Princeton University Press, 1984), and John G. Ruggie, *Constructing the World Polity: Essays on International Institutionalization* (New York: Routledge, 1998).

42. Claude, *Power in International Relations,* pp. 94–106.

entirely absent from world politics as yet, the sovereignty and independence of
the traditional "nation-state" is being rapidly eroded by the forces of globalization, including economic interdependence, democratization, and the growth in
the number and variety of international organizations.

In one sense, the whole debate misses the point: the processes of transformation at work in the world were not initiated in 1989. Change is a constant, not
something that occurs only at certain critical junctures in history. Even when a
single dramatic event like a major war or a revolution appears to change things
very suddenly, in retrospect the signs of an impending crisis almost always surface, often unnoticed or underestimated at the time, long before the crisis itself
occurs.

The underlying question is always this: Is the state still the primary actor in
international politics, or not? If nothing has replaced the state-based system, it
logically follows that there continues to be no governing authority capable of reg-
ulating the interactions of sovereign states. And if the system remains anarchic,
then it stands to reason that the basic patterns of interaction among these states—
including the resort to war—remain unchanged.

Let us imagine for a moment that a decade hence the United States is facing
several great powers on the rise and rather than being the lone "superpower"
dealing with lesser powers is forced to deal with these "new" rivals as equals.
Many Americans might be surprised and alarmed. They might wonder whose
fault it is, who let it happen. Some politicians, columnists, and professors would
be tempted to look around for a culprit, maybe a president or a political party.

In fact, it is likely, perhaps even inevitable, that this scenario will come to
pass, albeit not necessarily in ten years. The U.S. share in the world economy fell
to about 23 percent by 1980—less than one-half what it was in the late 1940s.[43]
The United States is still an economic giant without any equal—indeed, the U.S.
economy is equivalent to the combined economic might of the next four richest
countries (Japan, Germany, Britain, and France). However, power is far more
widely dispersed now than it was in the middle of the twentieth century, and this
trend shows no signs of slowing.[44]

Joseph Nye argues that international politics in the contemporary world
"resembles a complex three-dimensional chess game." Militarily, the world is
"largely unipolar" in Nye's view but "on the economic board, the United States is

---

43. It rose relatively in the 1980s, hovering around 25 percent, and climbed back to
slightly over 30 percent in the 1990s, as a result of what Federal Reserve Chairman Alan
Greenspan called the "irrational exuberance" of the stock market and a bubble economy. See
Eugene R. Wittkopf, ed., *The Future of American Foreign Policy* (New York: St. Martin's, 1994);
see also Joseph Nye, "The New Rome Meets the New Barbarians," *Economist,* Mar. 23, 2002,
p. 23.

44. Mearsheimer, *Tragedy of Great Power Politics,* esp. chap. 10.

not a hegemon, and must often bargain as an equal with Europe." Nye focuses the bulk of his analysis on transnational relations, or what he called the "bottom chessboard" involving entities and actors other than governments. Bankers, traders, and tourists share this chessboard with terrorists, hackers, and a host of other nongovernmental players.

> On this bottom board, power is widely dispersed, and it makes no sense to speak of unipolarity, multipolarity or hegemony. Those who recommend a hegemonic American foreign policy based on such traditional descriptions of American power are relying on woefully inadequate analysis. When you are in a three-dimensional game, you will lose if you focus only on the top board and fail to notice the other boards and the vertical connections among them.[45]

The crux of Nye's argument is based on what he calls "soft power," which means "the ability to get others to want what you want."[46] Hard power, by contrast, refers to coercion and intimidation—using economic and military instruments to bludgeon other countries into submission, cooperation, or, at the very least, acquiescence. Threats, of course, are credible only if strong words are backed by strong deeds—"sending in the marines" from time to time. For a government that relies primarily on the armed forces in the conduct of its foreign policy, periodic military intervention is necessary simply to keep up appearances.

There can be no doubt that the United States possesses enormous hard-power capabilities. The doubt arises in the area of soft-power resources in a competitive world in which economic power is measured in services as well as goods and producers are not confined or even seriously constrained by borders. Hard power and soft power can be mutually reinforcing in theory; in practice, however, the unilateral or too frequent or frivolous use of hard power inevitably undermines soft power—that is, the kind that is most useful on the lower chessboard where the real "battles" of the twenty-first century are most likely to be fought. We will return to this theme in a later chapter.

There is much talk in policy and academic circles now about America as the world hegemon. "A hegemon is a state that is so powerful that it dominates all the other states in the system."[47] The notion that any power in the world has the power to conquer or control the world is absurd on its face. One American

45. Nye, "New Rome Meets the New Barbarians," p. 24.

46. Ibid. For a full elaboration of this idea, see Joseph Nye, *The Paradox of American Power: Why the World's Only Superpower Can't Go It Alone* (New York: Oxford University Press, 2002).

47. Mearsheimer, *Tragedy of Great Power Politics*, p. 140. See also Robert Gilpin, *War and Change in World Politics* (Cambridge: Cambridge University Press, 1981), p. 29, and William C. Wohlforth, *The Elusive Balance: Power and Perceptions during the Cold War* (Ithaca: Cornell University Press, 1993), pp. 12–14.

scholar argues in a recent book, "[I]t is virtually impossible for any state to achieve global hegemony."[48] The main reason is the "stopping power of water":

> The principal impediment to world domination is the difficulty of projecting power across the world's oceans onto the territory of a rival great power. The United States, for example, is the most powerful state on the planet today. But it does not dominate Europe and Northeast Asia the way it does the Western Hemisphere, and it has no intention of trying to conquer and control those distant regions, mainly because of the stopping power of water. Indeed, there is reason to think that the American military commitment to Europe and Northeast Asia might wither away over the next decade. In short, there has never been a global hegemon, and there is not likely to be one any-time soon.[49]

These words were written before September 11, 2001, and the subsequent U.S.-led conquest of Afghanistan and Iraq. Some readers (and political analysts) may now question whether the United States "has no intention of trying to con-quer and control" lands beyond the Western Hemisphere. Intentions are ulti-mately unknowable. But if the makers of America's foreign policy are so rash as to believe the United States could (much less should) conquer and control the "distant lands" that lie across the world's two great oceans, they (and we) could be heading for serious trouble.

POWER POLITICS AND THE PURSUIT OF PRINCIPLES AFTER SEPTEMBER 11

Foreign policy was on the back burner during much of the 1990s as Americans were lulled into a sense of complacency by the demise of the other superpower—America's long-time nemesis. In addition, Americans were caught up in the euphoria of a soaring stock market and a booming economy. All that changed abruptly on September 11, 2001, when a series of terrorist attacks on the twin towers of the World Trade Center and the Pentagon—two symbols of American power—riveted the nation's attention on world affairs. Not since the Cuban Missile Crisis of 1962 had Americans felt so insecure, and not since the Vietnam War had they been so tuned in to foreign policy.

In the emotionally charged atmosphere that followed September 11, a new and untested president launched bold new policies and embraced preemp-tive action as part of a "war against terrorism." At the same time, he overhauled the machinery of government, creating a new cabinet-level Department of Homeland Security. These initiatives, designed to give the executive branch

---

48. Mearsheimer, *Tragedy of Great Power Politics,* p. 41.
49. Ibid.

greater law-enforcement powers at home and greater latitude for the use of lethal force abroad, were couched in moral principle. Hence, President George W. Bush declared that America's purpose was to overthrow repressive dictatorships in Afghanistan and Iraq, to contain an "axis of evil" that threatened world peace and stability, to prevent the spread of weapons of mass destruction, and to promote freedom and democracy. In the service of these noble aims, the White House would not hesitate to use all the internal security and military forces at its disposal. Indeed, the Bush administration would seek even greater police powers and would restructure the policy process to give a larger role to the attorney general (the head of the Justice Department) and the director of homeland security. In addition, the secretary of defense and the national security adviser would continue to be well positioned for countering any soft-power arguments that might emanate from the State Department.

In the days and weeks that followed the horrific events of September 11, the Bush administration set about preparing for the wars to come, first against Afghanistan for harboring terrorism and then against Iraq for allegedly building and planning to use weapons of mass destruction. After the first American invasion of Iraq in 1990–1991, a seasoned American diplomat wrote: "The Gulf War, in fact, illustrates the tendency of American foreign policy to define military actions not in the Clauswitzian sense of a 'continuation of policy by other means' but as the final phase of policy beyond which there is only victory or defeat."[50] The first President Bush, however, resisted calls for the ouster of the Iraqi tyrant, Saddam Hussein, because "it can be argued that such an outcome would have saddled the United States and its allies with responsibilities for the occupation and governance of Iraq that they were incapable of discharging."[51] Ironically, this is precisely what appeared to be happening in 2003 after the United States again invaded Iraq and this time marched all the way to Baghdad.

The tendency to look at external problems through ideological lenses, rather than political or diplomatic ones, can lead to trouble.[52] Arguably, the use

---

50. Stearns, *Talking to Strangers,* p. 7. The author elaborates as follows: "Our diplomacy was most effective when it was working to create and sustain a consensus supporting military action. When it came to the diplomatic and political ends to be served by the Gulf War, the attention of senior administration officials seemed to wander. . . . Diplomatic planning to anticipate the likely effect of the war (on the Iraqi Kurds and Shiite Moslems, or on Saddam Hussein himself) appeared to be almost nonexistent. The problems created for Turkey, first by the massive influx of Iraqi Kurds, then by stirring up the grievances of Turkish Kurds, seem to have taken the administration by surprise."

51. Ibid.

52. Ibid. Stearns argues that the U.S. government in 1990–1991 "should have shunned the language and tactics of total warfare and better weighed the political consequences of the policy it adopted." A similar criticism was also leveled against President George W. Bush in 2003.

of military force was necessary to stop Iraq's aggression and remove Iraqi forces from Kuwait in 1990–1991. But a critic might point out that it did not solve the riddle posed by Iraq's very existence in a strategic location—that is, in close proximity to Israel, the oil fields, and the Persian Gulf. To think of military force as a "solution" to such a problem can be misleading because it implies that there is a quick fix when there is not, as the United States discovered after the second invasion of Iraq in 2003.

How decision makers think about problems can influence the policies they adopt. Iraq under Saddam was like an illness that a well-trained physician can often manage but never cure. Thus, thinking in medical rather than strictly military terms may have avoided an unnecessary second Gulf War. The United States did not withdraw from the region after the first Gulf War (as we did from Europe after World War I), but we continued to rely heavily on unilateral force (military bases in Saudi Arabia and Kuwait, no-fly zones enforced by the U.S. Air Force, and an economic embargo), as well as multilateral diplomacy.

The value of military muscle in such circumstances has rarely if ever been lost on American presidents; the value of political expertise and analysis—the stuff of diplomacy—is less apparent. Under these circumstances, there is a risk that diplomacy will be depreciated at precisely those times when it is most needed. This risk was reflected in the new fighting vocabulary of American foreign policy after September 11. Phrases such as the "war on terrorism" and "weapons of mass destruction" were repeated over and over again like official mantras. America's enemies constituted an "axis of evil." President Bush allowed nobody to be neutral ("you're either with us or you're with the terrorists") and lapsed into the language of a barroom brawler ("bring 'em on"). He thus adopted "the language and tactics of total warfare."[53]

This approach, however, did not exclude the language of morality and religion. To brand the enemy as "evil" is to bring morality into the policy debate and throws the door wide open to religious interpretations, as well. The latter is particularly true when the "enemy" represents a religious tradition, Islam, often at odds with Christianity, and even more so when America's main nemesis—Osama bin Laden—is the very symbol of Islamism (a political-ideological outgrowth of Islamic fundamentalism). President Bush sought to assure Muslims that America was not declaring war on Islam, but he used evocative imagery and spoke in the most idealistic terms of planting freedom and democracy in the Arab world where it had never before taken root—what he called "nation building." In this manner, he wrapped military power in the mantle of moral principle and in so doing changed the rules of the game. But that part of the story will have to wait until we get to the final chapter.

---

53. See previous note.

CONCLUSION

American foreign policy can be fruitfully viewed as an ongoing search for the proper balance between moral principles and power politics, between high-minded ideals and narrow national interests. The tension between these two elements has contributed to both successes and failures in America's relations with the outside world.

American idealism and pragmatism are both rooted in the European intellectual ferment that gave rise to the scientific revolution and the Age of Reason (also known as the Enlightenment). These two countervailing tendencies are clearly present in the speeches and writings of the American Founders.

Pragmatists and scientists look at the world in much the same way. They demand proof and trust only empirical evidence to lead them to the truth. Knowledge is acquired gradually through a process of induction (analysis based on experimentation and careful observation). Society can be improved by applying scientific principles to everyday life, investing in basic research and development, and relying on the skills of engineers to put technology to work for the good of all. Conservatives tend to be pragmatists.

Idealists do not reject the findings of science, but they believe that science alone is inadequate to explain life's deepest mysteries or solve the world's worst problems—including war and poverty. They have always turned to theology and philosophy for answers. From at least the time of the Enlightenment, idealists have sought answers in reason rather than faith. They believe it is possible to learn the truth and acquire the wisdom to use scientific knowledge only through a process of deduction (analysis based on logic). In other words, idealists believe it is necessary to channel the findings of science using the insights of philosophy. Liberals tend to be idealists.

The tension between principles and power is always present in the great debates over the direction of American foreign policy and always has been. These debates often take the form of a tug-of-war between "liberals" and "conservatives" trying to win over public opinion.[54] This contest is usually fought using current issues as the battleground, but the real fight—the one that is rarely mentioned—is about how much weight to give to moral principles and how much to give to hard power in formulating foreign policy.

There can be a big difference between what policymakers are saying and what they are thinking. Similarly, there is a difference between words and deeds. Declaratory policy and "public diplomacy" (or what Marxists call propaganda) are often not the best guides to the intentions and motives of those in power. This

---

54. Because these terms are used in various (and often arbitrary) ways, I have put them in quotation marks.

is true everywhere, of course, but it complicates the analysis of American foreign policy more than that of other great powers precisely because of the ever-present tension between power and principle. When Americans hear the president invoke liberty and democracy as reasons for going to war, few doubt the president's veracity or question the validity of the reasons. After all, millions of Americans fought in World War I (more than 116,000 died) and believed President Wilson when he told them it was "to make the world safe for democracy." Not even Wilson's severest critics doubt that he meant what he said or that he really did mean to make the world safer and more democratic.

In sum, the dialectic of power and principle complicates the analysis of foreign policy for precisely the same reason that it complicates the formulation of that policy. The producers of policy are cut from the same basic cloth as the consumers. They, too, can feel conflicted over what to do and how best to do it. They, too, are subject to being pulled in opposite directions. When decision makers cannot decide, or have difficulty doing so, for whatever reason(s), the consequences can be serious indeed. When what is good for the country is not the same as what is morally good, a liberal president might have great difficulty being tough enough. The danger for a conservative president might lie in the opposite direction—being so tough that even our allies jump ship. As the following chapters will show, American has fallen victim to both of these hazards at different times and in 2003 is living with the consequences of one of the worst examples in recent memory.

2

Ideals and Self-Interest

The American Way

OVERVIEW

Chapter 2 covers the origins of American foreign policy more deeply. The term "exceptionalism" is defined, and I ask why generations of Americans have believed that the United States is special—an exception—in a world where the "law of the jungle" is the rule. I then consider the role of pragmatism in the foreign policy calculations of America's early decision makers and note that the first diplomats for the new American Republic had to do a kind of balancing act. Next, I examine the Monroe Doctrine and the idea of "manifest destiny." President Monroe's famous pronouncement—the first of many "doctrines" in American foreign policy—signals the beginning of a successful drive for regional hegemony in the Western Hemisphere. "Manifest destiny" was one of the great political buzzwords in the history of American foreign policy. It was a kind of moral fig leaf intended to cover the embarrassing truth about America's westward expansion—namely, that it was a land grab on a grand scale, not a divinely ordained mission. That this truth was embarrassing, however, says something important about the role of morality in American foreign policy. Exactly what it says is explored in the conclusion.

There would be three major themes in American foreign policy between 1787 and 1898: independence, freedom of the seas (foreign trade), and westward expansion.[1] The huge wave of immigrants would not wash onto America's shores until the second half of the nineteenth century, but the seeds of the American "melting pot" were sown at the time of the American Revolution. The words of Emma Lazarus, "Give me your tired, your poor, your huddled masses yearning to breathe free," have long resonated with a deep sense of moral destiny in the hearts of the American people. This belief in America's mission—raised to a new level as a result of the tectonic global power shift after World War II—has its roots in a political ethos canonized in the Constitution and Bill of Rights.

THE FOUNDERS AND FOREIGN POLICY

The early Americans produced a generation of political thinkers who created a kind of secular religion but who wisely did not reject or rule out the possibility of a higher being in the process (as, for

---

1. Robert H. Ferrell, ed., *Foundations of American Diplomacy, 1775–1872* (New York: Harper Torchbooks, 1968), see esp. pp. 1–20.

CHRONOLOGY, 1774–1898

1774	British Parliament passes a series of so-called Coercive Acts
1775–83	War of Independence (American Revolution)
1787	Northwest Ordinance opens a vast new region for statehood
1789	The French Revolution sparks turmoil that affects all of Europe for the next quarter of a century; George Washington inaugurated as first president of the United States
1793	Eli Whitney invents the cotton gin
1796	John Adams elected second president of the United States
1801	Thomas Jefferson elected third president of the United States by act of Congress
1803	In Europe, Napoleonic Wars escalate
1807	Congress votes construction of National Road
1808	Economic depression; James Madison elected fourth U.S. president
1812	War of 1812; Madison reelected president
1816	James Monroe elected fifth U.S. president
1830	Indian Removal Act
1831	Nat Turner slave rebellion in Virginia
1844	Samuel Morse sends first telegraph
1860	Abraham Lincoln elected sixteenth U.S. president
1861–65	American Civil War
1869	Transcontinental railroad completed
1898	Spanish-American War

example, Karl Marx would do later). The new "science of politics" they created revolves around the central idea of the Enlightenment: reason rather than received truth, blind faith, or superstition is the path to human progress.[2]

Far from being moralistic, the Founders expressed a brand of realism that would almost certainly have led to self-defeating pessimism about the prospects for "progress towards perfection." But the new science of politics saved the day by providing a pragmatic solution, one that sought to correct for the flaws in human nature by means of a system of checks and balances.

The idea of democracy was also a political expedient—good strategy as well as good "science." As an ideology of liberation it could be translated into an action program (the Revolutionary War) and given concrete institutional expression (the Constitution and Bill of Rights). Ironically, the myth of the American Revolution as an idealistic act of political creation goes a long way toward explaining the lasting appeal of "America" to the world, and the reality of a durable political system based on a pragmatic act of political engineering explains its stability and longevity.

America the Exceptional

Nothing said to this point diminishes the importance of idealism as a force in American foreign policy. Democracy and liberty have a universal appeal that transcends individual self-interest and personal gain. Aside from those corrupted by power or blinded by political ambition (absolute rulers and demagogues), the link between freedom and justice is readily apparent to all but the most morally obtuse. The American Founders were well aware of it and drew inspiration from it. Moreover, they used it to inspire the nation and unite the colonists in the drive for independence. The men who made the "miracle at Philadelphia" happen— George Washington, Thomas Jefferson, and James Madison, to name but three of the most prominent—were realists but not cynics.

Whatever the precise ratio of myth to reality, there are few events in history that compare with the American founding as an example of enlightened political action free of demagoguery, recriminations, purges, and the like. It is hard to exaggerate the role of this single event in shaping the political culture of the United States. It would be foolish to ignore it. I argue that the contradictions in American foreign policy—past and present—cannot be explained adequately without reference to the idealism in the words of the Declaration of Independence and the Preamble to the Constitution, irrespective of the realism that comes through when we go behind the scenes at Philadelphia or read between the lines of the document the authors hammered out there.

---

2. Thomas M. Magstadt, *Understanding Politics: Ideas, Institutions, and Issues,* 6th ed. (Belmont, Calif.: Wadsworth, 2003), pp. 63–64.

Idealism is an integral part of America's identity and collective self-image, its sense of its own exceptionalism. Americans truly believe America is exceptional—nobler, better, and more blessed than other nations on this earth. Exceptionalism in this case denotes a crucial difference between the Old World and New World, between Europe and America. Europe was moved by power; America was moved by principle.

The idea that America is different from other countries is not entirely baseless: America *is* exceptionally prosperous. In part, this economic success is a function of geography and geology: protected by oceans on both flanks and rich in natural resources, the United States has enjoyed certain natural advantages. But American supremacy is also a function of politics. In the minds of the Founders, promoting "the general Welfare" and securing "the Blessings of Liberty" were flip sides of the same coin. They believed with the English philosopher Adam Smith that a market economy was the best way to ensure the greatest good for the greatest number, and the institutions they initiated reflected this belief.[3]

Exceptional Pragmatism

Prosperous societies have at least one thing in common: political stability. A stable political system is impossible without a good measure of either repression or justice. Historically speaking, repression has been the "solution" of choice in most places until quite recently. The American Founders chose the other course. The concept of representative democracy they embraced was associated with *injustice* (as are virtually all revolutions). The specific injustice ("taxation without representation") is beside the point. Recognition of the link between democracy and justice is the key to understanding why the American Founders chose a form of liberal democracy over monarchy (the only other real choice at the time). But these two ideals, to repeat an earlier point, were rooted in a shockingly "realistic" assessment of human nature.

In choosing limited government (indirect rule with a highly selective franchise), the Founders laid the foundations for an expanding middle class without suddenly throwing the doors wide open, so to speak. Indeed, the original "liberal democracy" was limited in ways that appear extremely illiberal in today's world. For example, it did not grant equal rights to women, who were not allowed to vote in "the land of the free" until 1919. Worse still, the Bill of Rights (belying its name) did not abolish slavery—the most egregious deprivation of liberty ever practiced anywhere. The reason was not that Jefferson, Adams, and others were indifferent to the plight of the slaves or unaware of the wrong slavery represented

---

3. By a remarkable coincidence, Adam Smith published his famous *Inquiry into the Nature and Causes of the Wealth of Nations* in the same year, 1776, as Jefferson wrote the Declaration of Independence.

but, rather, that allowing slavery in the South was the only way to get the southern colonies to ratify the Constitution. In other words, the Founders placed pragmatism above principle. Indeed, they were no less pragmatic in conducting foreign policy than they were in domestic affairs.[4]

Before we consider how America managed to maneuver through the treacherous shoals and reefs of international politics in its first decade or two of existence, we need to remind ourselves that luck—whether good or bad—is often a big factor. For the United States, the fact that the French Revolution occurred at precisely the same time as America was launching its new Republic was a stroke of good luck with few parallels, or greater consequences, in history. It meant that for the next two decades Europe would be preoccupied with itself—that is, with the Napoleonic challenge to the European balance, and thus to Europe's conservative monarchies.[5]

America was exceptionally lucky, as well as exceptionally pragmatic. Not only did the French Revolution occur at an auspicious moment for young America, but it is also the case that geography and the "stopping power of water" greatly tilted the odds sharply in its favor.[6] These auspicious circumstances made it possible to pursue an unusual strategy of bowing out rather than participating in the European balance-of-power game.[7] This is a choice that exists only for a minor power removed from the central arena of international politics by a large body of water.

A Delicate Balancing Act

From its inception, the United States performed a delicate balancing act. America's early makers of foreign policy—who in some cases were also the professional

---

4. Ironically, a substantial body of opinion in the American academic community (often considered to be an "ivory tower") calls for a return to the "venerable American tradition" of pragmatism in public policy across the board. See, for example, John W. Kingdon, *America the Unusual* (New York: St. Martin's / Worth, 1999), pp. 88–95. Kingdon makes a point worthy of pondering: "Again, I think that too great an insistence on the 'American way' prevents us from learning from the experience of other countries. But more than that, it prevents us from being straightforward and sensible. . . . A little pragmatism can go a long way" (p. 95).

5. Ferrell, *Foundations of American Diplomacy*, p. 80.

6. John J. Mearsheimer, *The Tragedy of Great Power Politics,* (New York: Norton, 2001), pp. 114–128. The author notes, "neither of our insular great powers (the United Kingdom and the United States) has ever been invaded, whereas our continental great powers (France and Russia) have been invaded . . . twelve times since 1792. These continental states were assaulted across land eleven times, but only once from the sea. The apparent lesson is that large bodies of water make it extremely difficult for armies to invade territory defended by a well-armed great power." The British invaded the United States briefly in 1812, but the United States was not yet a "well-armed great power" at that time, whereas Great Britain was the preeminent sea power. Even so, the British promptly retreated and never returned—a testament to the stopping power of water.

7. Ibid. See esp. pp. 267–333.

diplomats responsible for its implementation—sought to balance democratic principles with a pragmatic pursuit of the national interest. On the one hand,

> Americans, from the earliest days of independence, have consciously sought to avoid European diplomatic models. We have seen ourselves, rightly or wrongly, as practitioners of a new diplomacy, born of the Enlightenment, in which the power of reason would replace military power and distinctions between personal and state morality would be narrowed if not entirely eliminated. The founders of the republic sought alternatives to the use of military force to achieve national objectives.[8]

On the other hand, our early diplomats were quite pragmatic when it came to pursuing the interests of the government they represented. Thus, the "sense of conducting ourselves differently from Europeans, of being more high-minded than they, more democratic and more scrupulous in our observance of international law, continued to permeate American diplomacy even after it became apparent that the United States was as capable of acting out of self-interest as any other state, and as likely to disregard international law when it did not suit the national purpose."[9]

America's first ambassadors enjoyed a great deal of latitude in the actual conduct of diplomacy (as opposed to policymaking). Franklin, for example, refrained from pressing the French monarchy into openly siding with the colonies (to the consternation of his colleagues), judging (correctly) that France would do so when it was good and ready—that is, when it was ready to go to war with Great Britain. This is the kind of judgment that can often best be made "on the ground" by a professional observer who knows the political terrain and the principal actors. For his part, Jefferson in Paris concentrated on America's commercial relations with France. Specifically, it was France's protectionist trade policies (especially the exclusion of American whale oil from the French market) that he sought to change. He largely succeeded in this undertaking, not by bullying or threatening France (which he was in no position to do) but by persuasion.[10] Moreover, it was *all* Jefferson: micro-management from afar was not a factor. The strategy (access for American products) was made in Washington; the tactics (how to get the king to play ball) were Jefferson's.

Franklin and Jefferson epitomize the diplomatic profession as it ought to be practiced; they accomplished a great deal in a foreign post at a time when the United States was still in its infancy, when lines of authority "back home" were therefore unclear, and when the emerging American nation was caught in the throes of a life-and-death independence struggle.

---

8. Monteagle Stearns, *Talking to Strangers: Improving American Diplomacy at Home and Abroad* (Princeton: Princeton University Press, 1996), p. 20.

9. Ibid., p. 21.

10. Ibid., pp. 21–31.

In our external relations, diplomacy (persuasion) was the only instrument available; military force (coercion) was not an option. By the same token, economic sanctions were not available when the colonies were still a confederation of agrarian proto-states and the British Royal Navy ruled the high seas. Hence, the "delicate balancing act" our early diplomats had to perform was doubly difficult because the country they represented was a newcomer and, as such, it was no match on the international stage for Europe's Great Powers.

YOUNG AMERICA, OLD WORLD

Making a virtue of necessity is the American way in foreign affairs. Its effect is to entwine power and principle so tightly that no one—not even the president—can separate the two. So it was in the beginning, when the United States under the steady leadership of George Washington deliberately embarked on a starkly different road in foreign affairs from the one chosen by the European powers.

In choosing to stay out of European power struggles, Washington and his nineteenth-century heirs were motivated by two primary concerns. First, there were hard facts to consider: on the one hand, the United States was the only democracy in existence (a negative); on the other, a vast ocean protected America from Europe's armies and insulated it from Europe's wars (a positive). In the late eighteenth century, the United States could expect to find no sympathy for liberal causes on the other side of the Atlantic. On the contrary, the French Revolution kindled fears of a liberal contagion on the Continent (not unlike Western liberal-democratic concerns about the possible spread of communism after the October Revolution). Meanwhile, young America faced formidable challenges of "nation building" in the postcolonial period.

In sum, the United States in the 1790s was isolated and alone in the world. This isolation was three-dimensional—political, geographic, and economic.[11] Political and geographic isolation was advantageous in the beginning, but economic relations with Europe were essential if America was to prosper. In his Farewell Address in 1896 President Washington put the matter bluntly: "The great rule of conduct for us in regard to foreign nations is, in extending our commercial relations to have with them as little political connection as possible."[12]

The United States was in an ideal position to bow out of Europe's struggles. The Great Powers were preoccupied with Napoleon in the decade before and after 1800. With hegemonic ambitions in the Old World and extensive

---

11. The economic isolation was due in part to the relatively weak trade and financial ties of nations in the eighteenth century compared with the present; it was also due in part to piracy and the practice of interdiction on the high seas in wartime—a practice that often did not spare or exempt neutral powers.

12. Ferrell, *Foundations of American Diplomacy*, p. 92.

holdings in the New, France was a potential threat to American interests, but the United States wisely left Europe's balance-of-power problem to the conservative monarchies (Austria, Prussia, Russia) and Great Britain to sort out. The strategy was simple and straightforward: stay on the sidelines and let the threatened European powers to check Napoleon. Bowing out would continue to serve the United States well throughout the nineteenth century, as the United States, brandishing its ideals like weapons of war, brashly set out to establish its hegemony in the New World.[13] (We explore the era of American expansionism in the next chapter.)

Thus, it made sense on pragmatic grounds for the United States to avoid "entangling alliances," but it made equal sense on moral grounds.[14] "Observe good faith and justice toward all nations," Washington advised. "Cultivate peace and harmony with all. In the execution of such a plan nothing is more essential than that permanent, inveterate antipathies against particular nations and passionate attachments for others should be excluded, and that in place of them just and amicable feeling toward all should be cultivated."[15] The confluence of geography, ideology, and politics, therefore, "contributed significantly to two important foreign policy traditions: isolationism and moralism."[16]

America as a Developing Country

At its start, the United States was interested only in trade with Europe. The commercial thrust of early American diplomacy can be seen in the nature of our international treaties between 1778 and 1899 (see Table 2-1). Over two-thirds of these agreements involved commerce or claims (mostly economic). Consular activities and extradition are routine diplomatic fare in large part. Although boundary

---

13. Anyone who doubts that the United States was "brandishing its ideals like weapons" needs only to read the speeches of nineteenth-century expansionists in Congress and the press. For example, in 1847 the *New York Herald* exulted that the presence of the American army in Mexico would guarantee the "regeneration" of the Mexican people; similarly, the *New York Sun* saw the conquest and annexation of Mexico as "the finger of Providence uplifted for the salvation of a people oppressed by tyrants and robbers." See Albert K. Weinberg, *Manifest Destiny: A Study of Nationalist Expansionism in American History* (1935; reprint, Chicago: Quadrangle Books, 1963), pp. 172–173. This fascinating study chronicles the wide array of moral and religious justifications proffered by imperialist politicians, newspaper editors, and others for a foreign policy aimed at regional hegemony (the ultimate goal of international power politics).

14. It was Thomas Jefferson who actually popularized the phrase "entangling alliances," although it is often inaccurately attributed to Washington.

15. Ferrell, *Foundations of American Diplomacy*, p. 92.

16. James McCormick, *American Foreign Policy and American Values* (Itasca, Ill.: Peacock, 1985), p. 6; see also John Spanier and Steven W. Hook, *American Foreign Policy since World War II*, 14th ed. (Washington, D.C.: Congressional Quarterly, 1985), pp. 10–18.

Table 2-1 Content of U.S. Treaties from 1778 to 1899	
Content	Number of treaties
Alliance	1
Amity and commerce	272
Boundary	32
Claims	167
Consular activities	47
Extradition	47
Multilateral	37
Territorial concessions	18
Total	621

Source: Calculated by the author from Igor I. Kavass and Mark A. Michael, *United States Treaties and Other International Agreements, Cumulative Index, 1776–1949* (Buffalo, N.Y.: Wm. S. Hein, 1975).

issues and territorial concessions tend to be controversial, they constituted less than 10 percent of the total.

Early Americans associated alliances with war and commerce with peace. We entered into a formal military alliance with France against the British in 1778, but the alliance was dissolved by mutual consent after twenty-two years. That would be the first and last peacetime military alliance in American diplomatic history prior to creation of the North Atlantic Treaty Organisation (NATO) almost exactly a century and a half later.

War was anathema to commerce. But staying out of war and keeping trade routes open proved to be a tall order for the young republic. The ink had not yet dried on the U.S. Constitution when the French Revolution exploded on the Continent, setting in motion a train of events that led inexorably to the convulsive Napoleonic Wars. It is easily forgotten that this turbulent era in European history coincided with the first crucial decades in American history. Indeed, the urgent logic of Washington's injunction against foreign entanglements in his Farewell Address can be appreciated only in the context of international politics in the 1790s—specifically, the gathering storm in Europe.

The rivalry between England and France was natural enough. As the pre-eminent naval power, separated from the Continent by the English Channel, Great Britain faced little or no danger of military invasion unless one of the European powers succeeded in conquering the others. This was precisely what Napoleon set out to do. The way he sought to do it, moreover, was particularly alarming to the British (although the myopic monarchs of the Continent failed to see the full dimensions of the threat).

Napoleon claimed to embody the will of the French people. In the name of "liberty, equality, and fraternity" he mobilized an entire nation for the first time in modern history. It was this popularization of war—the contemporary equivalent of the atom bomb—accompanied by a royal complacency on the Continent that gave Napoleon his big chance.[17]

In America, the rise of revolutionary France posed a two-pronged foreign policy problem. First, the French revolutionaries expected the Americans to back Robespierre's radical new "democratic" regime against its natural enemies, the monarchs of Europe.[18] In particular, they wanted the United States to honor the existing French-American military alliance in the event of war between France and Britain. Anything less would not only be a violation of the existing treaty but also an act of cynicism and ingratitude—cynicism because a popular uprising had overthrown a reactionary monarchy in France, ingratitude because the French in somewhat similar circumstances had sided with the Americans.[19]

Second, the British Royal Navy ruled the waves, including both the Atlantic and the Caribbean oceans. War had erupted between Great Britain and France in 1793 and, except for the nineteen-month interval from November 1801 to May 1803, raged almost continuously until 1815. This turbulence in Europe formed the backdrop of American foreign policy during the first twenty-five years of the nation's existence. When the British navy shut down enemy shipping on the high seas, both France and Spain responded by opening the West Indies they controlled to American merchant ships.

The British then invoked the Rule of 1756, holding that trade not open in peacetime could not be legally opened in wartime. For a time, American sea-trading companies got around this rule by transshipping goods—that is, by

---

17. On this complacency, see Gordon A. Craig and Alexander L. George, *Force and Statecraft: Diplomatic Problems of Our Times,* 2nd ed. (New York: Oxford University Press, 1990), pp. 25–27. On Napoleon's "popularization of war," see Robert E. Osgood and Robert W. Tucker, *Force, Order, and Justice* (Baltimore: Johns Hopkins University Press, 1967), pp. 51–52. According to these two distinguished scholars, Napoleon "transformed warfare into a national crusade, involving not just tactical maneuver and attrition of the enemy's supply lines but annihilation of the enemy's forces, occupation of his territory, and even political conversion of his people. With universal conscription and comprehensive material and economic mobilization, he created a 'nation in arms' " (pp. 51–52).

18. Maximilien de Robespierre was one of the key leaders of the radical Jacobin faction in the French Revolution. As the head of the secretive twelve-member governing body called the Committee of Public Safety that was formed in 1793 under the aegis of the National Convention, Robespierre directed the Reign of Terror with the aim of creating a utopian "republic of virtue." No one felt safe, including members of the Convention. In July 1794, they managed to overthrow Robespierre and sent him to the guillotine. In the end, he shared the same fate as Louis XVI, the hated monarch he had helped to overthrow.

19. I say "somewhat similar circumstances" because any facile attempt to draw an analogy between the American and French Revolutions breaks down quickly upon closer examination.

diverting cargo (sugar, for example) from the Caribbean islands to American ports, offloading and paying duty, then, having received all or most of the duty back, reloading and carrying the "laundered" goods on to France or Spain. London halted this lucrative trade in 1805, much to the consternation of American sea merchants and the Jefferson administration. The British practice of "impressing seamen"—seizing sailors from American ships at sea and forcing them to serve in the British navy—added insult to injury. Nonetheless, there was precious little the United States could do about it short of provoking another war with Great Britain (which the prudent Jefferson was loath to do). The war did eventually come, in 1812, but not before Jefferson, keen to exhaust every possibility short of war, made an ill-fated attempt at economic coercion (a total trade embargo on Europe).

In sum, America's early national leaders consciously sought to distinguish the way the United States conducted its diplomatic affairs from the European model. The Americans made treaties of amity and commerce with Prussia, Sweden, Tripoli, and Tunis, among others. They seized the opportunity presented by France's war with Britain to get the Louisiana Territory at a fire-sale price ($15 million) in 1803.[20] They got far more land on the cheap in the Louisiana Purchase than most military aggressors have ever gained by force of arms. They annexed Texas in 1845 and obtained another chunk of territory from Mexico through the Gadsden Purchase in 1853. Finally, they bought Alaska at a fire-sale price in 1868. Remarkably, with one major exception (Texas), they acquired all this territory by diplomacy rather than war.

Ironically, none of these early diplomatic successes would have been possible in the absence of the balance-of-power rivalries that were being played out in Europe during the turbulent years between the French Revolution (1789) and Napoleon's final defeat at Waterloo (1815). The alliance with France was paramount, but the Netherlands, Russia, and Spain also weighed in on the side of America against Europe's preeminent naval power, Great Britain.[21]

Today, when the United States outranks all rivals, it is easy to forget that America was originally a small nation, sparsely populated, and surrounded by territory claimed by the Great Powers of Europe. Washington, Adams, and

---

20. Presidents Adams and Jefferson, who were both diplomats in Paris before they were chief executives in Washington, deserve credit. Although historians understandably credit Jefferson, David McCullough, a Pulitzer Prizing–winning biographer, notes, "Were it not for John Adams making peace with France, there might never have been a Louisiana Purchase." David McCullough, *John Adams* (New York: Simon and Schuster, 2001), p. 586.

21. Walter Lippmann, *U.S. Foreign Policy: Shield of the Republic* (Boston: Little, Brown, 1943), p. 12; see also Alexander DeConde, *A History of American Foreign Policy*, vol. 1: *Growth to World Power (1700–1914)* (New York: Scribner's, 1978), pp. 28–29.

Jefferson could not afford to forget it. (See map of North America circa 1800 in the front of this book.)

1812: An Honest Mistake

The United States declared war on Great Britain in 1812 to uphold America's rights as a neutral power and to save face. The British had repeatedly violated America's territorial waters, seized hundreds of American merchant ships, and impressed American sailors. (Similarly, France had seized American ships and imprisoned American seamen in French ports.)

The Americans had been given ample provocation to declare war, but under Washington, Adams, and Jefferson had prudently avoided doing so—and for good reason. Britain was the superpower of the nineteenth century. America was still in its infancy. Whether it would remain intact or break up was a question that would not be answered until the Civil War, nearly six decades later. Thus, the contest in 1812 was one between a David and a Goliath.

Free trade and commerce were vital to the United States. Britain and France were at war; London imposed a "paper blockade" upon the Continent and moved aggressively to establish control over maritime commerce, capturing neutral violators on the high seas and allowing safe passage only to merchant ships granted special licenses. The infamous British orders in council were the legal expression of this policy.

The War of 1812 was divisive in the United States. President James Madison was scholarly by nature and certainly no warmonger. However, tense relations with England had taken a turn for the worse shortly after Madison was sworn into office. Thinking he had a deal with the British ambassador, David Erskine, Madison had obligingly (but, as it happened, prematurely) suspended "nonintercourse" with England only to be rebuffed by the British foreign secretary, George Canning. Then, too, expansionist war hawks in Congress, eager to grab Florida and Canada, were spoiling for a fight. The declaration of war, however, was far from unanimous. It passed by a comfortable margin (79 to 49) in the House, but a change of only four votes would have defeated it in the Senate. The British government actually rescinded the orders in council two days before the Senate vote, but the news had not yet crossed the Atlantic.

America's first declared war can best be characterized as an honest mistake. We were not fighting for our lives, but for our rights. It is a peculiarly "American thing" to do that—to mix ideals and self-interest so that there is no way to separate these motives. In any event, our rights are indistinguishable from our interests, as individuals and as a nation.

The War of 1812 ended inconclusively in 1814 with the signing of the Treaty of Ghent. Ironically, the British Royal Navy became America's guardian angel from that day forward.

EUROPE, KEEP OUT!

Napoleon met his Waterloo the following year (in 1815), thus ending the long war in Europe. It was to be the last major war fought in Europe in a century. Just as the European war had been the bane of American neutrality so the coming era of European peace would be a boon to American isolationism. The "isolationist impulse" in American diplomatic history is inseparably linked to America's westward expansion in the first half of the nineteenth century. The true story of how America built a continent empire and justified it has been obscured by the more romantic myths surrounding the frontier, the pioneers, and the ever-popular theme of "cowboys and Indians." In reality, America's success in "winning the West" was rooted in international relations—specifically in the stabilization of the European balance-of-power system after 1815. In a fortuitous twist of fate, Britain's role as the "keeper" of the balance in Europe turned out to be a windfall for the United States. Next we consider how and why Anglo-American national interests eventually converged.

The Monroe Doctrine

Spain's decline as a great power set the stage for the Monroe Doctrine. The background to this historic development is studded with revolutions in Spanish America as well as in Spain and Italy. Had these revolutions occurred after 1945 instead of 1815, they would have been called "national liberation movements." There are striking similarities. They were inspired by ideology (liberalism or republicanism) and supported by a foreign government (the United States). American support during the presidency of James Monroe was moral rather than material in nature. It remained within certain cautious limits even after the enunciation of the Monroe Doctrine in 1823.[22]

The reasons for caution had nothing to do with a lack of enthusiasm for anticolonialism and everything to do with the danger of great power intervention in the Western Hemisphere.[23] In the aftermath of the long war against Napoleon, Europe's conservative monarchies (Austria, France, Prussia, and Russia) were determined to crush any attempt to sow the seeds of revolution in Europe. Thus, in 1821 Austria brutally suppressed uprisings in Italy, and two years later France

---

22. On this point, see Thomas M. Bailey, *A Diplomatic History of the American People,* 7th ed. (New York: Appleton-Century-Crafts, 1964), pp. 188–189.

23. Here is how Secretary of State John Quincy Adams described President Monroe's reaction to the French invasion of Spain: "I [Adam] find him . . . alarmed, far beyond anything that I could have conceived possible, with the fear that the Holy Alliance are about to restore immediately all South America to Spain. [Secretary of War John] Calhoun stimulates the panic, and the news that Cadiz has surrendered to the French has so affected the President that he appeared entirely to despair of the cause of South America." *National Intelligencer,* June 2, 1821, 3:1, quoted in Bailey, *Diplomatic History,* pp. 178–179.

invaded Spain in order to keep the Spanish despot Ferdinand VII from being top-pled. Next, Europe turned its attention to Spanish America, where, as already noted, the spirit of rebellion was spreading like a contagion and upstart "states" were declaring their independence.

True to form as a "revolutionary state," America was the first to extend diplomatic recognition to these newcomers on the international stage. Secretary of State John Quincy Adams made heroic efforts to get the British to follow suit, but to no avail. British reluctance was tactical rather than philosophical: in real-ity, London was hardly less opposed than Washington to European intervention in the New World. Indeed, British foreign secretary George Canning sought a secret collaboration with the United States in this enterprise as part of a larger balance-of-power "game" he was playing, and Canning gave himself all the credit for declaring Spanish America off limits to Europe.[24]

When the Monroe Doctrine was first unveiled, it might well have been empty bravado without British backing. As Secretary of State Adams put it, the naval power of the United States was to that of Great Britain "as a cockboat in the wake of the British man-of-war."[25] Although it was never formalized, there clearly existed an Anglo-American understanding that in retrospect was an important step toward the enduring special relationship that exists to this day. But, as Walter Lippmann noted, "it was never avowed." As a result, "To this day most Americans have never heard of it."[26]

Nonetheless, the Monroe Doctrine did serve clear notice where the United States stood on the question of European intervention in the Western Hemisphere. Monroe chose the occasion of the president's regular annual mes-sage to Congress (December 2, 1823) as the time and place to declare that "the American continents, by the free and independent condition which they have assumed and maintain, are henceforth not to be considered as subjects for future colonization by any European powers."[27] These words were embedded in a long speech devoted largely to domestic affairs. The fact that fear of European inter-vention was very much on Monroe's mind is evident from the following passage:

---

24. Canning's famous quip "I called the New World into existence to redress the balance of the Old" may have been boastful and self-serving, but it is also highly revealing because it illustrates how keen Great Britain was to keep its European rivals out of the Western Hemisphere.

25. John Adams, *Memoirs*, 6:179, cited in Dexter Perkins, *A History of the Monroe Doctrine* (Boston: Little, Brown, 1955), p. 43. Perkins notes on p. 68, "It is, after all, anachro-nistic in the highest degree to give greater weight to the immature American democracy in 1823 than to the power whose prestige was never greater, whose force was never more impressive, than eight years after the defeat of Napoleon at Waterloo."

26. Lippmann, *U.S. Foreign Policy*, p. 18.

27. James D. Richardson, ed., *A Compilation of the Messages and Papers of the Presidents: 1789–1897*, 10 vols. (Washington, D.C., 1896–1899), 2:209.

The political system [monarchy] of the allied powers is essentially different . . . from that of America. . . . We owe it, therefore, to candor and to the amicable relations existing between the United States and those powers to declare that we should consider any attempt on their part to extend their system to any portion of this hemisphere as dangerous to our peace and safety.[28]

Monroe's message was crystal clear: America would view "any interposition" by a European power "for the purpose of oppressing" the newly independent states of the Western Hemisphere "as the manifestation of an unfriendly disposition toward the United States."[29] This fragment of the speech is the one most often quoted and best remembered. But the rest of the passage has been largely ignored or forgotten:

Our policy in regard to Europe which was adopted at an early stage of the wars which have so long agitated that quarter of the globe, nevertheless remains the same, which is, not to interfere in the internal concerns of any of its powers; *to consider the government de facto as the legitimate government for us* [italics added].[30]

This passage contains two principles—noninterference and "no fault" recognition—that American presidents treated with disdain during the cold war.[31] Implicit in these two principles is a third, namely, that the newly independent states of Latin America were not at liberty to form alliances with European Great Powers against the United States.

The Monroe Doctrine is a landmark in American history. Arguably, the policy it promulgated merely summed up basic principles (noncolonization, nonintervention, and noninterference) already well established by 1823.[32] Nonetheless, Monroe and Adams made these principles explicit and in so doing audaciously warned the European powers to keep hands off the Americas. The United States thus stepped out onto the world for the first time. In so doing, "the president and

---

28. Ibid., 2:218.

29. It is only fair to note that as a "superpower" in the second half of the twentieth century, the United States frequently broke its own rules of noninterference. That is to say, by intervening at will in developing countries we did unto others as we would not have had others do unto us during a similar stage in our national history.

30. Richardson, *Compilation of the Messages and Papers*, 2:218–219.

31. What I mean by "no fault" here is that normally the act of exchanging ambassadors with a foreign government does not imply approval or disapproval of the regime's leadership, policies, or ideology. Especially (though not exclusively) in foreign affairs, governments typically deal with political facts first and treat moral preferences with less immediacy—hence Monroe's reference to "de facto" recognition.

32. DeConde, *Growth to World Power*, p. 130. DeConde identifies a fourth principle, "the no-transfer principle," not explicitly stated in Monroe's speech but "expressed in supporting documents."

Secretary Adams both knew that British policy opposed European intervention in Spanish America . . . [and] could, therefore, make their bold pronouncement without fear and without force of their own."[33] Clearly, any policy of isolationism did not include Latin America, did not mean that America would remain passive in the face of international actions it found threatening. Neither did it mean that relations between the United States and the new republics of Latin America would be close, neighborly, or even amicable.[34] Exactly what it did mean was spelled out in stages during the last three-quarters of the nineteenth century.

Manifest Destiny

American imperialists (politicians, entrepreneurs, journalists, and others) concocted a variety of theories, concepts, and pretexts for westward expansion—natural right, geographical predestination, destined use of the soil, true title, a mission of regeneration, natural growth, political gravitation, inevitable destiny, the white man's burden, paramount interest, political affinity, self-defense, international police power, and world leadership.[35] The notion of manifest destiny in its many permutations was a means of assuaging the national conscience by stretching America's principles to cover its expansionist policies in the nineteenth century.

At the beginning of the nineteenth century, the United States of America consisted of sixteen states, the original thirteen plus Kentucky, Tennessee, and Vermont. At the end of the century, the number had grown to forty-five states. The change in the number of states is impressive but understates the extent of the territorial expansion that occurred during this period. Ohio was added in

33. Ibid. On this point, Lippmann states, "The prohibition [against intervention] was directed at Spain, France, Russia, and Austria. President Monroe undertook this momentous engagement after he had consulted Madison and Jefferson. They approved it only after Canning, the British Foreign Secretary, had assured the American Minister, Richard Rush, that Britain and the British navy would support the United States. For the Founding Fathers understood the realities of foreign policy too well to make commitments without having first made certain they had the means to support them." Lippmann, *U.S. Foreign Policy*, p. 17.

34. News of Monroe's "trumpet blast" did not exactly electrify Latin Americans. DeConde writes, "They knew that if any outside force had saved their independence, it was the British fleet, not Monroe's blast on the republican trumpet. When several of the new states, among them Colombia, Brazil, and Mexico, approached the United States for an alliance or assistance based on Monroe's idea, the immediate practical emptiness of the doctrine became clear. The United States turned them down." DeConde, *Growth to World Power*, p. 131. See also Perkins, *History of the Monroe Doctrine*, p. 68.

35. Weinberg, *Manifest Destiny*. The book is actually organized around these themes so that, for example, the author devotes an entire chapter to the use of "natural right" as a justification for imperialism.

1803, the same year as the Louisiana Purchase, but there was still a vast expanse of real estate east of the Mississippi that had not yet been settled, to say nothing of reaching statehood. By the time the United States declared war on Spain in 1898, the roles of David and Goliath (America and Europe) had been reversed: having expanded beyond the Mississippi, beyond the Rocky Mountains, and all the way to the Pacific Ocean, the United States dwarfed Spain. In fact, America was physically larger than all the West European powers put together, and far larger than any single European state with the exception of Russia. By 1898 the United States stretched from the Atlantic to the Pacific and spanned four time zones. Many western states made the states "back East" appear diminutive by comparison. Texas alone is five times bigger than the state of New York, the largest of the original thirteen. And although Alaska would not be admitted to statehood until 1956, the Alaskan Territory, purchased from Russia during Abraham Lincoln's presidency, was even larger than Texas.

In 1846, after President James Knox Polk informed the British, who also claimed Oregon, that the joint occupation of the disputed "Oregon Country" would end in twelve months, the two governments reached a compromise, fixing the present boundaries. In that same year, the United States annexed Texas, which had seceded from Mexico following more than a decade of rebellion; Texas came bundled with New Mexico, parts of Colorado, Kansas, Oklahoma, and Wyoming. Naturally, the annexation touched off a war. Following its military defeat in 1848, a humbled Mexico ceded Arizona, California, Nevada, and Utah, as well as part of Colorado, New Mexico, and Wyoming, to the victors. In 1853, with memories of the recent war still fresh, Mexico "sold" southern Arizona and New Mexico to the United States (known in history as the Gadsden Purchase). The external boundaries of the "continental United States" were thus established at mid-century; hereafter, there was nothing to prevent waves of pioneers and settlers from staking claims to the American West—nothing, that is, except for the *internal boundaries* defined by the Native Americans who lived there. Now the stage was set for the great drama of the American frontier that would unfold in the half-century between the Mexican War (1848) and the Spanish-American War (1898).

This is not the place to re-tell the story of "how the West was won" or to recount the wars and massacres associated with the winning.[36] Suffice it to say, that it was not a walk in the park. Any romantic notions about an American age

---

36. See especially Dee Brown, *Bury My Heart at Wounded Knee* (New York: Holt, 2000); Nicholas Black Elk, *Black Elk Speaks: Being the Life Story of a Holy Man of the Oglala Sioux* (Lincoln: University of Nebraska Press, 2000); and Anthony Wallace, *Jackson and the Indians: The Tragic Fate of the First Americans* (Cambridge: Harvard University Press, 2001).

of innocence are quickly dispelled by even a cursory look at the way "whites" treated "reds" (the aboriginal populations of North America) in the nineteenth century.[37] In the growing body of revisionist (reverse-image) literature on this era, words like "tragic," "appalling," "rapacious," and "brutal" pop up over and over again. The point is not to demonize the politicians of this era or the pioneers or the United States Cavalry but to highlight the aggressive approach to territorial expansion that occurred under the guises of isolationism and neutrality. For example, the United States was hardly neutral in the Texas revolution.[38] Nor did the isolationist impulse prevent the expansionists in Congress from justifying the outward push against the ever-receding frontier though it entailed risks. Indeed, in the course of the westward expansion, the United States had more or less hostile encounters with England, France, Russia, Spain, and, of course, Mexico. At the century's end, the Spanish-American War confirmed that isolationism and expansionism were not mutually exclusive.

The idea of "manifest destiny" implied that American imperialism was either historically inevitable or morally imperative or both. In fact, it was neither. In the words of one prominent scholar: "The American drive for hegemony was successful. Indeed, . . . the United States is the only state in modern times to have gained regional hegemony. This impressive achievement, not some purported noble behavior toward the outside world, is the real basis of American exceptionalism in the foreign policy realm."[39] In retrospect it is clear that manifest destiny was an ideology of convenience rather than conviction. Eager to make the practice of imperialism compatible with the principles of liberal democracy, advocates of expansionist policies instinctively recognized the propaganda value of moral sugarcoating. The era of American global ascendancy was about to dawn. We explore this "dawning" in the next chapter.

---

37. In earlier periods, Native American populations were also decimated, but the death toll was more often an unintended result of European intrusion and immigration (especially English, French, and Spanish) than caused by deliberate violence. As the Pulitzer Prize–winning evolutionary biologist Jared Wilson notes, "The main killers were Old World germs to which Indians had never been exposed, and against which they therefore had neither immune nor genetic resistance. Smallpox, measles, influenza, and typhus competed for top rank among the killers. As if these had not been enough, diphtheria, malaria, mumps, pertussis [more commonly known as whooping cough], plague, tuberculosis, and yellow fever came up close behind." Jared Wilson, *Guns, Germs, and Steel: The Fate of Human Societies* (New York: Norton, 1997), pp. 210–212.

38. Thomas Bailey characterizes U.S. policy toward Texas as a case of "flagrant unneutrality": "Civilized governments are under moral obligation to have adequate neutrality laws and to enforce them. As the Texas revolution probably would not have succeeded without American support, Mexico had a genuine grievance against the United States." Bailey, *Diplomatic History*, p. 241.

39. Mearsheimer, *Tragedy of Great Power Politics*, p. 236.

AMERICAN WARS

The United States fought four wars in the nineteenth century—with Great Britain (1812), Mexico (1848), the Confederacy (1861–1865), and finally, Spain (1898). Three of these wars were declared; the Civil War was the only exception. Lincoln's desire to prevent European states from recognizing the Confederacy was one major reason for not asking Congress for a formal declaration of war against the South. This "domestic disturbance" had a foreign policy dimension that has often gone unnoticed.

The Civil War

In the nineteenth century, the textile industry was vital to Great Britain's trade-based economy. At the outbreak of the Civil War, British textile workers accounted for fully one-fifth of the British labor force. The South supplied roughly 80 percent of the cotton fiber for this thriving industry. "If the American supply should suddenly be cut off, the most important industry in England would be paralyzed, and the economic life of the British Isles would suffer a crippling blow."[40] Not surprisingly, therefore, the British public sympathized with the South in the Civil War. The British government recognized the state of belligerency between the North and South, and the British chancellor of the exchequer, William Gladstone, even spoke of the Confederate "nation" on at least one occasion. Nonetheless, when push came to shove the British remained on the sidelines and, no less important, made certain that France did too.

The closest the British came to intervention in the Civil War involved a plan of mediation that never materialized. Emperor Napoleon III of France, however, had other ideas:

> Jealous of the growing might of the United States, he was evidently eager to establish an American balance of power by dividing the powerful republic. More immediately important was the fact that he had just undertaken to establish a French puppet empire in Mexico. A permanent division of the United States into North and South, with possible Southern support as a reward for his intervention, would insure the success of his Mexican gamble. On the other hand a victory for the North would jeopardize his ambitious scheme.[41]

The British blocked French intervention despite the apparent compatibility of interests between the two European powers. In the end, the British interest in containing France outweighed the British interest in promoting a divorce between North and South. Otherwise put, Great Britain was more committed to maintain-

---

40. Ibid., p. 333.
41. Ibid., p. 338.

ing the balance of power in the Old World than to redressing the balance in the New World. Moreover, the British clearly saw these two "balances" as being interconnected and, in effect, chose to uphold the integrity of the Monroe Doctrine, a long-term political-military strategy that trumped short-term economic gains.

Imperialism is never without costs, risks, and dangers. In the case of the United States, the Civil War can be counted as one of the costs of American expansionism in the nineteenth century. President Lincoln's aim was to keep the Union from splitting asunder, not to end slavery. The issue that precipitated the secessionist movement in the South was none other than the addition of new states in the West and whether these states would enter as "free" or "slave" states. If they entered as free states, it was just a matter a time before an abolitionist majority in Congress would cast slavery into the dustbin of history.

The Spanish-American War

The balance of power in the Americas did shift decisively in the nineteenth century, a shift that was to prove irresistible and irreversible after the Civil War. The United States was fast emerging as a great power in its own right, the first major non-European power of the modern age. As if to remove all doubt, the United States declared war on Spain in 1898; in reality, it was part of a larger expansionist drive to gain control over territories outside the North American continent. The immediate object was Cuba, but the United States attacked Spain first in the Philippines! It was "an odd way to free Cuba, but in warfare an elementary rule is to hit the enemy wherever he is vulnerable."[42]

Sailing into the troubled waters of the Caribbean and the Pacific, and with an eye on the Isthmus of Panama, the United States made a spectacular debut on the world stage in 1898. American jingoists and propagandists beat the drums of war. Preachers prayed for the benighted natives of islands Americans knew nothing about. Politicians made fiery speeches laced with transparent rationalizations for armed aggression. Under the moral cover of "manifest destiny" and "the white man's burden," the United States developed a deep-water navy spurred on by a new doctrine of sea power popularized by a navy captain named Alfred Thayer Mahan.[43]

---

42. Ibid., p. 468.

43. Weinberg, *Manifest Destiny*, pp. 259–260. For a detailed account of the "white man's burden" concept in the 1890s, see pp. 283–323. The author discusses the influence of Darwinism and (false) analogies between biology and society involving the concept of "natural growth" on pp. 191–223. For a brief appraisal of Mahan's role in recasting the military-strategic theory underpinning American foreign policy, see Selig Adler, *The Isolationist Impulse: Its Twentieth Century Reaction*, paperback ed. (New York: Free Press, 1966), p. 28. According to Adler, Mahan "earned international fame by delineating the relationship in history between sea power and national greatness. Command of the sea, wrote Mahan, was necessary if the United States wished to become a great power and insure its future prosperity and security" (p. 28).

Mahan argued that landlocked nations were destined to shrivel and die on the vine. The fact that land "is almost all obstacle, the sea almost all open plain" meant that sea powers alone would have access to world markets and the resources needed to grow. Accordingly, he urged the United States "to cast aside the policy of isolation which befitted her infancy" and to undertake her "inevitable task and appointed lot in the work of upholding the common interest of civilization."[44] According to one noted historian, "In this bold stand, Mahan took a position far in advance of his fellow-imperialists who usually wished to work expansionism into the framework of isolationism."[45]

FROM ISOLATIONISM TO HEGEMONY

Far from being at odds with an isolationist mentality, expansionism can be seen as "a major expression of isolationism." According to this interpretation, Americans "adopted expansion as a means of freeing the United States from the entanglements threatened by European neighborhood."[46]

In pursuing imperialist aims, the United States was not behaving differently from other sovereign states, however. The European powers, including France, Germany, Great Britain, the Netherlands, and Portugal, were building far-flung colonial empires in the Middle East and North Africa, sub-Saharan Africa, South Asia, East Asia, and the Pacific Rim. The crucial difference between the American and European imperial experiences is that in the former case the territories acquired were largely contiguous (Alaska, Hawaii, and American Samoa were notable exceptions), and in the latter they were geographically removed (often remote) from the ruling state. This difference is significant in a military-strategic sense but not in a moral sense.

The Monroe Doctrine—the first of many foreign policy "doctrines" as it turned out—opened the door to an assertive foreign policy in the New World, and the concept of manifest destiny was a transparent fig leaf for a foreign policy designed to serve America's expansionist ambitions. At the same time, the United States remained aloof from Europe's struggles and rivalries, except to express sympathy for the cause of liberal democracy wherever it was on the move.

At the beginning of the nineteenth century, the population of the United States stood at roughly 5.3 million, somewhat smaller than the population of Mexico. By the end of the century, there were nearly 5.6 Americans for every Mexican. Between 1850 and 1900, the U.S. population more than tripled, due largely to a massive influx of European immigrants, climbing from about 23 million at mid-century to almost 76 million at the turn (see Table 2-2).

---

44. Quoted in ibid., Adler, *The Isolationist Impulse.*
45. Ibid.
46. Ibid., Weinberg, *Manifest Destiny.* p. 454.

Table 2-2 The American Hegemon

	1800	1830	1850	1880	1900
Population (thousands)					
United States	5,308	12,866	23,192	50,156	75,995
United Kingdom	15,717	24,028	27,369	34,885	41,499
Mexico	5,765	6,382	7,853	9,210	13,607
Canada	362	1,085	2,436	4,325	5,371
Relative share of world wealth (%)					
United States	n.a.	12	15	23	38
United Kingdom	n.a.	47	59	45	23

Sources: UK population figures are from B. R. Mitchell, *Abstract to British Historical Statistics* (Cambridge: Cambridge University Press, 1962), p. 608; figures for the United States, Mexico, and Canada are from B. R. Mitchell, *International Historical Statistics: The Americas, 1750–1988,* 2nd ed. (New York: Stockton, 1993), p. 4. Data on world wealth are from J. David Singer and Melvin Small, *National Material Capabilities Data, 1816–1985* (Ann Arbor, Mich.: Inter-University Consortium for Political and Social Research, 1993).

Note: Mexico became an independent state in 1821; Canada became independent in 1867. Also, the census years varied somewhat in Mexico and Canada. For example, the mid-century census was taken in 1851 in Canada and in 1854 in Mexico.

Not only did a demographic sea change occur in the Western Hemisphere, but also a cartographic one, as the rapacious new Republic carried the stars and stripes across the Mississippi and redrew the political map of North America. (See map of North American westward expansion in the front of the book.) Finally, the United States also won the race to industrialize, sprinting past even the mighty United Kingdom by 1900 (see Table 2-2). The United States "had the most powerful economy in the world and it had clearly achieved hegemony in the Western Hemisphere."[47]

In sum, America came of age as a Great Power in the second half of the nineteenth century. The urge to expand, however, was evident even before the United States became a federal republic in 1789. At first, expansionism (another name for imperialism) raised both moral and military issues for the United States. The military obstacles almost miraculously fell away in the nineteenth century. The conservative monarchies of Europe were preoccupied with checking each other and thus maintaining a balance on the Continent. The United Kingdom was content to hang onto Canada (until 1867) and found ample opportunities in Africa and Asia.

47. Mearsheimer, *Tragedy of Great Power Politics,* p. 235.

During the second half of the nineteenth century, the balance of power shifted in favor of the United States as demographic and economic indicators for that period clearly show. By the end of the nineteenth century the United States was a full-fledged Great Power with a territorial empire stretching from ocean to ocean. Neither Canada to the north nor Mexico to the south posed any threat to the United States. America had achieved the rare status of regional hegemon in the Western Hemisphere.

This achievement signified a massive acquisition of land and power. The United States could not have transformed itself from a small federal republic into a continent-wide empire without the use of offensive military force. Defensive military power does not raise moral problems for democracies, but offensive military power certainly does. By definition, democracies emphasize *consent* and decry coercion in political life.[48] In the moral reckoning of most Americans, land grabs are associated with the ways of autocracy, not democracy. Old Europe settled disputes on the battlefield; America embraces the rule of law.

The choice between power and principle was an impossible one for a nation with a conscience and an opportunity for conquest. The answer was to conquer in the name of principle rather than power, to justify conquest on exculpatory moral or religious grounds rather than admit to incriminating political motives.[49] It did not matter what the rest of the world believed about America's motives in 1900; what mattered was what America believed about itself. America's principles might have become an obstacle to its success as a great power; instead, these principles facilitated conquest because principles inspire in a way that naked power cannot. And America's power was built not only on tangible assets but also on intangibles—on pride and patriotism.

This formula worked liked magic in the nineteenth century. Some historians look back on that era as a time when America turned its back on the ideals of the Founders. To be sure, there were contradictions and hypocrisies aplenty in the politics of American imperialism. Nonetheless, America did not forget its principles in the nineteenth century, nor did it distort them. Rather, it distorted reality in order to keep its principles alive. It would be for later generations of Americans to discover the dangers in this approach.

CONCLUSION

At its founding, the United States was a loosely knit collection of former British colonies huddled along the eastern seaboard of North America, a weak fledgling

---

48. Even Theodore Roosevelt, the president who made "big stick" diplomacy his trademark, "became troubled over the relation of democracy to empire" in his later years. Howard K. Beale, *Theodore Roosevelt and the Rise of America to World Power* (1956; reprint, New York: Collier Books, 1967), p. 388.

49. Weinberg, *Manifest Destiny.*

whose very existence as a liberal democracy threatened—and was in turn threatened by—the autocratically ruled Great Powers of Europe. In the early decades of its existence, the United States attempted to bow out of the balance of power without, however, cutting itself off from Europe's markets.

The Old World was all about power, and its rulers (Europe's absolute monarchs) abhorred the New World's principles. The ingenious way America's Founders dealt with this predicament was to make a virtue of necessity. Whatever young America did to survive in a hostile world would be wrapped in the concealing cloth of principle. The nation's survival was not immediately endangered, thanks in part to the French Revolution—Europe's turmoil was America's good fortune. The stopping power of water was another piece of luck.

The ocean that separated Europe and the Western Hemisphere was a mixed blessing, however. Trade and commerce were essential to the American republic from the start, but the obstacles were formidable. Establishing a trade regime that facilitated international commerce, kept economics and politics separate, and protected neutral ships on the high seas was essential.

Because the United States lacked the tangible elements of power, its leaders stressed the intangible elements—above all, the moral and legal principles of Western civilization and the ideals of the Enlightenment. This moral strategy had a certain pragmatic basis—America's early decision makers had good reason to hope the appeal to Enlightenment values would resonate in Europe precisely because these values were quintessentially European in origin.

The notion of American exceptionalism, however defined, has at times given the United States an important edge in foreign affairs. America rarely questions the rightness of any cause it champions, any land it invades, any war it fights. This self-assurance in a morally ambiguous world is a source of strength hardly less important than America's arsenal of deadly weapons. Where it came from is a supreme irony, because the origins of this uniquely American power source trace back to the early days of the Republic, when America was weak and vulnerable. Like a defense lawyer who argues the law when the facts weigh against the accused, the Founders argue eloquently that moral principles must guide politics within *and among* nations, as though power had no place in a properly ordered world. In fact, they had led a revolution for independence rather than liberty, but they had a keen understanding of the need for a new kind of political rhetoric and they wisely chose the language of liberty.

Washington, Adams, and Jefferson could not have imagined how future generations of American politicians—often individuals of lesser intellect and little learning—would manipulate and misuse this idealism in the pursuit of personal as well as national power maximization. The latter was clearly the motive behind the brutal and relentless westward expansion into lands inhabited by

Native Americans, who posed no threat and, in fact, were largely defenseless against the "guns, germs, and steel" of the invaders.[50]

What made America's westward expansion possible was a peculiar series of linked circumstances. Maintaining a balance of power in Europe was in America's national interest because an all-conquering European state (a hegemon) might have attempted a comeback in the New World. However, it so happened that after the defeat of Napoleon in 1815, none of the several European land powers was a potential regional hegemon until the rise of a unified German state tilted the balance in Germany's favor. It was equally fortunate that the United Kingdom was an effective offshore balancer. This meant that the United States could pursue its goal of regional hegemony without fear of outside interference. America's westward expansion—the completion of the work of the American Revolution—owed its success to the British Royal Navy as much as to the U.S. Cavalry. This point is generally glossed over in the legends of "frontier America."

Foreign policy is always a balancing act for Great Powers. Keeping would-be aggressors in check while maximizing one's own power is the primary objective. For most state actors, the choice is between balancing and buck-passing: that is, a participant in the international system normally must confront a would-be aggressor or pass the buck (if there are other Great Powers who can catch it). In the nineteenth century, as we have seen, America was able to bow out of Europe's power struggles altogether. This strategy ceased to be viable after America emerged as a great power—indeed, the most dynamic great power of all. Thus, as we will see in a later chapter, the United States would attempt to pass the buck in World War I before stepping in as the offshore balancer when the British faltered in that role. In other words, America would have no choice but to "play the game" in the twentieth century.

In sum, the United States grew from an isolated fledgling Republic in 1800 into a Great Power in 1900. In so doing, power and principle mutually reinforced America's bid for regional hegemony. America was constrained less by its principles than by its pragmatism in the nineteenth century. Where power and principle conflicted, America's leaders were adept at rationalizing the nation's actions. This skill was essential to America's success as a rising great power, but, as we will see in subsequent chapters, it has a serious downside as well.

---

50. Diamond, *Guns, Germs, and Steel.*

3

Hegemony and Insolvency
The Burdens of a Great Power

OVERVIEW

This chapter spans the period from the Spanish-American War to World War I. I raise the question of solvency in foreign policy and argue that America experienced growing pains in the first half of the twentieth century: it was the greatest of the Great Powers but it had still not completely shed the isolationist mindset associated with the early days of the Republic. I explore the origins of America's interventionist policies in Latin America during the presidencies of William McKinley and Theodore Roosevelt. Finally, I examine the foreign policy of Woodrow Wilson and ask whether Wilson was the soft-headed idealist his critics have often made him out to be. By looking at his actions, as well as his words, I conclude that Wilson was definitely a political realist before the American entry into World War I in 1917. Even after World War I, I find, Wilson's commitment to the League of Nations and the idea of "collective security" was the result of a marriage of idealism and realism—in other words, although the notion of "collective security" called for daring diplomacy, it did not represent a total departure from political realism, as is often supposed.

Foreign policy is the stuff of international politics. Conversely, the international system shapes the foreign policies of participating states. When power ratios in the world order change, the effect can be similar to the shifting of the earth's tectonic plates. Tremors are certain and a massively destructive upheaval is possible. Earthquakes commonly occur along old "fault lines" and stress gives rise to new ones. These fault lines are often invisible to all but the best-trained eyes. The analogy to the international system is striking.

At the end of the nineteenth century, the subterranean "plates" along a major political fault line on the European Continent were beginning to cause tremors. The line ran between the dynamic new state, Germany, which threatened to upset Europe's equilibrium, and a declining old one, France.[1] The British interest was to act as the "keeper of the balance." But whereas Great Britain ultimately was able

---

1. The German Empire was founded in 1871. Otto von Bismarck became the German chancellor. The allied German states had just defeated France on the battlefield. It had taken the German forces barely six weeks to defeat the French. This war not only humiliated France but also greatly diminished its power and prestige; the new German Reich annexed Alsace-Lorraine as a result of this war.

CHRONOLOGY, 1900–1918

1900   Boxer Rebellion in China

1901   President McKinley is assassinated; Vice President Theodore Roosevelt becomes nation's youngest president (the twenty-sixth)

1902   Great Britain, Germany, and Italy blockade Venezuelan ports

1903   United States acquires territory for Panama Canal; Orville and Wilbur Wright make first successful airplane test-flights at Kitty Hawk, N.C.

1904   Roosevelt Corollary of the Monroe Doctrine enunciated; outbreak of war between Russia and Japan

1907   Hague Conference elaborates the rules of war and international arbitration procedures

1908   Central authority begins to crumble in China; Henry Ford introduces Model T

1910   Japan annexes Korea

1911   First transcontinental airplane flight; revolution in China

1913   Woodrow Wilson becomes twenty-eighth president; United States blockades Mexico in support of revolution

1914   World War I breaks out; Wilson declares U.S. neutrality

1915   United States lands troops in Haiti (treaty makes Haiti virtual U.S. protectorate); first transcontinental telephone call

1916   United States establishes military government in Dominican Republic

1917   United States enters war in Europe; October Revolution overthrows monarchy in Russia; Lenin takes charge of new Bolshevik-led government in November and purges all rivals for power

1918   Armistice signed November 11 ending World War I; civil war breaks out in Russia

to carry off this role in the past, it would take the intervention of an insular *non-European* power, the United States, to subdue the German Reich and prevent the establishment of a hegemonic state on the Continent.[2]

The United States was reluctant to break the tradition of nonentanglement in European affairs, reluctant to turn its attention from the Western Hemisphere to Europe. As a rising insular state, America would soon discover that its freedom to choose a foreign policy divorced from Europe, was constrained by circumstances and exigencies beyond its control. A new *global* international system was rapidly eclipsing the old Eurocentric balance-of-power system. The two parts of Europe, east and west, were moving farther apart. The United States and Russia were soon to supplant Great Britain and France as archrivals. The new challengers, Germany and Japan, would make spectacular but ultimately disastrous bids for dominance in Europe and Asia, respectively.

In the aftershock of two massive political upheavals (aptly named "world wars") caused by the east-west fault slip on the Continent, the very foundations of American foreign policy would crack and finally crumble away. The story of this transformation begins with the run-up to World War I.

THE CONCEPT OF SOLVENCY

Solvency is basic to the success of all public policy, be it foreign or domestic. In foreign affairs, solvency exists when a nation's commitments accurately reflect its vital interests and do not exceed its capabilities. By a quirk of fate, it did not become a serious issue in the nineteenth century, owing to

> the adoption by Monroe, Jefferson, and Madison of the concert with Great Britain. By that act of statesmanship the foreign policy of the United States became solvent—its foreign commitments were in accord with its vital interests and the means to sustain the commitments were more than adequate. Then, and only then, did foreign relations cease to be great domestic issues: with respect to the strong powers of the world, American relations were firmly settled.[3]

---

2. For an intriguing historical interpretation along these lines based on a systemic theory of international politics, see Ludwig Dehio, *The Precarious Balance: Four Centuries of the European Power Struggle,* trans. Charles Fullman (New York: Vintage Books, 1962), esp. pp. 264–266; originally published in German in 1948. Dehio sees geopolitics and balance-of-power considerations as the keys to explaining modern European history. He argues that Europe unwittingly spawned the "young powers" (especially the United States) through competition for colonies across the seas. These upstarts eventually displaced the old European powers and thus moved the center stage of world politics off the Continent for the first time since the dawn of the modern state system in about the sixteenth century.

3. Walter Lippmann, *U.S. Foreign Policy: Shield of the Republic* (Boston: Little, Brown, 1943), pp. 82–83.

In this incisive passage, Walter Lippmann revealed the secret of America's success in the seminal period between the enunciation of the Monroe Doctrine in 1823 and the end of the Spanish-American War in 1898—the age of American expansionism and manifest destiny. In surveying the period between the Spanish-American War and World War II, Lippmann concluded that American foreign policy slid into insolvency after 1899: "Accordingly, the nation has been deeply divided throughout this period. It has been divided on the issues of imperialism, on intervention in the first World War, on participation in the settlement of that war, on reconstruction after that war, on measures to prevent the second World War, on preparedness for it, on intervention in it, and on what course to take when it ends."[4] Insolvency in foreign affairs, in Lippmann's view, was the cause of domestic political dissension during this period, much as bankruptcy in a corporation will cause "demoralizing dissension about income and expenditures." Lippmann acknowledged that the analogy was not exact: "Nevertheless there is a grim accounting if the budget of foreign relations is insolvent. The accounting is in war. Insolvency in foreign policy will mean that preventable wars are not prevented, that unavoidable wars are fought without being adequately prepared for them, and that settlements are made which are the prelude to a new cycle of unprevented wars, unprepared wars, and unworkable settlements."[5]

The question of solvency did not spring full blown until the outbreak of World War I, but the winds of change were stirring, and occasionally gusting, from 1898 to 1914. William McKinley, Teddy Roosevelt, William Howard Taft, and Woodrow Wilson resided in the White House during this period. Roosevelt and Wilson—so different in demeanor, outlook, and temperament—both followed in the footsteps of McKinley. The imprints of these footsteps were visible in many places beyond the borders of the continental United States. This fact would be closely linked to another: in the half-century between 1898 and 1945, the United States would find itself at war with European powers three times, twice on European soil. What course Washington, Jefferson, Madison, and Monroe would have chosen in the circumstances is impossible to know, but they would probably puzzle over the strange twist of history that led to America's "entanglements" in Europe, Asia, and everywhere else on the face of the earth.

LATIN AMERICA: BIG STICK DIPLOMACY

The treaty with Spain that ended the war, signed in Paris on December 10, 1898, was a watershed in American history. Under its terms, a humiliated Spain gave up sovereignty over Cuba and ceded the Philippines, Puerto Rico, and Guam outright to the United States. Spain's abject submission was greeted with less than

4. Ibid.
5. Ibid., p. 84.

universal enthusiasm in the U.S. Congress. In fact, it touched off one of the most acrimonious foreign policy debates in American history.

The anti-imperialists included such illustrious names as Charles William Elliot, president of Harvard University; E. L. Godkin, editor of the *Nation* and the *New York Evening Post;* William James and Charles Eliot Norton, both distinguished Harvard professors; James Russell Lowell, founder and co-editor with Norton of the *North American Review;* Samuel Gompers, president of the American Federation of Labor; former president Grover Cleveland and his secretary of war William Endicott; the famed steel magnate and philanthropist Andrew Carnegie; and Mark Twain. The anti-imperialists also had powerful allies in Congress, most notably Thomas B. Reed, the brilliant and fiercely independent Republican Speaker of the House from Maine.[6]

The anti-imperialists pointed out that the United States had never before acquired overseas territories that were not contiguous and that could not therefore be readily converted into new states. The Philippines and Puerto Rico were remote and densely populated lands, home to alien peoples, languages, and cultures. We had entered the war ostensibly to free Cuba, critics pointed out, and ended up "some 8000 miles away trying to rivet shackles on 7 million protesting peoples."[7] The Senate debate was both historic and highly vitriolic. It turned into a showdown and foreshadowed others to come. The anti-imperialists denounced and inveighed against annexation on a high moral and philosophical ground and warned darkly of unintended future consequences. In the indomitable Tom Reed, they had a trump card, too. But in the end even Speaker Reed could not resist the tidal wave of expansionist fervor that swept across the nation in the late 1890s.[8]

The Spanish-American War signaled the end of the domestic consensus over American foreign policy and the beginning of a new era. For the first time in our history perennial questions would arise about the solvency of a doctrine-driven interventionist approach to international politics that in the nation's second century would severely erode the moral, political, and military constraints that were a hallmark of its first 100 years.

---

6. See Barbara Tuchman, *The Proud Tower: A Portrait of the World before the War, 1890–1914* (New York: Macmillan, 1966), pp. 117–167.

7. Thomas M. Bailey, *A Diplomatic History of the American People,* 7th ed. (New York: Appleton-Century-Crofts, 1964), p. 475.

8. The "passionately antiwar" Reed held firmly to his position until the last two days of March 1898, when the publication of the report on the investigation into the sinking of the *Maine* "forced . . . the Speaker . . . to surrender to the onslaughts of the rapidly increasing interventionist forces." Walter LaFeber, *The New Empire: An Interpretation of American Expansion, 1860–1898* (Ithaca: Cornell University Press, 1963), p. 402.

Cuba: "The Monroe Doctrine is Gone!"

In the debate over annexation, anti-imperialists condemned a foreign policy at odds with the Declaration of Independence and the spirit of the American Revolution. The United States had fought against foreign tyranny and was now acting like a foreign tyrant itself. Tyranny begets tyranny: soon it would infect our own domestic life. Besides, opponents argued, the United States already had plenty of land; colonial dependencies would be a liability more than an asset. Equally prophetic was the argument that by meddling in the Far East (that is, outside the Western Hemisphere) the United States was violating its own principle of noninterference. "The Monroe Doctrine is gone!" bellowed Senator George Hoar of Massachusetts.[9]

In retrospect it is clear that the Spanish-American War was the first giant step toward a worldwide policing (or "conflict management") system maintained and operated by the United States during the cold war. In the words of Albert Beveridge:

> Fate has written our policy for us; the trade of the world must and shall be ours. . . . We will cover the ocean with our merchant marine. We will build a navy to the measure of our greatness. . . . American law, American order, American civilization will plant themselves on those shores hitherto bloody and benighted but by those agencies of God henceforth to be made beautiful and bright.[10]

It is ironic that Cuba was the object of so much controversy at the turn of the century. Almost exactly six decades later Fidel Castro would lead a popular revolution against a corrupt Cuban dictatorship backed by the United States. Victorious, Castro would create a socialist state and throw himself into the arms of America's archrival, the Soviet Union. This would prove to be the most serious challenge to the integrity of the Monroe Doctrine in American history.

The imperialists (who were in the majority) countered with bravado and moralistic incantations. They felt God had anointed America. Thus, it was our divine mission to spread civilization and Christianity in the world. Rudyard Kipling, the famed British poet who came to be revered by American imperialists, waxed eloquent:

> Take up the White Man's burden—
> Ye dare not stoop to less—
> Nor call too loud on Freedom
> To cloke your weariness.

---

9. Ibid.
10. Quoted in Tuchman, *Proud Tower*, p. 154.

The *Omaha World-Herald* ran an editorial that aptly concluded: "In other words, Mr. Kipling would have Uncle Sam take up John Bull's burden," precisely what the United States did in the coming century: Great Britain had been the "keeper of the balance" in Europe, now the United States would play that role on a global scale. The role was strikingly similar, but the stage was far larger and the stakes much higher in the twentieth century. At the turn, the curtain was just beginning to go up.

The Panama Canal: Testing Big Stick Diplomacy

In 1900 the idea of building a canal across the Isthmus of Panama, the narrow land bridge connecting Central and South America, was not new. But it was given a big boost in the 1890s by two wars—one fought in Asia and one in the Caribbean. Japan's victory over China in 1895, which set off alarm bells in Europe and the United States, "gave urgency and cogency to the demand for the Isthmian Canal and to Captain Mahan's contention that Cuba in the Caribbean as well as Hawaii in the Pacific were necessary for the Canal's strategic defense." In the Senate, Henry Cabot Lodge echoed Mahan's argument that Cuba would be a future "necessity."[11]

The running Senate debate over American foreign policy in the 1890s is one of the most memorable in history, one that presaged the events and outcomes of the Spanish-American War.[12] The United States emerged from that war as an Asian power with new interests and assets to protect. The war itself had demonstrated the importance of a canal. The journey from Puget Sound around South America to Cuban waters was three times the distance that it would have been had there been a shortcut through the Panamanian isthmus. In the years between 1850 and 1900, the United States had extended its western border all the way to the Pacific, which in itself was a compelling reason to pursue the canal project.

However, the problems it raised were complicated both technically and politically. Imagine digging a "ditch" between the Caribbean Sea and the Pacific Ocean through miles of swampy, mosquito-infested terrain in tropical heat with

---

11. Ibid., pp. 145–146.

12. The debate ranged well beyond the U.S. Capitol. Newspaper editors in those days jumped into political fights with a vigor we can barely imagine in these times of editorial timidity, shrinking readership, and vanishing independence. Distinguished members of the academic community also weighed in. President Charles William Eliot of Harvard, for example, chose a Washington forum to denounce jingoism as "offensive" and declare it "absolutely foreign to American society, . . . yet some of my friends endeavor to pass it off as patriotic Americanism." Eliot was not alone in his vehement opposition to the militarism advocated by Mahan and a growing imperialist chorus. "The building of a navy and the presence of a large standing army mean . . . the abandonment of what is characteristically American. . . . The building of battleships is English and French policy. It should never be ours." Ibid.

century-old technology! Politically, the problem was twofold: first, the real estate involved belonged to Colombia, not the United States. Second, Great Britain also had a vital interest in the project, one that the United States had recognized diplomatically and legally in 1850.[13]

The British, who were the only power on earth in a position to block American designs on Panama, decided to bow out. The Hay-Pauncefote Treaty signed in November 1901 gave the United States a free hand to build, operate, and *fortify* a canal. Britain's assent to fortification was the key; it would be an American canal under American control.

On November 3, 1903, Panama rose up against Colombia, declaring itself sovereign and independent; the United States recognized the new state of Panama three days later, as American warships blocked Colombian forces from landing to quell the revolt. Colombia refused to recognize the independence of Panama but was powerless to obtain redress or compensation of any kind. It was in Panama that "big stick" diplomacy was first put to the test. Teddy Roosevelt's famous words "I took Panama" were not mere bombast. They were true. What is more, they revealed an attitude that over time hardened into set policy. Given the resulting tendency of North Americans to trample on the territorial rights of South Americans, it is small wonder that "Yankee, go home!" became a common sentiment down there.

When the canal opened in 1914, Europe was careening into World War I. France would fall to Germany in short order, and two European empires (Russia and Austria-Hungary) would collapse. While Europe was self-destructing, the United States was "taking care of business" in its own immediate sphere of interest. In the spring of 1914, with the Mexican Revolution in full swing, U.S. forces occupied Vera Cruz. War was narrowly averted, but tensions continued to build. Following a cross-border raid by Francisco "Pancho" Villa in March 1916, President Woodrow Wilson ordered a punitive military incursion into Mexico under the command of Gen. John J. Pershing. U.S. troops stayed in Mexico for nearly a year but eventually withdrew, having failed to accomplish anything except to inflame anti-"gringo" sentiment in Mexico.

By this time, the United States had made its intention of acting as the hemispheric "policeman" crystal clear. When Venezuela defaulted on its foreign debt in 1902 and turmoil threatened European nationals, Great Britain, Germany, and Italy intervened. At first the United States acquiesced, but when history began to repeat itself the following year in the Dominican Republic, the pugnacious American president and hawks in Congress were ready for a face-off. In May 1904

---

13. Under the Clayton-Bulwer Treaty (April 19, 1850) both parties pledged to cooperate in any efforts to facilitate construction of a canal and never to fortify or seek to exercise control over it. Article I of the treaty stipulated that neither party would "occupy" or "colonize" or establish "dominion" over "any part of Central America."

President Roosevelt decided that the United States would not interfere with any government that paid its debts and kept its house in order, but that misconduct and malfeasance justified intervention "by some civilized nation, and in the Western Hemisphere the United States cannot ignore this duty." He argued: "If we are willing to let Germany or England act as the policemen of the Caribbean, then we can afford not to interfere when gross wrongdoing occurs. But if we intend to say 'Hands off' to the powers of Europe, sooner or later we must keep order ourselves."[14] Historians would come to know this new policy as the "Roosevelt Corollary" to the Monroe Doctrine.

The Roosevelt Corollary was a harbinger of a great change in American foreign policy, one that reflected the changing world order as well as the growth of American power. During the course of the nineteenth century, the United States had gradually and imperceptibly rotated 180 degrees from being a postrevolutionary, anticolonial state in sympathy with popular revolutions suspicious of the Great Powers to being a Great Power itself. Having thoroughly satisfied its appetite for territory, America was preoccupied with maintaining order and perpetuating the status quo. But at the turn of the century, the process of reinventing America's role in the world was just beginning.

THE NEW FRONTIER: OPENING DOORS IN ASIA

At the end of the nineteenth century, the United States became entangled in Asian politics. "We are face to face with a strange destiny," wrote a *Washington Post* editor in 1898. "The taste of empire is in the mouth of the people even as the taste of blood in the jungle. It means an imperial policy, the Republic renascent, taking her place with the armed nations."[15] In the space of only two decades, the United States made the transition from continental-regional power to world power and from a strategic policy of quasi-isolationism, territorial expansion, and nonacceptance of the status quo to one of interventionism in defense of the status quo.

When the United States broke out of its self-imposed isolation in the Western Hemisphere, it looked toward Asia, not toward Europe. In the mid-nineteenth century, the overwhelming majority of European-Americans knew nothing about Asia except that it existed and that its peoples and cultures were "different." It was an exotic, inscrutable place on the other side of a vast ocean that was at once an invitation to adventurers and traders and a barrier to invasion

---

14. The quotations are from Roosevelt's letters to Secretary of State Elihu Root, May 20 and June 7, 1904, cited in Henry F. Pringle, *Theodore Roosevelt: A Biography* (New York: Harvest Books, 1931), pp. 294–295.

15. Robert Endicott Osgood, *Ideals and Self-Interest in America's Foreign Relations: The Great Transformation of the Twentieth Century* (Chicago: University of Chicago Press, 1953), p. 48.

and conquest. Japan was the sole Asian power to participate in an arena of intense international competition as a player rather than a pawn.

Japan's Rising Sun

When Commodore Matthew C. Perry steamed into the picturesque Bay of Edo (present-day Tokyo) in the summer of 1853, the Japanese were astonished; they had never seen a steamship. Thus casually began the U.S. relationship with Japan, a country that was poised to undergo a transformation of world-historical impact.

Japan was a provincial feudal-agrarian society in the 1850s. Neither Perry nor anyone else imagined that by the end of the century Japan would be well on its way toward becoming a modern, unified, and militarily powerful state without equal in Asia.[16] In 1895, when Japan fought China for control of Korea and won, it "caused a sudden recognition of Japan as a rising power in the East and startled Kaiser Wilhelm into coining a phrase, *die Gelbe Gefahr* ("the Yellow Peril").[17] Only the "triple intervention" of France, Germany, and Russia prevented Japan from colonizing Port Arthur and the Korean Peninsula. A decade later, Japan fought and defeated Russia, demonstrating its prowess as a naval power as well as the "samurai spirit" of its soldiers.

The story of Japan's transformation is beyond the scope of this book.[18] Suffice it to say that its significance for world history—as well as for international relations in our own time—is enormous. Together with America's coming of age, the Japanese ascent to Great Power status signaled the end of an era, the last stage in the relatively short life span (less than three centuries) of an international system in which Europe was center stage, America was a British understudy, and Asia was offstage. Gone were the days when Europe ruled the world.

China's Falling Star

China, unlike Japan, was an empire in decay in the second half of the nineteenth century. Power abhors a vacuum. The political disintegration of China created temptations and opportunities that proved irresistible for the Great Powers of Europe, as well as the United States and Japan. The emergence of Japan as a potential East Asian hegemonic state lent a sense of urgency to the efforts of France, Germany, Great Britain, Russia, and the United States to maneuver for

---

16. Ironically, the Japanese eventually came to view Perry as a hero. On July 14, 1901, forty-eight years to the day after he first knocked on the door, the Japanese government erected a monument in his honor in Tokyo Bay.

17. Tuchman, *Proud Tower*, p. 145.

18. For a succinct description of this transformation, see Paul Kennedy, *The Rise and Fall of the Great Powers* (New York: Vintage Books, 1989), pp. 206–209.

trade concessions and spheres of influence in China. The burgeoning Chinese market was tantalizing enough, but the desire to preempt Japan's conquering and colonizing whatever parts of North Asia it wanted (especially Korea and Manchuria) gave impetus to the European powers.

When the Boxer Rebellion broke out in 1900, it prompted "the dispatch of a full-scale international relief expedition, mounted by British bluejackets, Russian Cossacks, French colonial infantry, Italian Bersaglieri and detachments of the German and Austro-Hungarian armies, as well as Japanese guardsmen and United States marines."[19] Note that this "expedition" was launched without the aid of an umbrella international organization. But everyone wanted access to China, including the United States.

The American interest in Asia at the turn of the century illustrates how the end result of a policy is seldom evident at its inception. The acquisition of the Philippines in 1898 gave the United States a significant presence in Asia and a stake in the outcome of any present or future conflict in the region. But Americans did not suddenly "discover" China in the 1890s. In fact, the United States had piggybacked on the British policy of extracting extraterritorial rights and special economic privileges from a crumbling Chinese imperial government ever since the British forced the door to China open in 1842.[20] We pursued a "me-too" policy that betrayed a deep-rooted tendency toward hypocrisy in foreign affairs:

> [B]y our own revolutionary tradition we were conscientiously opposed to colonialism, suspicious of European machinations, a bit holier-than-they in our early abstention from empire and even from power politics. Yet at the same time by demanding most-favored-nation treatment we were quick to enjoy all the semi-colonial fruits of extraterritoriality. . . . The result was to encourage in our traditional policy a disconcerting split between humanitarian ideals and strategic realism.[21]

As a "player" in the contest for access to the lucrative and limitless market that China represented in the minds of westerners, the United States was, in a sense, on the side of the angels. It was in America's national interest to defend the "territorial and administrative integrity" of China. Whether idealism had anything at all to do with it is highly debatable.[22]

---

19. John Keegan, *The First World War* (New York: Vintage Books, 1998), pp. 14–15.

20. John King Fairbank, *The United States and China*, 3rd ed. (Cambridge: Harvard University Press, 1971), pp. 283–295. Fairbank detected a "curious ambivalence" in our early China policy, which he elaborated as follows: "The principal reality was the unequal treaty system but since this had been fought for and was still maintained by British and French arms, the United States government felt little primary responsibility for it. Our principal thought was to get our share of privilege and opportunity, a me-too policy" (p. 289).

21. Ibid., p. 290.

22. The confusion of principles and propaganda may be accidental or intentional, but either way its practical value in the realm of "public diplomacy" (the polite term for propaganda) cannot be denied.

The British, however, had the biggest stake by far in the Open Door policy. If China were to be carved up into a patchwork of colonized territories, British commercial interests would suffer most.[23] Once again, the United States enjoyed the benefits of the long-standing Anglo-American entente.[24] However, by the turn of the century, the scale of relative costs and benefits was tilting toward equipoise.

The trailblazers on the U.S. path beyond the hemispheric perimeter were Presidents William McKinley (1897–1901) and Theodore Roosevelt (1901–1909) and Secretary of State John Hay (1898–1905). Secretary Hay made overtures to the European powers regarding China's status. His Open Door Notes in 1899 are famous for attempting (unsuccessfully) to restrain the imperialistic appetites of the Europeans. But what is seldom mentioned is that America's new acquisitions in the Pacific "outstripped those of the other powers": "While the Germans were securing a naval base at Kiaochow in Shantung and the Russians at Port Arthur, we got potential bases in Hawaii, Samoa, and the Philippines. Similarly while the European powers were seeking spheres of interest for commercial exploitation in China, we annexed an Asian archipelago. This American expansion is all the more significant because it was so largely unpremeditated in the public mind."[25]

America's China policy prior to the Communist victory in 1949 was synonymous with the Open Door doctrine that consisted of two main tenets: the integrity of China and equal treatment. In practical terms the latter meant that all foreigners would enjoy "equal opportunity" and "competition" would be "fair." The United States made passive attempts to reinforce the "integrity" element of the Open Door doctrine in 1915 and again in 1930 by a policy of nonrecognition—that is, we refused to recognize Japan's control over any territory formerly ruled or presently claimed by China. This doctrine, however pious, proved powerless to stop Japanese advances in the 1930s as did Secretary of State Cordell Hull's attempt at moral deterrence using the principle of nonintervention. In the time after World War II and right down to the present day, of course, we have embraced interventionism with few, if any, geographic or other constraints.

---

23. In the 1890s, when French, German, and Russian encroachments in China became an issue, Great Britain controlled as much as 80 percent of China's foreign trade. See Alexander DeConde, *A History of American Foreign Policy,* vol. 1: *Growth to World Power (1700–1914)* (New York: Sribner's, 1978), p. 326, and Fairbank, *United States and China,* p. 296.

24. The mere fact that the United States had not used force to gain concessions in China did little to soften Chinese impressions of America. The mandarins who advised the Chinese emperor on foreign affairs were wise to American complicity in British policy. See Warren Cohen, *America's Response to China: An Interpretive History of Sino-American Relations* (New York: Wiley, 1971), p. 30.

25. Fairbank, *United States and China,* pp. 295–296.

WORLD WAR I: REPLACING THE OLD ORDER

Few would dispute the historian John Keegan's verdict that World War I was "tragic and unnecessary." Prior to August 1914, nobody saw it coming. Hostilities of some sort perhaps, a skirmish in the Balkans, maybe even a showdown at sea between Britain and Germany to induce the kaiser to abandon the decade-long naval arms race.[26] But nobody could imagine the kind of war that was coming, the murderous killing power of modern weapons, the fighting spirit of Europe's new armor-clad nationalism, or the treachery and lethal stupidity of monarchs, politicians, and military commanders who would allow it to happen.

The fate of millions of young men was sealed in the first month of the war. In the wake of the bloody but indecisive battle of the Marne came the "slow deadly sinking into the stalemate of trench warfare."[27] The death toll would be staggering, on a scale not witnessed at any other time or place in human history, "sucking up lives at the rate of 5,000 and sometimes 50,000 a day, absorbing munitions, energy, money, brains and trained men" like a monstrous, bloodthirsty sponge.[28] August 1914 was a deadly month, but it was only a dress rehearsal.

> By the end of 1914, four months after the outbreak of the Great War, 300,000 Frenchmen had been killed, 600,000 wounded. . . . By the end of the war nearly two million Frenchmen were dead. . . . The heaviest casualties had been suffered by the youngest year-groups: between 27 per cent and 30 per cent of the conscript classes of 1912–1915. . . . Among the five million wounded of the war, moreover, several hundred thousand were numbered as "*grands mutilés*," soldiers who had lost limbs or eyes. [29]

German war losses were on a comparable scale. More than a third of all German males between the ages of nineteen and twenty-two when the war broke out were killed. For each year of the war the death rate averaged 465,000. In all, more than 2 million Germans died "in the war, or of wounds in its aftermath."[30] Proportionately, however, Serbia sacrificed the largest number of its citizens in the war, roughly 15 percent of the total population, compared with 2–3 percent of the British, French, and German populations.

World War I was a fight-to-the-death of the kind that George Washington and Thomas Jefferson did not countenance when they warned against getting involved in Europe's imbroglios. Indeed, President Woodrow Wilson vigorously

---

26. On the Anglo-German naval rivalry, see Sidney B. Fay, *The Origins of the World War*, vol. 1: *Before Sarajevo* (New York: Free Press, 1966), pp. 233–245.
27. Barbara Tuchman, *The Guns of August* (New York: Dell, 1962), p. 487.
28. Ibid., p. 488.
29. Keegan, *First World War*, pp. 6–7.
30. Ibid., p. 7.

sought to avoid direct involvement, and did so until mid-1917, ignoring earlier pretexts and provocations. American neutrality was not rewarded, however. The sinking of the *Lusitania* in 1915, with loss of American life, outraged the public. After two years of unsuccessful negotiations, in March 1917, the Germans renewed unrestricted warfare, sinking three American ships homeward bound. On April 6, 1917, at Wilson's request Congress declared war.

In the two decades following the war with Spain, the United States had built a world-class navy, but the army was inexperienced in combat and unimpressive on paper, numbering only 107,641 men. There was no "military-industrial complex" in existence at that time, no powerful arms industry lobby in Washington: indeed, the army had to rely on European (largely French) heavy weapons, including tanks, artillery, and airplanes. Only the U.S. Marine Corps was battle ready to any degree in the spring of 1917.

But the power of the American economy and the spirit of its people had never before been tested in a major foreign war when the country was united in common cause. The Civil War had demonstrated the willingness of American soldiers to fight and die for a cause they believed in, but that was a fratricidal contest, fought half a century earlier, with little value as an inkling of what American entry into this war might mean. Hence, a top-ranking German naval officer, Admiral Eduard von Capelle, could tell the budgetary committee of the German parliament on January 31, 1917, that "America from a military point of view means nothing and again nothing and for a third time nothing."

By March 1918, "nothing" had materialized into 318,000 American soldiers on French soil. By the war's end the enlisted strength of American ground forces numbered nearly 4 million men.[31] The United States went from "nothing" to being Germany's worst nightmare in the time-span of a single year.

WILSON'S NEW WORLD ORDER

The United States belatedly entered the Great War on the Continent not for moral or even political reasons, but out of a sense of military-strategic necessity.[32] Walter Lippmann (writing in the maelstrom of World War II) put the matter succinctly in 1943: "in the first World War it was no longer possible for the United States to be neutral towards Germany when in 1917 she threatened, by conquering Britain, to become our nearest neighbor." Lippmann argued that in the twentieth century America's next-door neighbors, geo-strategically speaking, were Britain, Japan, and Soviet Russia. In other words, the Monroe Doctrine would

---

31. Keegan, *First World War*, p. 373.
32. Arthur Link, for example, notes "Wilson's apparent fear that the threat of a German victory imperiled the balance of power." Arthur S. Link, *Wilson the Diplomatist: A Look at His Major Foreign Policies* (Chicago: Quadrangle Books, 1965), p. 88.

remain in effect, but a policy of isolation backed by a strategy of "passive defense" would no longer suffice to protect America's hemisphere of interest.[33]

Collective Security and the League of Nations

Wilson's concept of a new world order represented a radical departure from the old one. The impulse behind his ardent search for an alternative to the balance-of-power system was understandable enough. To Wilson and many of his contemporaries the so-called "balance" was inherently unstable and the "system" was in actuality a "war system" rather than a structure well suited to maintain the peace.[34] The Founding Fathers were right about Europe's proclivity toward war. That proclivity had not disappeared or even declined in the century between the Napoleonic Wars and World War I, contrary to what defenders of this equilibrium theory say. There had been many small wars in Europe during this period, culminating in the most destructive and deadly conflagration ever. In this context, President Wilson's quest for an alternative to the balance of power appears noble and imperative.

The causes of World War I in Wilson's view can be extrapolated from the characteristics of the international system that produced it.[35] These most notably included the European political-diplomatic ploy of forging behind-the-back alliances and engaging rivals in arms races. The Anglo-German naval arms race, according to this view, had acquired a life and momentum of its own and contributed in no small measure to the tinderbox that was Europe in 1914.

This was the background to Wilson's famous dictum calling for "open covenants openly arrived at." The most basic cause of war, in Wilson's view, was the balance-of-power system itself. Wilson relentlessly laid bare the inadequacies of the old system, but he was by no means the first or only public figure here

---

33. Lippmann, *U.S. Foreign Policy,* pp. 92–93. For the broader argument Lippmann makes see chap. 6 in its entirety, pp. 81–113.

34. For a lucid discussion of the logical and empirical problems entailed in the balance-of-power concept, see Inis Claude Jr., *Power and International Relations* (New York: Random House, 1962), pp. 11–93.

35. On a personal note, when I was researching my doctoral dissertation at the Library of Congress in the late 1960s, I met an elderly gentleman who possessed an encyclopedic knowledge of World War I and who was there at the library day in and day out doing research on the causes of that cataclysm. It turned out that he had been traveling or studying in Europe when the war broke out and he still carried vivid memories of the events that for my generation were "only" history—so vivid, in fact, that he was endeavoring to write the definitive book on the causes of the Great War. Unfortunately, he was still trying to get "the big picture," as he put it, fully half a century later! The anecdote is revealing, not so much as an example of "writer's block" on a grand scale, but as a glimpse of the disorienting psychological effect and cognitive confusion the "war to end wars" evoked in the minds of thoughtful people everywhere.

and abroad to advocate collective security. On the contrary, according to the author of an award-winning study, "there had emerged by the end of World War I, a reasonably coherent doctrine of collective security, a body of thought which prescribed a new system for the management of power in international relations."[36]

Exactly what did Wilson have in mind? In theory, collective security sounds like a practical alternative to the self-operating balance-of-power system:

> [T]he concept of collective security involves the creation of an international system in which the danger of aggressive warfare by any state is to be met by the avowed determination of virtually all other states to exert pressure of every necessary variety—moral, diplomatic, economic, and military—to frustrate attack upon any state. The expectation of collective resistance to aggression is conceived as a deterrent threat to states which might be tempted to misuse their power and as a promise of security to all states which might be subject to attack. The scheme is collective in the fullest sense; it purports to provide security for all states, by the action of all states, against all states which might challenge the existing order by the arbitrary unleashing of their power.[37]

Wilson called for "a new and more wholesome diplomacy" and put the European powers on notice that in the future they would have to "take an entirely new course of action" if they expected America to play an active role in world affairs.[38] Wilson *was* talking about revolutionary change, but the charge that Wilson was oblivious of the realities of force in foreign policy is false on the evidence. Indeed, he argued that instead of the vagaries of an unstable "balance" there needed to be "a force . . . so much greater than the force of any nation . . . or any alliance hitherto formed or projected that no nation, no probable combination of nations could face or withstand it."[39]

President Wilson distilled his foreign policy into the famous Fourteen Points in an address before a joint session of Congress on January 8, 1918. They included open diplomacy, freedom of the seas, general disarmament, removal of trade barriers, a fair and impartial settlement of colonial claims, as well as the liberation of Belgium and self-determination for the Russian people. Point Fourteen—the League of Nations—was the key, however, because it alone could guarantee the kind of future world Wilson imagined.

The League of Nations ultimately failed, but not because Wilson failed to recognize military power as a key element in his blueprint for a new world order,

36. Claude, *Power and International Relations*, pp. 109–110.
37. Ibid., p. 110.
38. James Brown Scott Jr., ed., *President Wilson's Foreign Policy* (New York: Oxford University Press, 1918), p. 191, and D. H. Miller, *The Drafting of the Covenant* (New York: Putnam's, 1928), 1:42. Both quotes are cited in Claude, *Power and International Relations*, p. 111.
39. Quoted in Scott, *President Wilson's Foreign Policy*, p. 248.

as many "realists" have charged. No American president has been more maligned and misrepresented than Woodrow Wilson for his alleged failure to give the role of coercive force in world politics its due. Wilson's critics frequently cite the references to "moral force" in his speeches.[40] These same critics typically ignore passages like the following:

> We cannot do without force. . . . You cannot establish freedom, my fellow citizens, without force, and the only force you can substitute for an armed mankind is the concerted force of the combined action of mankind through the instrumentality of all the enlightened Governments of the world. This is the only conceivable system that you can substitute for the old order of things which brought the calamity of this war upon us and would assuredly bring the calamity of another war upon us.[41]

Critics have heaped scorn on Wilson's "idealistic" approach to foreign policy in part because the League of Nations failed to stop German, Italian, and Japanese aggressions in the prelude to World War II. In fact, the whole idea of collective security *as Wilson conceived it* was never tried.[42] When the League of Nations was put to that test in the 1930s, the United States was not even a member, a fatal flaw in that system.

Wilson understood that to be effective a system based on collective security rather than self-defense, arms races, secret treaties, and exclusive alliances would require collaborative action on the part of sovereign states unaccustomed to a great deal of coordination or cooperation in political-military affairs. There would have to be an organizational framework of some sort, a league of *all* the important nations. The membership would have to be universal for the intended enforcement mechanism to work. When President Wilson sponsored the League of Nations he assumed that the United States would play a prominent role in the new organization.

Wilson spent the last days of his political life desperately trying to sell the idea of the League to a skeptical America, but his blueprint for a new world order had powerful detractors in Washington. A Democrat, he faced a Republican majority led by the redoubtable Henry Cabot Lodge in the Senate. Wilson's troubles at home became manifest when he was at the Paris Peace Conference in the spring of 1919, and Senator Lodge was busy undermining the treaty before it had been finalized. In March, Lodge presented his "Round Robin" resolution to the

---

40. Claude, *Power and International Relations,* pp. 103–106.

41. Ray S. Baker and William E. Dodd, eds., *Public Papers of Woodrow Wilson,* vol. 2: *War and Peace* (New York: Harper and Brothers, 1925–1927), p. 51, cited in Claude, *ibid.,* p. 101.

42. Claude, *Power and International Relations,* p. 154. As Claude astutely points out, "The pretense that the actual League was the Wilsonian League was never quite discarded."

Senate signed by thirty-seven legislators declaring that the League of Nations "in the form now proposed to the peace conference" was unacceptable.[43]

The main stumbling block for opponents of the treaty (and the League) was Article 10, which pledged every League member "to respect and preserve as against external aggression the territorial integrity and existing political independence" of every other member. Only slightly less controversial were other elements, which established machinery for the arbitration of international disputes and decreed that an attack against one member state would "*ipso facto* [automatically] be deemed to . . . [be] an act of war against all the other Members" to be followed by an immediate economic blockade and a joint decision as to the precise nature of the military response.

History's dramas are often exercises in poetic justice. Yesterday's "comedy of errors" becomes tomorrow's tragedy. The Senate's rejection of the Versailles Treaty sealed the fate of the League and helped set the stage for World War II. It did so for a variety of reasons, not least of which was this: it signaled America's turning away from international liberalism and presaged the breaking waves of isolationism, protectionism, and parochial nationalism that followed in the wake of the 1929 stock market crash.

President Wilson's health failed at a critical moment in American history, but cruel fate does not fully explain his failure to win the political battle for the Treaty of Versailles and the League of Nations in the United States Senate or before the court of American public opinion. A full explanation must take into account the political culture of isolationism that lingered even in the aftermath of the Great War, as well as the personal political ambitions, convictions, and machinations of Senator Lodge and other Republican leaders in Congress. And, in fairness, it must take account of Woodrow Wilson's own deficiencies as a politician, statesman, and strategic thinker.

The Politics and Morality of Collective Security

Wilson was the unfortunate victim of his own rhetoric. He was most eloquent and persuasive when he talked about morality and power, as he often did. "The force of America is the force of moral principle. . . . [T]here is nothing else that she loves, and . . . there is nothing else for which she will contend."[44] Whatever World War I meant to Europeans, for Americans it must be a "war to end wars." Even his war message to Congress reflects his penchant for lofty language and righteous motives: "[war] for democracy, for the right of those who submit to authority, to have a voice in their own governments, for the rights and liberties of

---

43. Link, *Wilson the Diplomatist,* p. 129.
44. Quoted in John Morton Blum, *Woodrow Wilson and the Politics of Morality* (Boston: Little, Brown, 1956), p. 84.

small nations, for a universal dominion of right by such a concert of free peoples as shall bring peace and safety to all nations and make the world itself at last free."[45] The United States would enter the war to make the world "safe for democracy" in a universal sense, not just for American democracy. This kind of thinking (and talk) was one of the acorns that sprouted into the oak tree of "containment" after World War II. Not only was it strategically unlimited in its implications for foreign affairs, but it also was tactically unwise from the standpoint of domestic politics.

Wilson was expecting a lot, calling on the American people to do a sudden about-face, to go from isolationism to all-out internationalism with no questions asked. Unfortunately, he was presenting a big new idea that begged too many questions and left a befuddled public at the mercy of politicians with less-than-pure hearts.

Precisely what sort of questions did collective security raise? Philosophically, it was a formula for a static world, an international system based on the perpetuation of the status quo indefinitely if not infinitely. The real world is dynamic: rulers come and go, allegiances shift, empires rise and fall, territories change hands. Wilson clearly did not intend this result, did not want to block *all* possibilities for political change, but the fact is that transfers of power, transitions and transformations in world history, have almost always been closely associated with violence—war, revolution, or some other form of conflict.[46]

Collective security raised other serious theoretical and practical questions as well. For example, activation of enforcement mechanisms under the Covenant required unanimous approval by the League's members. If one state opposed League action, the organization would be sidelined in a crisis. In effect, this is what happened in the 1930s. Also, the operation of a system based on collective security assumed that "aggression" is easily defined and identified. In truth, the League's members were never able to agree on a definition of aggression, much less on what constituted an act of aggression within the meaning of the Covenant's key enforcement provisions.[47]

In theory, collective security works best if there exists a rough equality among the major powers or at the very least if there is no ascendant superpower capable of defeating any combination of opposing powers in a showdown. Collective security could work even with a superpower in the picture provided the

---

45. Quoted in Link, *Wilson the Diplomatist*, p. 89.

46. For example, Wilson argued that Communist-inspired revolution in Russia and by implication elsewhere was a mass response to grievous wrongs and that the threat it posed to democracy would not go away unless the root causes were removed—force would not do the trick. In Wilson's own words, trying to stop a revolutionary movement by troops in the field is like using a broom to hold back a great ocean." Ibid., pp. 117–118.

47. For a lucid critique of collective security, see Claude, *Power and International Relations*, pp. 150–204.

superpower belonged to a world organization devoted to maintaining the peace and fully accepted its rules, aims, and procedures. If, however, the superpower opposed the world organization or pursued policies based on national rather than international interests, collective security would by definition fail.

In practice, these conditions were not met after World War I, nor have they ever been met. Alas, it is unlikely that they ever will be.

The "great debate" occasioned by Wilson's decision to champion the League of Nations and with it a new international system based on collective security is framed in tragedy, both personal and political. Wilson suffered a severe stroke on September 25, 1919. The stricken president was paralyzed on the left side of his face and body. Politics, like life itself, is often moved in one direction or another by an accident. Wilson's stroke could hardly have come at a worse time. The fate of the Versailles Treaty in the Senate, like Wilson's very life, was hanging in the balance. His mind was far less severely impaired than his body, but "the disease had wrecked his emotional constitution and aggravated his more unfortunate traits."[48]

Faced with Republican opposition in the Senate, Wilson redoubled his resolve not to compromise on collective security (Article 10 of the Covenant). He rejected Lodge's fourteen reservations, which had been rubber-stamped by the Senate Foreign Relations Committee and then approved by the full Senate—highlighting the key role Congress can play in the foreign policy process when it chooses to do so. It was a standoff that doomed the treaty, the League, and ultimately the peace.

In sum, President Wilson was a visionary in the best sense of the word, but he was not a diplomat and he lacked the political instincts of a "born politician." On the critical issues embodied in the Treaty of Versailles and League of Nations he refused to compromise either with Republicans in the Senate or with allies in Europe. In 1920 he asked that the election be "a great and solemn referendum" on the League. In the words of one astute observer, "It would be difficult to imagine a more egregious error."[49]

The Republicans won the election in a landslide, but not because the electorate was dead-set against the League. There is often a voter backlash against the party in power: eight years of having a Democrat in the White House gave the Republican candidate, a virtual unknown named Warren G. Harding, a big advantage going into the presidential race. Moreover, the sacrifices associated with the war and public disillusionment associated with its untidy and divisive end would inevitably be blamed on the Democrats and on Wilson personally.

---

48. Link, *Wilson the Diplomatist,* p. 150.
49. Selig Adler, *The Isolationist Impulse: Its Twentieth Century Reaction,* paperback ed. (New York: Free Press, 1966), p. 104.

Wilson unwittingly gave the isolationist wing of the Republican Party a big boost. There were distinguished internationalists among the Republicans, including William Howard Taft, Charles Evans Hughes, and Elihu Root, but most of them despised Wilson and were thus predisposed to find fault with his policies.

As the Republican standard-bearer, Harding had equivocated on foreign policy (and virtually everything else). The 1920 election therefore was "of prime importance in the history of isolationism—not because of the way the people voted, but because of the dangerously simple popular interpretation of the result."[50] Voters believed that a vote for Harding was a vote for the League with reservations, but two days after the election the president-elect pronounced the issue of joining as "dead as slavery." Harding interpreted his election as a mandate against the League.

Sideshow: The Intervention in Russia

The October Revolution in Russia coincided with the American entrance into World War I. It set off alarm bells in Western democracies (especially France and Great Britain) because its leader, Lenin, stridently denounced capitalism and "bourgeois democracy." France and Great Britain dispatched military forces to Russia to help the counterrevolutionary "Whites" defeat the "Reds" in the civil war that was raging there. Reluctantly, President Wilson succumbed to pressure from the French and British and joined in the Allied intervention.[51] American troops landed at Archangel and Vladivostok in little more than token numbers and remained in Russia for only a limited time.

America's role in this episode was a relatively minor one, but it is noteworthy for two reasons. First, this military intervention was not led by the United States but, rather, by America's two major European allies. The United States was dragged into it as a reluctant partner. After World War II, these roles would be reversed (with the notable exception of the Suez Crisis in 1956). Second, the intervention not only helped set the stage for cold war but was also the opening scene in the first act of a long drama pitting Soviet Russia against the Western democracies. The curtain would not go up on the second act until 1947. When it did, both the stage and actors had changed beyond recognition. Germany and Japan were crushed, France and Great Britain were crippled, the United States was a superpower, and the Soviet Union had become a formidable challenger.

---

50. Ibid., p. 109.

51. Wilson was not inclined to intervene in the Russian Revolution and, in fact, quite naively welcomed it as a sign that the Russian masses had always longed for democracy! See George F. Kennan, *Russia and the West: Under Lenin and Stalin* (New York: Mentor, 1961), pp. 23–24.

LOSING THE PEACE: THE TRAGEDY OF VERSAILLES

In 1918, as World War I was approaching its culmination, the key issue for the Allies was whether to agree to an armistice with Germany pending the negotiation of a final settlement (peace treaty) or, instead, to demand Germany's "unconditional surrender." France and Great Britain favored the former course of action, and the United States favored the latter. Why were the French and British more anxious to end the war than the "idealistic" American president? War-weariness was, of course, a factor. But power politics also played a major part. Strategically, the longer the war dragged on, the bigger America's voice would be in determining the final outcome. France and Great Britain, therefore, both had a strong incentive to end the war as quickly as possible.[52]

Each of the Allies had a different set of objectives as well as one common aim: defeating Germany. How a war is ended, on whose terms, and with what sort of postwar limits on the future war-making capacity of the vanquished is hardly less important than who wins and who loses on the battlefield. World War I superbly illustrates this point. Great Britain was eager to ensure British naval superiority over Germany and, in general, British preeminence on the high seas. The French were (understandably) preoccupied with guarantees against any future land invasion along France's common frontier with Germany. France's natural ally against Germany on the Continent was Russia, but Russia was in the throes of the Bolshevik Revolution and would not be a fit ally in the postwar era. The United States had no territorial ambitions or strategic interests in Europe beyond creating a framework for peace and stability in a region that had once again proved to be the world's most volatile arena of conflict.

A complete examination of the Allies' divergent aims in the war is beyond the scope of this book.[53] The key point for our purposes is that the Versailles Treaty, which has often been denounced by historians as a harsh peace settlement that set the stage for the next war by imposing onerous conditions ("war guilt," disarmament, indemnities, and reparations) on Germany, did not do the one thing that might have made World War II impossible: it did not break up the German state. Bismarck's united Germany was the behemoth of the Continent. It had been in existence for less than thirty-five years when World War I broke out. The Hapsburg Empire disintegrated after the war, as did the Ottoman Empire, and the future of the Russian Empire was in grave doubt. The tragedy of Versailles, thus, was not about what the Allies did with Germany but what they did not do when they had the chance.

---

52. A. J. P. Taylor, *The Origins of the Second World War* (Greenwich, Conn.: Fawcett, 1961), p. 26.

53. Taylor brilliantly dissects the Allies' motives at the end of World War I in ibid., pp. 22–44.

In fairness, this tragedy cannot be laid at Wilson's doorstep alone; there was plenty of blame to go around. Wilson's principle of self-determination left him reluctant to oppose the right of Germans to live together in one state, although the Allies did insist that the rump state of Austria remain separate from Germany. The idea of a punitive peace, moreover, ran counter to the liberal ideal of a world of free and independent states engaging in free trade and settling disputes by arbitration rather than resorting to war. If Germany were not readmitted to the community (and comity) of nations, what incentive would Germans have to play by the rules of a new world order constructed along these lines?[54]

The problem was that the Allies did impose a harsh peace but left an intact Germany (minus Danzig and pieces of territory given to the new state of Poland) on its own to fulfill its obligations with no means of enforcement short of economic sanctions or war. But the enforcement machinery of the League Covenant required a triggering event. So long as Germany did not attack a League member (which it was in no position to do in the 1920s), there was no legal mechanism to initiate concerted action by the League. In fact, after 1925, when Germany was permitted to join the League, such action by, say, France acting unilaterally would have obligated the League to come to Germany's aid.

The Allied failure to break up Germany and America's failure with the League were two strikes against Wilson's plan for an international system to ensure perpetual peace. The third strike—the deathblow—was the panic induced in the West by the Great Depression in the 1930s. The severe economic crisis induced the major powers to turn inward to a more extreme degree than they otherwise would have done. But the United States had lapsed into a familiar isolationist mood even before the stock market crash on October 29, 1929.

CONCLUSION

Declaring war on Spain in 1898 was America's debut on the world stage. Prior to the Spanish-American War, the United States had not asserted itself beyond the Western Hemisphere. Between 1898 and the outbreak of World War I in 1914, the United States looked mainly south and west, to Latin America and Asia, rather than Europe. The acquisition of virtual colonies in the Caribbean (Cuba, Puerto Rico) and the Pacific (Hawaii, the Philippines) meant that the United States would for the first time in its history need a navy to project its growing power overseas.

The emergence of Germany and Japan as Great Powers coincided with America's coming of age. The balance of power was shifting in Europe and Asia. America alone had no rivals in its region of the world. In Europe, the Great Powers were engaged in an arms race. In Asia, Japan, China, and Russia engaged in a fierce competition for control of Korea and Manchuria. Japan fought and

---

54. Ibid., p. 32.

won wars with China (1895) and Russia (1904–1905). The outlines of future Great Power rivalries involving China, Germany, Japan, Russia, and the United States were thus forming at the start of the twentieth century.

As a Great Power with far-flung interests, the United States could no longer pursue a strategy of bowing out in Europe or Asia. When war clouds gather, Great Powers often seek to pass the buck rather than confront an aggressor, because war carries great costs and risks. The United States sought to avoid war in Europe as long as possible.

Accordingly, President Woodrow Wilson kept the country out of World War I for three years. In doing so, he pursued a classic strategy of passing the buck. He hoped (with good reason in 1914) that the coalition of England, France, and Russia would be able to defeat Germany without any help from the United States. When America finally intervened, it was only after the United Kingdom appeared to be failing in its traditional role of "offshore balancer." Thus, the United States played the role of backup offshore balancer in World War I.

Even Wilson's sophisticated critics—historians and biographers—have too often failed to notice the pragmatic side of Wilson's actions as opposed to his words. Wilson did not plunge the country headlong into the European war in 1914. Indeed, "No American troops were sent across the Atlantic to help prevent World War I or to stop the fighting after war broke out."[55] Wilson would surely have been content to let the European powers fight it out had Germany under Kaiser Wilhelm not been poised to win the war.

The strategy Wilson pursued following the outbreak of World War I was a classic example of Realpolitik: pass the buck if possible; intervene to preserve the balance of power if necessary. The United States did not get into World War I to create peace in Europe but rather to prevent a dangerous rival from achieving regional hegemony.

Moreover, Wilson did not push for an early end to World War I as we might expect from a president with pacifist tendencies, even though he was pressured by France and Britain to do so. Wilson the "idealist" had argued the case for imposing an "unconditional surrender" on Germany—in war, the supposed dove had the heart of a hawk.

Wilson's determination to find an alternative to the anarchic international system was rational but, as it turned out, politically unrealistic. The idea of "collective security" operating within the framework of a universal international organization had never been tried. The concept did not preclude national armies nor did it require the pooling of national sovereignty. Wilson's belief that sovereignty and security could be separated and that sovereign states would trust the League to keep the peace turned out to be false.

---

55. John J. Mearsheimer, *The Tragedy of Great Power Politics* (New York: Norton, 2001), p. 265.

Wilson reasoned that in the aftermath of a bloody and destructive general war the world would be ready to try something new that offered the hope of preventing such wars in the future. He also reasoned that the United States, as the richest and mightiest Great Power, would have to play a leading role in the new international organization if it was to have any chance of succeeding. Finally, he wanted to ensure that the United States would not retreat into an isolationist shell after the war (as it, in fact, did). The cause of Wilson's failure was an analytical error rather than any excess of idealism: he failed to understand that the tremendous force of nationalism would quickly rekindle old rivalries and fuel a fierce competition for power in Europe and Asia.

The 1920 election and the fate of the League point to the conclusion that democracy and foreign policy often do not mix very well. A president might have the best of plans, aims, and intentions, and yet fail miserably in foreign affairs. Presidents can stumble because they face a hostile Congress or a Senate majority controlled by the opposing party. Presidents can also be brought down by public opinion, which is often fickle and ill informed. When the opposition party and public opinion join forces, the result is deadly for a sitting president's pet policies. Above all, a president is unlikely to be effective as commander in chief and "chief diplomat" unless he or she is also effective as politician and manipulator of public opinion at home.

Alexis de Tocqueville, the nineteenth-century French observer of American democracy, astutely observed that democracies are "decidedly inferior to other governments" in the conduct of foreign relations. The latter

> demand scarcely any of those qualities which are peculiar to a democracy; they require, on the contrary, the perfect use of almost all those in which it is deficient. Democracy is favorable to the increase of the internal resources of a state; it diffuses wealth and comfort, promotes public spirit, and fortifies the respect for law in all classes of society.... But a democracy can only with great difficulty regulate the details of an important undertaking, persevere in a fixed design, and work out its execution in spite of serious obstacles.[56]

A more fitting epitaph for Woodrow Wilson's foreign policy is hard to imagine.

---

56. Alexis de Tocqueville, *Democracy in America* (New York: Vintage Books, 1945), 1:243. The translation has gone through several iterations. It was originally translated by Henry Reeve and revised by Francis Bowen. The 1945 edition was further corrected and edited by Phillips Bradley and includes Bradley's historical essay, editorial notes, and bibliographies.

$$4$$

Between Wars
Collective Security and Delusions of Peace

OVERVIEW

This chapter covers the years between World War I and World War II, when the United States reverted to isolationism. First we look at the causes and consequences of this policy both in the 1920s, when American diplomacy, under Republican leadership, was given to legalistic gimmickry such as the Kellogg-Briand Pact outlawing war, and in the 1930s, when the Great Depression strongly reinforced America's protectionist and isolationist tendencies. Next is an examination of U.S. foreign policy in the period leading up to the outbreak of World War II. I point out that as in World War I the United States passed the buck as long as possible, and I argue that the United States committed American forces to the war in order to prevent Germany and Japan from becoming regional hegemons, not to keep the peace. The chapter ends with some conclusions about the relative role of power and principle in explaining America's foreign policy in the turbulent period between 1919 and 1939. I argue that Americans were disinclined to play the rough game of international power politics or to make personal sacrifices for the sake of abstract ideals during the interwar years. Despite Woodrow Wilson's ambitious attempt to reinvent the international order by creating a League of Nations to promote perpetual peace through collective security, the United States did not learn the hard lessons of life as a major power in time to help prevent the outbreak of another world war.

In 1914, after the bombing of Vera Cruz, President Wilson declared that "the United States had gone down to Mexico to serve mankind." Wilson did not bother to explain precisely how "mankind" would benefit from U.S. intervention in Mexico. During World War I, Wilson advised American naval cadets "not only always to think first of America, but always, also, to think first of humanity." Wilson typically chose his words carefully. He was extremely literate and not given to self-contradiction. There had to be some logic in his tendency to equate what was good for America with what was good for the world. And indeed there was. The United States, he explained to the assembled cadets, had been "founded for the benefit of mankind."[1]

It was probably this conviction that inspired Wilson's heroic efforts after World War I to place America in the vanguard of the movement to create a new world order based on a radical proposal for organizing international relations.

---

1. Quoted in Edward Hallett Carr, *The Twenty Years' Crisis 1919–1939: An Introduction to the Study of International Relations,* 2nd ed. (New York: Harper Torchbooks, 1964), pp. 78–79. The quotations are from Ray S. Baker and William E. Dodd, eds., *Public Papers of Woodrow Wilson,* vol. 1: *The New Democracy* (New York: Harper and Brothers, 1925–1927, pp. 104 and 318–319.

CHRONOLOGY, 1919–1939	
1919	Paris Peace Conference; Treaty of Versailles concluded, creating League of Nations
1920	U.S. Senate rejects League of Nations Covenant; Nineteenth Amendment ratified (giving women right to vote); beginning of licensed radio broadcasting
1921	Warren G. Harding elected twenty-ninth president;
1928	Herbert Hoover elected thirty-first president
1929	U.S. stock market crash
1930	Smoot-Hawley Tariff passed; protectionist policies stifle world trade
1931	Empire State Building opens in New York City; Japan occupies Manchuria
1932	Franklin Delano Roosevelt elected thirty-second president
1933	New Deal legislation passed
1935	German troops occupy the Rhineland; League of Nations votes to impose sanctions on Italy under Article XVI
1936	Italian army occupies Addis Ababa (Ethiopia's capital); League of Nations collapses; Spanish Civil War follows extreme-Right rebellion led by Gen. Francisco Franco
1937	Hostilities between Japan and China escalate, spark international crisis
1938	Munich Conference; Germany absorbs Sudetenland (German-speaking part of Czechoslovakia)
1939	Germany seizes and subjugates Czechoslovakia; Italy invades Albania; Germany attacks Poland; Great Britain and France declare war on Germany; United States declares neutrality

COLLECTIVE INSECURITY (1919–1935)

As a peace settlement, the Treaty of Versailles was a spectacular failure for the simple reason that it settled almost nothing and satisfied almost no one. It left France, Germany, and Japan deeply dissatisfied and the United States teetering precariously between internationalism and isolationism.

The United States led the effort to devise a scheme for the payment of German reparations and hosted the Washington Conference in 1921–1922 that, among other things, fixed the ratio of naval armaments among the major powers.[2] These diplomatic efforts masked the harsh reality behind postwar American foreign policy—the United States and Europe had once again parted ways. At the beginning of the 1920s, America failed the first litmus test of internationalism—joining the League of Nations; by the end of the decade, America failed the second test—supporting the new World Court.[3] No country that refused to participate in these two institutions could claim full membership in the international community.

Great Britain and France were the ultimate guarantors of the peace in Europe, but they were not in perfect accord. France continued to be dissatisfied with the Versailles arrangements, fearing a future invasion by a resurgent and revenge-seeking Germany. The British were more complacent. The war was over. Germany had been defeated; its navy had vanished. If any continental power was in a position to bully the others, it was France. Italy was a puny counterweight on Europe's southern flank, and Soviet Russia in the east, having lost the Baltic states and being totally isolated by a combination of ideology, politics, and geography, was none at all.

When France invaded and occupied the Ruhr in 1923 in clear violation of the Versailles Treaty and its obligations under the Covenant, the League of Nations was tested for the second time and failed. The first test had come earlier in the same year, when Mussolini bombarded and landed troops on the Greek island of Corfu. The League had failed that test as well.[4]

This was the background to the famous Locarno Pact of 1925 by which Great Britain signed a mutual guaranty of the French and Belgian borders with Germany. An earlier attempt to fill the gap in international security resulting from the absence of the United States, Russia, and Germany from the League, the so-called Geneva Protocol (strengthening League provisions for the pacific settlement of disputes), had failed when Great Britain balked. The "spirit of Locarno" perhaps did more than anything else—more even than the League of Nations itself—to create a sense of security (false though it was) among the European powers.

---

2. The conference had four important results: (1) the Four-Power Pacific Treaty (France, Great Britain, Japan, and the United States provided a mutual guarantee of each other's rights to Pacific holdings); (2) the Shantung Treaty (Japan returned Kiachow to China); (3) the Nine-Power Treaty (guaranteed China's territorial and administrative integrity, reiterating the Open Door principle); and (4) naval armaments treaty (provided for a ten-year freeze on large warships and established a ratio for capital ships of 5:5:3:1.67:1.67 among the United States, Great Britain, Japan, France, and Italy, respectively).

3. Selig Adler, *The Isolationist Impulse: Its Twentieth Century Reaction*, paperback ed. (New York: Free Press, 1966), pp. 186–194.

4. Ibid., p. 202.

The Locarno treaty, like the League, was fatally flawed.[5] The British guaranteed only the western frontiers of Germany. Germany signed the treaty and eventually joined the League but never explicitly promised not to attack its neighbors to the east and south. France sought further security in a treaty with Poland and the states of the Little Entente, built the string of fortifications from Switzerland to Belgium (the Maginot Line), and reorganized the army.

A decade after the end of the "war to end wars," the balance of power appeared to be in equipoise. Nineteen twenty-eight was an election year and all was well in America—or so it seemed. The Democrats nominated Alfred E. Smith. Most Democrats were more interested in winning an election than defending internationalism or fighting lost causes.[6] The party's diehard faction of League supporters now seemed quixotic, anachronistic, and insufficiently pragmatic: "By 1928, Republican neo-isolationists had won tacit acceptance from the Democratic opposition . . . and substantial difference in our foreign policy between the parties all but disappeared."[7] This accidental "bipartisanship" was ahead of its time and highly unfortunate, even apart from the fact that it drove the last nail in the coffin of collective security. Ironically, it sealed the fate of the League at the apex of its apparent success.

The Illusion of Peace

Germany's admission to the League in 1926 represents a high-water mark in that body's prestige and apparent success. Up until this time, it was still possible to view the League as a club run by the victorious powers designed to maintain postwar status quo in Europe. Giving Germany a place of honor at the League's table (both in the Assembly and as a permanent member of the Council) "would . . . give the League a fresh start on a more impartial basis."[8] Germany's path to the League, however, was not smooth. Brazil, Poland, and Spain, non-permanent members of the Council, demanded equal treatment, causing a momentary paralysis in the process. Germany was ultimately admitted, but there was a price to be paid: Brazil and Spain withdrew from the League in disgust. Spain returned in 1928, and the League reached a milestone: in Europe, only the Soviet Union remained outside of the organization.

Incredibly, the United States was little more than a bystander in these important diplomatic events. What we were doing at this time might as well have

---

5. For a commentary on the Locarno Pact's defects, see E. H. Carr, *International Relations between the Two World Wars, 1919–1939* (1947; reprint, New York: Harper Torchbooks, 1966), pp. 96–97.

6. Adler, *Isolationist Impulse*, pp. 196–200.

7. Ibid., p. 196.

8. Ibid., p. 99.

been left undone. The American secretary of state, Frank Kellogg, followed the lead of the French foreign minister, Aristide Briand, in forging one of the most widely ridiculed treaties of all time. The result was the infamous Kellogg-Briand Pact, signed at Paris in 1928, by which all the major powers renounced aggressive war. The pact, however, made no provisions for sanctions and so was purely symbolic. Moreover, for all the signatories who were League members (all but the United States) it was redundant and as such diluted the moral authority of the Covenant. It was not America's finest hour.

In the period after the Washington Conference, only the United States among the major powers virtually stopped building the types of warships not covered by the 1922 treaty, including cruisers, destroyers, and submarines. The numbers of warships five signatories built or put into the pipeline between 1922 and 1930 says it all. For every ten new warships built or planned by Japan and France, for example, the United States built less than one. Surprisingly, Italy laid down more new warships than Great Britain, which nonetheless built almost seven times as many as the United States.[9] It was a portent of the gathering storm in Europe that Germany and Russia did not approve the treaty, which at the insistence of France preserved the rights and obligations of previous treaties and continued to bar the way to German arms equality.

The Disarmament Delusion

President Herbert Hoover's answer to the new naval arms race was to join with the British prime minister, Ramsay MacDonald, in calling a second disarmament conference for the purpose of plugging the huge loophole in the first one by placing upper limits on all types of warships.[10] The United States came away from this conference having across-the-board parity (on paper) with Great Britain in warships of all categories (not just battleships and carriers), and the Japanese gained parity in submarines but nothing else. Ultra-nationalists in Japan were up in arms, so to speak; one of them assassinated the Japanese prime minister. Rather than heeding such straws in the wind and preparing the nation for the possibility of a future showdown with the rising dictators of Europe and Asia, President Hoover made an astonishing proposal to the fifty-one-nation World Disarmament Conference at Geneva, Switzerland, in February 1932: abolish all offensive weapons and substantially reduce land armaments. The newspaper headlines read, "THANK HEAVEN FOR HOOVER," but the idea, floated only a few short years before the onset of a new hell on earth, never got off the ground.

---

9. Senate Doc. 202, 78th Cong., 2nd sess. Cited in Thomas M. Bailey, *A Diplomatic History of the American People*, 7th ed. (New York: Appleton-Century-Crofts, 1964), p. 648. The numbers are as follows: Japan—125; France—119; Italy—82; Britain—74; United States—11.

10. Ibid., p. 651.

In hindsight, Hoover's disarmament overtures appear utopian and naive, but in the context of the Great Depression they looked different. Americans were understandably preoccupied with the domestic crisis that caused the loss of jobs, savings, and farms on an unprecedented scale. Banks closed and bankruptcies soared. Hoover's proposals offered the prospect of cuts in public spending and tax relief at a time when ordinary people looked in vain for any signs of hope. Nor was it only an American crisis. The ripple effects spread and became a world economic crisis, a curse for the democracies, but a blessing for the demagogues and warmongers waiting in the wings.

The Business of Diplomacy (and Vice Versa)

The United States emerged from World War I an economic titan. In 1914 America was a debtor nation. That changed overnight owing to the horrific destruction, hardships, and economic dislocations caused by the conflict in Europe. By 1919 the United States boasted the most powerful economy in the world, one that was unscathed by the war and generated more exports than any of its war-ravaged competitors. The United States also emerged from the war as the world's chief moneylender and banking center, having lent allied governments more than $7 billion before the armistice and another $3.5 billion after it. This substantial debt owed to the U.S. Treasury became a source of serious tension between Washington and several key European powers, including France and Italy. Debtor nations, struggling to restore public confidence and rebuild their battered economies, clamored for debt cancellation.

If the war had been a bane for Europe, in both economic and humanitarian terms, it was a boon for the United States. As the Allied powers engaged the German armies on the battlefield, the United States economy was humming, exporting huge quantities of foodstuffs, munitions, and other necessities to Belgium, France, Great Britain, and Italy, among other countries, paid for with credits financed at home by the sale of Liberty Bonds. The powerful wave of prosperity thus stimulated by the war continued to carry the American economy on its crest until 1929, when it crashed into the reefs and rocks of Wall Street. By that time, private investors, awash in profits generated by the booming U.S. economy, had exported capital to the tune of $12 billion. On the eve of the Great Depression, foreign entities (mainly governments and banks) owed the American government or investors roughly $20 billion—a staggering sum in the 1920s.

Europeans argued that they had borne the brunt of the fighting for thirty-two months before America's belated entry into the war and American credits were really wartime subsidies rather than actual loans. America's economy had flourished while Europe's floundered. Americans had supplied food, guns, medicine, and blankets while they (the Allies) were doing all the fighting. Millions of

Europeans had made the supreme sacrifice. "Was gold more precious than blood?"[11]

The idea of canceling war debts had few if any backers in the United States. First, these debts would not be canceled for American taxpayers unless the U.S. Treasury tossed its outstanding bonds into the Potomac. The *Literary Digest* hit the nail on the head in 1926: "All those who would like to see America cancel the European debt are requested to mail in their Liberty bonds."[12] A third of the money former Allies owed America was the result of debts incurred *after* the war. Moreover, the British, French, and others spent lavishly on armaments and other things. Finally, the Europeans fared far better in the peace settlement, making off with German ships, colonies, and oil-rich mandates in the Middle East, as well as large IOUs in the form of German reparations and indemnities. The United States, it was said, got nothing out of Europe except its army.[13]

The 1920s was a Republican decade in American politics. President Calvin Coolidge epitomized the dominant ideology of the day when he told an assembly of newspaper editors, "The business of America is business."[14] Given the traditional Republican abhorrence of high taxes and "Big Government" and its close ties with Big Business, it is perhaps not surprising that all three Republican administrations of this era were ill-disposed to liberalize immigration rules, lower tariff barriers, or forgive foreign debts. In retrospect, these head-in-the-sand policies appear foolhardy and shortsighted, but at the time they were very popular (as evidenced by Republican successes at the polls).

When America refused to cancel Europe's debts, the Europeans, led by France, insisted on tying debt repayments to German reparations. Washington balked, but the system that evolved in the period 1921–1933 did, in effect, create just such a "financial merry-go-round": U.S. investors made loans through Wall Street bankers to the Weimar Republic (Germany), which in turn made reparations payments to France and Great Britain, enabling Paris to make debt payments to London and both to make installments on outstanding war debts to the United States Treasury. This circular arrangement had more to do with politics and diplomacy than economics or government finances.

The American people did not understand international economics, did not see the relationship between U.S. protectionist trade policies in the 1920s and the war-debt issue. They failed to realize that the one-time Allies would not be willing or able to pay back the money they had borrowed if American markets were closed to European exports.

---

11. Bailey, *Diplomatic History*, pp. 656–657.
12. *Literary Digest,* Sept. 18, 1926, p. 17. Quoted in Bailey, *Diplomatic History*, p. 659.
13. Ibid., pp. 659–660.
14. Coolidge spoke these words before the Society of American Newspaper Editors on January 17, 1925.

But that is exactly what happened: the "Irreconcilables" and isolationists now in control of Congress erected high tariff barriers in the early 1920s.[15] After the shock of the Wall Street stock market crash in 1929 and the rapid onset of the Great Depression, the politics of panic and hysteria replaced the politics of reason and drowned out the faint voices of moderation. Congress, still controlled by the Republicans, passed the severely protectionist Smoot-Hawley Tariff, which raised already high rates even higher, in the summer of 1930.[16]

Faced with the decision whether to sign or veto the bill, President Hoover found himself under tremendous pressure from both sides. Thirty-eight nations sent wires to Washington protesting. More than a thousand economists petitioned the president to kill the measure. Hoover's decision to sign it was the worst thing he did during his four years in the White House. The economists were right: the tariff was the death knell of international debt repayment and foreign trade. It would invite retaliation and all-around protectionism, bringing the international economy to a virtual standstill and deepening the Depression, not only in America but also worldwide. Worst of all, it would encourage the natural myopia of nations in crisis, making it possible for Germany to escape almost unnoticed from the Versailles system of rule and restrictions, to rearm and prepare for a new war of aggression. It was, of course, the League's job to enforce these rules, but the League, fatally flawed by America's absence from the outset, virtually dissolved in the panic-stricken, topsy-turvy world of the 1930s.

The single-minded pursuit of domestic prosperity in America during the Roaring Twenties, like the counterculture trends in fashion and the fine arts, was a reaction to the horrors and sacrifices of World War I. It was a decade of self-contradiction: exploration and rebellion in style and social mores, conservatism and reversion to tradition in mass opinion, public policy, and politics in general. Above all, it was a time when enduring economic principles (for example, a competitive system of international trade relations) were sacrificed for shortsighted economic reasons (high tariffs designed to keep foreign products out of American markets).

The scandals of the Harding administration and the political dominance of Big Business are mirrored in our time by corporate scandals, a revolving door that allows a privileged elite to move back and forth between Washington and Wall Street, compulsive corporate secrecy, a lack of governmental transparency often expressed (or disguised) as an obsession with security, and collusive ties between government and business. This situation will not improve without far-reaching

---

15. The Irreconcilables were a group of hardcore Republican legislators who were dead-set against Woodrow Wilson's policies, in particular the League of Nations and the World Court.

16. According to one noted diplomatic historian, "The existing rates of 1922 were already so high as to discourage many European imports, with which Allied debt payments could be made, and the new law added bricks to the wall." Bailey, *Diplomatic History*, pp. 664–665.

political reforms of the kind undertaken in America a century ago in what historians call the Progressive Era.

Even under the best of circumstances, the worst decisions are often made in times of crisis, precisely when the calm voice of reason is most crucial. One of the lessons of the 1920s is that when domestic politics is corrupted by unscrupulous public servants or distorted by the unchecked power of special interests, foreign policy is likely to be one of the first and costliest casualties. At the beginning of the twenty-first century, all signs pointed to the conclusion that Americans would have to relearn this lesson the hard way.

Holiday for Hitler

Tensions between the United States and Europe reached the breaking point on December 15, 1932, when the six debtor nations, including France and Belgium, defaulted outright. President Hoover had declared a one-year holiday (moratorium) on reparations and war debts in the summer of 1931. Hoover acted not out of a generosity of spirit but rather to forestall a total collapse of European economies that would have obliterated any chance of international debt repayment after a banking crisis hit Austria and quickly spread to neighboring Germany. Hoover belatedly came around to the view that debt relief was a necessary step toward a solution to the financial crisis looming in Europe, and he was able to bring Congress along for a time.

The Europeans, too, had to be persuaded to give ground on the issue of German reparations payments. They did so, in fact moving to cancel all but a token amount on the assumption—unwarranted as it turned out—that the United States would reduce their "war-debt" burden commensurately.

It was not to be. The public and Congress—led by newspaper tycoon William Randolph Hearst and Senator William E. Borah of Idaho—were outraged at the notion of American taxpayers, in effect, paying Germany's reparations bill. Senator Borah, the "lion of Idaho," was the original Irreconcilable who had led the opposition to the Treaty of Versailles, the League of Nations, and the World Court on the grounds that it would dilute American sovereignty and entangle the United States in embroilments abroad that were none of our business. In the past, Borah had favored disarmament (as a way to save taxpayers' money and stay out of trouble) and the Kellogg-Briand Pact (outlawing war), as well—all populist stands that resonated in the insular and isolationist interior of the country. Now he was dead set against any debt forgiveness and extracted a pledge from Hoover that the United States was "not a party to, nor in any way committed to any such agreements."[17]

---

17. W. S. Myers, ed., *The State Papers and Other Public Writings of Herbert Hoover* (Garden City, N.Y.: Doubleday, Doran, 1934), 2:235.

This episode was the beginning of a rapid deterioration in Washington's relations with its erstwhile allies—that is, with the very European democratic states that would be America's natural allies in any future confrontations with totalitarianism, whether from the Left (communism) or the Right (fascism). The fateful sequel came at the London Economic Conference convened in June 1933 to consider a full range of international economic issues from debt to tariffs to currency stabilization. The new American president, Franklin Delano Roosevelt, a Democrat with a pedigree, had refused to budge from the basic position of his Republican predecessor on the first two issues (debt and tariffs) but expressed interest in the third (currency stabilization). With the conference in full swing, however, he changed his mind, dispatching a blunt radio message to the diplomatic assembly in London rebuking the conferees for focusing on the currency issue rather than "fundamental economic ills." Roosevelt's about-face was met with shock, dismay, and anger; European leaders bitterly denounced America's callous attitude and vacillation (as they saw it) and lost trust in its new president at a moment of great peril not merely to economic recovery but to the very survival of democracy in Europe.

The failure of this conference and the disunity it fostered in effect gave Adolf Hitler a green light by virtually eliminating any risk that Nazi aggression would become the catalyst for a strong anti-German alliance. A few months later, Germany withdrew from the Geneva Disarmament Conference and the League of Nations, Hitler's first steps toward the launching of a massive rearmament that would transform Nazi Germany into a military behemoth—and the Western democracies' worst nightmare—in five short years.

In April 1934, Congress passed the Johnson Act (named for its Irreconcilable sponsor, Sen. Hiram Johnson of California), banning loans or credits of any kind to governments in default to the United States. Two months later, all the European debtor nations except Finland officially defaulted. Europeans hurled epithets at the United States, including "vampire" and "bloodsucker." It was one of the all-time low points in North Atlantic relations, and it came at a time when ominous, dark clouds were building in Europe and Asia.

In 1931 Japan had invaded Manchuria and seized control of several important towns, eventually establishing the puppet state of Manchukuo. It ignited an undeclared war between China and Japan that changed the political landscape of the Far East and presaged the all-consuming conflagration to come. In 1932 the Chaco War between Bolivia and Paraguay broke out; that war would not end until 1935, the year in which Italy invaded Ethiopia, an act of naked aggression known in history as "the rape of Ethiopia." It gave the League Council little choice but to declare that Italy had "resorted to war in disregard of her obligations under Art. XII," and impose sanctions. By this time, Germany, Japan, and Spain had all quit the League. The following year, Nazi Germany would renounce the Locarno

Pact and reoccupy the Rhineland, and the Spanish Civil War would erupt, splitting all Europe into fascist and antifascist camps.[18]

The League of Nations was little more than an empty shell by 1935. Old patterns of state behavior had reappeared with a vengeance, a process that had started already in 1919 before the ink on the Covenant was dry. The classical balance-of-power system based on diplomatic maneuver, coalition formation (alliances), and arms races was back in full swing. During the heyday of the collective security system (1919–1935), no fewer than sixteen major international treaties and alliances were negotiated, with five in October 1925 alone. It was a paradox and a danger signal that apparently made no impression on American policymakers at the time.

BACK TO THE FUTURE (1936–1941)

Faced with a hostile Europe, Roosevelt reverted to a sphere-of-influence policy predicated on a bifurcated world and placing Europe in the other "half." It was the worldview enshrined in the Monroe Doctrine.

Roosevelt's first term began on a diplomatic high note in U.S. relations with Latin America. The president and his secretary of state, Cordell Hull, embraced the good-neighbor policy enthusiastically, negotiating reciprocal tariff reductions with Latin American states and supporting a nonintervention pact, in effect "reversing completely the preventive interventionism of his distant cousin, Theodore Roosevelt."[19] The second year of his presidency, 1934, was a milestone in U.S. relations with Cuba: the United States signed a treaty releasing Cuba from the humiliating restraints of the Platte Amendment (giving the United States control over Cuba without corresponding obligations). By the same token, FDR cemented close ties with Canada in the years before World War II and settled a potentially nasty dispute with Mexico after the Mexican government evicted and expropriated the assets of foreign oil companies in 1938.

With the war in Europe gathering its deadly momentum, the good-neighbor policy paid off. In the past the Monroe Doctrine had always assumed British naval

---

18. The Spanish Civil War involved a fight-to-the-death between right wing (fascist) and left wing (Marxist) forces and thus mirrored the polarization of social classes, economic interests, and political factions that was occurring at this time in many European countries. Hitler's Germany backed the extreme Right, and Stalin's Russia backed the extreme Left. Francisco Franco, the Spanish general who led the revolt against the republic, became Spain's dictator in 1939 and remained in power until his death in 1975. For an excellent account of this epic struggle, see Hugh Thomas, *The Spanish Civil War* (New York: Harper and Row, 1961). For a critically acclaimed literary account, see Ernest Hemingway, *For Whom the Bell Tolls* (New York: Scribner's, 1940).

19. Bailey, *Diplomatic History*, p. 683. The Senate unanimously approved this pact.

supremacy in the North Atlantic. Now, with Germany threatening the British Isles, that assumption was in jeopardy. The most immediate fear in the United States was that bits of European colonial holdings in the Western Hemisphere would fall into enemy hands (especially Hitler's) and become bridgeheads and springboards for attacks on neighboring states. In these perilous circumstances, the United States and Latin America reached a remarkable consensus on what was to be done. At Havana, Cuba, a setting fraught with symbolism, they agreed to take over and jointly administer endangered colonies of European powers *preemptively if necessary*. The so-called Act of Havana even went so far as to allow the United States to move in temporarily on its own and without prior approval in an emergency.

FDR managed to mend Uncle Sam's fences in the Western Hemisphere in the years preceding America's entry into World War II because Congress and public opinion approved. The good-neighbor policy was consistent with the isolationist impulse that gripped the nation during the interwar period. It was firmly grounded in the foreign policy tradition of Washington, Jefferson, and Monroe. It was a "feel good" policy that fed a false sense of security and failed to face up to the real evils at loose in the world.

The Neutrality Laws

President Roosevelt's election signaled a new approach to public policy emanating from the White House. FDR favored proactive government. Well-traveled and personally at home in Europe, he was an internationalist both culturally and philosophically. Democrats running for Congress rode into Washington on FDR's coattails in 1932, giving the new administration a large Democratic majority in both the House and the Senate. Nonetheless, from March 4, 1933, when he took the oath of office, until December 7, 1941, when Japan attacked Pearl Harbor, FDR fought an uphill battle with conservatives and isolationists. The "hill" was Capitol Hill. The fact that he vetoed more legislation during his first two terms in office than any other president in American history is one measure of the insolvency of American foreign policy during these turbulent years.[20]

Antiwar sentiment in America rose to new heights in 1934–1935. The Senate held hearings to investigate charges that bankers and munitions makers had made huge profits during 1914–1917, when the United States was officially pursuing a policy of strict neutrality. The Nye Committee (named after Sen.

---

20. Roosevelt was the last president to be inaugurated in the month of March; in 1937 he became the first to be inaugurated in January. FDR exercised his veto power 635 times during his four terms; Grover Cleveland is the only other president to use the veto so aggressively, killing 584 pieces of legislation in his two nonconsecutive terms. Significantly, both presidents served during an economic depression.

Gerald P. Nye of North Dakota) contributed to the rising crescendo of public opposition to rearmament and outrage at press revelations about the so-called "merchants of death" who allegedly enriched themselves by "fomenting wars so as to sell military hardware."[21]

Congress passed the first in a series of neutrality laws in 1935 and followed up with several more in 1936 and 1937. The 1935 law, a reaction to the Ethiopian crisis, stipulated that the president could ban the sale or transportation of arms to all belligerents in a war. Much to Roosevelt's chagrin, Congress did not give him the flexibility to supply arms to the victim but not the aggressor. In light of the fact that public opinion overwhelmingly favored strict neutrality, FDR reluctantly signed the bill.

This era in American history illustrates how excessive caution (the polar opposite of reckless risk-taking) can backfire in foreign policy. The mood of America from top to bottom became increasingly defensive and introverted. In turning its back on the rest of the world, America sought to avoid the risks and hazards of international power politics and was unwilling to "get involved" even after such gross violations of moral principle as Italy's invasion of Abyssinia (Ethiopia) or Hitler's assault on the Jews clearly indicated that democracy and totalitarianism were on a collision course.

The Neutrality Act of 1936 went even further in tying the president's hands, banning war loans to all belligerents without exception and without regard to the political or moral circumstances. If, for example, France or Great Britain were to come to the aid of Ethiopia, the president would have to cut off munitions and loans to them. In deference to the Monroe Doctrine, the law exempted any Latin American state at war with a European or Asian state.

Congress passed additional neutrality legislation in 1937 to deal specifically with the situation in Spain. Both Hitler's Germany and Mussolini's Italy had taken sides in the Spanish Civil War, supporting the right-wing, pro-Catholic, anticommunist Gen. Francisco Franco against the so-called Loyalists, who were in turn supported by leftists and the Soviet Union. The major 1937 law enacted "permanent neutrality" and extended the ban on treating with belligerents to parties involved in a civil conflict. It also outlawed travel on belligerent ships.

Although Congress tightened the neutrality noose in stages between 1935 and 1937, it left FDR one loophole. The president could list certain commodities that belligerents would be allowed to buy on a "cash-and-carry" basis. In effect, this meant that a belligerent with a strong navy, a merchant fleet, and enough hard currency could obtain American goods. The terms were simple: no credit, no "home delivery." Few nations outside of the Western Hemisphere

21. See H. C. Engelbrecht and F. C. Hanighen, *Merchants of Death: A Study of the International Armament Industry* (New York: Dodd, Mead, 1934). Quoted in Bailey, *Diplomatic History*, p. 700.

were in a position to take advantage of this opportunity. Great Britain, of course, was one of the chosen few.

Lend-Lease

International events moved rapidly after 1935. In North America, the "dirty thirties" started with the Great Depression that spread to Europe. In Asia, Japan had launched its career of aggression by invading Manchuria. The rape of Manchuria preceded the rape of Ethiopia by several years and in hindsight signaled a complete breakdown in the rules of international conduct and the total collapse of the ambiguous half-and-half global order that had evolved after the last war. By the end of the decade, World War II was in full swing in Europe, Japan was on the march in Asia, and the United States was beginning to stir, despite the isolationist bloc in Congress.

After Germany invaded Poland on September 1, 1939, a full-scale conflict was set into motion. Two days later, the British and French declared war on Germany. In the United States, public opinion was overwhelmingly anti-German, but there was no popular enthusiasm for direct American involvement. In these circumstances, President Roosevelt's hands were tied—almost.

Almost, but not quite: in the immediate aftermath of Hitler's attack on Poland, FDR asked Congress to repeal the arms embargo. The 1937 Neutrality Act had recently expired; in its place the president proposed continuation of the cash-and-carry rule and establishment of North Atlantic danger zones barred to American ships and citizens. A heated debate between noninterventionists and Roosevelt's supporters ensued on Capitol Hill. A Gallup Poll taken in September 1939 found public opinion evenly divided on whether or not to repeal the arms embargo. Both sides in this controversy wanted to stay out of the war. The only question was how best to accomplish this purpose.

Hitler's attack on Denmark and Norway in the spring of 1940, followed by attacks on Belgium, Holland, Luxembourg, and France, elicited sharply worded protests from Washington and a gradually escalating series of acts that had the cumulative effect of ending all pretense of American neutrality. FDR's dilemma was a derivative of politics, not policy: 1940 was an election year and the American people were still divided over foreign policy. The issue was still at this late date not so much a question of ends (few favored entry into the war in 1940) but, rather, of means (how to stay out *and* help Great Britain stay afloat following the fall of France).

In Washington, the machinery of government now began to awaken. Congress passed a military conscription law in September 1940—the first ever in peacetime—and the United States announced the famous "destroyer-base deal," which gave the embattled British navy fifty much-needed warships in return for rent-free leases on sites for naval bases in the eastern North Atlantic (in the

Bahamas, Bermuda, and Newfoundland, among other places). FDR made this "deal" by executive agreement, bypassing Congress completely. Then, following his victory in the election of 1940 (when he was on a precedent-shattering third term), he pushed his "lend-lease" bill (cleverly numbered "1776") through Congress.

Lend-lease was ingenious. It allowed the president to give billions of dollars worth of munitions and supplies to the Allies while keeping the pretense of neutrality and, at the same time, to avoid the war-debt issue that had proven so contentious after World War I: the United States, FDR assured wary post-Depression taxpayers, was not *giving* anything away, merely lending arms and equipment. In theory, we would get the stuff back or get repaid after the war. In practice, of course, much of the "stuff" of war is used up (perishables, fuel, and medicines, as well as bullets, bombs, and other ordnance) or destroyed in the fighting. Instead of presenting America's allies with the bill after the war, America would funnel billions of dollars into Western Europe's recovery.

THE FAILED SEARCH FOR SOLVENCY

In World War I we stayed out too long and left the arena too soon. When we called it quits in Europe, we withdrew into the fortress of America.

The interwar years were marked by a frantic all-round search for national security in a changed international order that had not been tested. Worse still, the main mechanism of the new system, the League of Nations, was flawed from the start. The insolvency of the League was masked for a time, but the maneuvering and jockeying that went on among the European powers in the 1920s was a clear indication that the League members believed they needed reinsurance.

There was also a lack of solvency in American foreign policy that was manifested in various ways. First, there was controversy and a conspicuous absence of domestic consensus going all the way back to the Spanish-American War, as we have seen. Second, America's power and interests greatly exceeded America's willingness to make commitments and sacrifices. Hence, the United States was the richest state in the world but devoted a far smaller percentage of its national wealth to military spending than the other Great Powers. This penny-pinching approach to defense and America's navel-gazing self-absorption—so clearly reflected in the isolationist rhetoric of its leaders—combined to negate any deterrent effect the United States might have had on Germany and Japan.

Politicians and voters alike were loath to acknowledge overarching national interests when doing so might require the United States to make firm commitments. The country overwhelming preferred to stay out of Europe's business, to keep Asia's doors open to American products, and to maximize its independence and freedom of action.

In the twenties, we stayed out of the League of Nations, adopted protectionist economic policies, and sank back into a delusional state of semi-isolationism.

In the thirties, as the international system came undone, we retreated into the storm cellar of neutrality, hoping to stay there safe and sound until the storm had passed. Despite the fact that the United States was by far the most powerful country in the world, Germany and Japan produced nearly ten times more aircraft in 1935 than did American arms manufacturers, a pattern that kept repeating itself for the rest of the decade (see Table 4–1).[22] Instead of passing, the storm worsened until we had no choice but to take active steps to meet the danger.

CONCLUSION

The frequent charge that the League of Nations failed is true, but it begs the question: when did it fail? The League's first failure occurred in 1920 when the U.S. Senate rejected the Treaty of Versailles ending World War I. The League had little chance to succeed in its primary role of war prevention without the active participation of all the Great Powers, especially the United States. Blaming the League of Nations for failing to prevent the outbreak of World War II misses the point: the League was a creature of the Great Powers. The failure of the League, then, was a failure of the Great Powers—and not only the United States.

The Great Powers of Europe did not trust the League, but they also failed to act *outside* the League—preferring instead to pass the buck rather than form an effective balancing coalition against Nazi Germany in the late 1930s. It is possible that the very existence of the League created a false sense of security, but it is more likely that the Great Powers (including the United States) would have behaved in essentially the same way had there been no League.

Would the course of history have changed if the United States had joined the League? As Lord Acton noted, "history does not disclose its alternatives." Even so, it is a question too titillating to ignore. Certainly American participation in the League would have given that body the stamp of legitimacy it lacked without the world's largest power. More important still is what it would have said about the American role in the postwar world and about the political maturity of the American people. One thing is clear: the long-term maintenance of any stable order among competing Great Powers was impossible without the participation of the greatest of them all, the United States.

Nothing ever guarantees peace in this world. However, some things left undone—for example, the failure of the United States to join the League in the early 1920s or to lead the effort to stop Germany in the mid-1930s—can grease the skids of war. That is the ultimate lesson of American foreign policy in the interwar years.

---

22. Paul Kennedy, *The Rise and Fall of the Great Powers* (New York: Vintage Books, 1989), p. 324.

Table 4-1 National Income and Defense Spending of the Powers in 1937			
	National income (billions of dollars)	Defense spending (% of total national income)	Annual defense spending (billions of dollars)
British Empire	22	5.7	1.25
France	10	9.1	0.91
Germany	17	23.5	3.99
Italy	6	14.5	0.87
Japan	4	28.2	1.13
USSR	19	26.4	5.01
United States	68	1.5	1.02

Source: Paul Kennedy, *The Rise and Fall of the Great Powers* (New York: Vintage Books, 1989), p. 332.

The American retreat into isolationism after World War I was an attempt to have the benefits of Great Power status without assuming the burdens. What was missing from the foreign policy equation was not due to a deficiency in material resources but to a defect of wit and will and a failure to translate latent power into military might. This disparity between America's role as a Great Power on the one hand and its reluctance to play that role on the other led to a state of foreign policy insolvency. After President Wilson's attempt to abolish the balance of power failed, the United States passed the buck to the French, the British, and finally, to the Soviet Union. But events conspired to force the United States to choose between confronting Japan and Germany or allowing them to conquer Asia and Europe, respectively (see Chapter 5).

One thing that was conspicuously absent in foreign policy debates in the decade after 1928 was debate—real debate. As previously noted, debate over fundamental issues, principles, and alternative courses was largely abandoned for political reasons in 1928—not the high politics of policy differences over how best to serve the national interest but the low politics of how to win elections. As a result, few voices were raised in opposition to protectionism and isolationism.

The perennial tension between power and principle was resolved by ignoring the claims of both. Americans, ever-mindful of the horrors of the last war, sought to avoid a costly arms race that might again lead to armed conflict in a faraway place and, faced with the hardships of the Great Depression, were loath to support external commitments that might well entail personal sacrifices for the sake of abstract ideals. Ideals such as peace and freedom are more than mere abstractions, of course, but it is human nature to take them for granted unless they are denied or under imminent threat. The public perception of the threat to the American way of life in the 1930s focused primarily on internal circumstances; ironically, this trance-like introversion, by helping to clear the way for Hitler's bid to conquer Europe and Japan's to conquer Asia, set the stage for a massive assault on the fundamental principles of political life on which democracy itself is predicated.

Out of the tragedy of World War II grew an intellectual movement that came to be known as political realism. Walter Lippmann, quoted in the previous chapter, was one of this movement's leading lights. Other key figures of the realist school included the famed British historian E. H. Carr and an American political scientist whose academic disciples taught a generation of students and future policymakers, Hans J. Morgenthau.[23] Political realists adopted a Machiavellian stance toward moral questions.[24] Often maligned as morally obtuse or indifferent, these thinkers were instead committed to seeing the world as it is rather than as it ought to be out of a conviction that misplaced idealism in international politics more often leads to grief than to good. In this conviction they were inspired by the causes and consequences of World War I and often used Woodrow Wilson as a kind of object lesson to "prove" that the road to hell is paved with good intentions. But the fault lay less with President Wilson than with the failure of his successors to maintain a solvent foreign policy.

In sum, the failings of American foreign policy in the first four decades of the twentieth century had multiple causes and no paucity of culprits. Policymakers did not correctly calibrate America's response to the changing power distribution in the international system. Politicians pursued local interests at the expense of national interests. The electorate was too self-absorbed, too preoccupied with internal affairs, and too slow to recognize the futility of isolationism, the need to make timely commitments, and the urgency of building military capabilities on a matching scale. It is a story all too familiar to observers of the contemporary scene.

23. Edward Hallett Carr, *The Twenty Years' Crisis: 1919–1939: An Introduction to the Study of International Relations*, 2nd ed. (New York: Harper Touchbooks, 1964); and *International Relations*; Hans J. Morgenthau, *Politics among Nations: The Struggle for Power and Peace*, 5th ed. (New York: Knopf, 1973), and *In Defense of the National Interest* (New York: Knopf, 1951).

24. Niccolò Machiavelli (1469–1527), Italian statesman and political philosopher, is the author of *The Prince*, a shockingly unsentimental handbook (still in print) on how to acquire and hold onto political power. Machiavelli has often, mistakenly in my view, been condemned as an advocate of an immoral approach to politics—namely, that the "ends justify the means."

5

The Cold War
Containment and Deterrence

OVERVIEW

World War II sounded the death knell of isolationism in America. This chapter opens with a discussion of the circumstances and consequences of America's decision to declare war on Japan in 1941. I examine America's role in the fight against the Axis powers in Asia and Europe and in the shaping of the postwar international system. Next the origins of the cold war and the genesis of the policy of containment are discussed. I then examine the concepts "massive retaliation" and "deterrence," giving special attention to the second Berlin Crisis and the Cuban Missile Crisis. I also look at the evolution of nuclear diplomacy and the advent of "mutual deterrence." Finally, I discuss the strategy of flexible response and relate this strategy to the ill-fated decision to wage a major war in Vietnam.

Japan attacked the United States on December 7, 1941. Calling it "a date that will live in infamy," President Roosevelt asked Congress for a declaration of war on the following day.[1]

Pearl Harbor was a watershed. Uncle Sam's entrance into World War II signaled the end of an era. In political terms, it turned the tables, putting the isolationists on the defensive. It was the end of the policy of isolationism (actually a set of policies) that had long treated noninvolvement in the political affairs and military imbroglios of Europe and Asia as the norm. Nostalgia for the "good old days" did not vanish overnight—indeed, isolationist longings still surface from time to time—but World War II fundamentally and forever changed the political culture of foreign policy in the United States.

Change was necessary but came with no guarantees. The end of the war brought new challenges, such as defining U.S.-Soviet postwar relations; aiding Europe's reconstruction and establishing peaceful, stable, democratic states in Germany and Japan; and working through the United Nations to smooth the

---

1. The speech can be read in its entirely at http://bsn.boulder.co.us/government/national/speeches/spc.html.

1941   Japan attacks Pearl Harbor on December 7; United States declares war on Japan, Germany, and Italy

1942   Japanese Americans interned in detention camps

1943   "Big Three" (Roosevelt, Churchill, Stalin) meet at Tehran (Iran)

1945   Yalta Conference; Harry Truman becomes the thirty-third president of the United States; Soviet army occupies Bulgaria, Czechoslovakia, Hungary, Poland, and Romania, as well as Northern Iran; United States drops atomic bombs on Hiroshima and Nagasaki

1946   Churchill gives "Iron Curtain" speech; George Kennan sends famous Long Telegram

1948   First Berlin crisis; United States recognizes newly created state of Israel

1949   Birth of North Atlantic Treaty Organization

1950   Republican senator Joseph McCarthy conducts anticommunist witch hunt

1952   Dwight D. Eisenhower elected thirty-fourth president of the United States; United States explodes first hydrogen bomb in Pacific Ocean

1954   Birth of Southeast Asia Treaty Organization (SEATO); in landmark case, *Brown vs. Board of Education*, U.S. Supreme Court declares racial segregation in public schools unconstitutional

1955   Soviets create Warsaw Pact

1956   Egypt nationalizes Suez Canal, provoking Israeli attack; Congress passes Highway Act (provides federal aid to states to build nationwide interstate highway system)

1957   USSR becomes the first country to launch a satellite (Sputnik) into outer space

1958   Birth of European Economic Community (better known as the Common Market)

1959   Fidel Castro seizes power in Cuba; Alaska becomes forty-ninth state

1960   Congo gains independence from Belgium leading to first superpower crisis in sub-Saharan Africa; France "goes nuclear"—starts building national nuclear strike force over strong U.S. objections; John F. Kennedy becomes the thirty-fifth president

1961   Bay of Pigs invasion; Soviets become first to put a man in space (Yuri Gagarin orbits the earth)

1962   American astronaut John Glenn orbits the earth in Mercury capsule; Cuban Missile Crisis

1963   Partial Nuclear Test Ban Treaty signed; President Kennedy assassinated in Dallas; Vice President Lyndon Johnson succeeds him

process of decolonization in Africa and Asia. These challenges would call for new directions, new solutions, and, above all, new thinking. A proactive foreign policy would make far greater daily demands on the American people than an inactive or reactive one. Even more than the new and unprecedented demands such a policy would place on material and financial resources were the burdens it would place on political leadership. America's economy would be tested and would prove equal to the test; it was a different kind of resource that would be called into question, the very resource that America exhibited in such great abundance at its founding, namely, political wisdom. In retrospect, the two-hundred-year history of American foreign policy witnessed periodic shortfalls in that vital resource, which nonetheless did not prevent the steady growth in American economic and military power. As demonstrated in Chapter 4, at no time was the lack of wisdom and foresight more costly than during the years between the two world wars.

Recall that Woodrow Wilson had tried to commit the United States to a new direction in foreign affairs, to imbue the American people with a new world-view, and above all to ensure that we would never again look the other way when despotism and aggression posed a threat to democracy, freedom, and stability. Wilson's best efforts were not enough. After his premature departure from the Washington scene and the defeat of his philosophical bedfellows in the 1920s, World War I came to be viewed as an exception to the norm (staying out of Europe's conflicts) rather than the incubator of a new norm (defining the national interest in global rather than essentially hemispheric terms). Isolationism returned with a vengeance—and with terrible consequences.

A clear majority of the American people were disenchanted with Europe's propensity to start wars and anxious not to get sucked into another one anytime soon. A Gallup Poll in January 1937, for example, found that two-thirds of Americans did not favor either side in the Spanish Civil War.[2] After Japanese warplanes sank an American gunboat (the *Panay*) in December 1937, the U.S. House of Representatives narrowly defeated (by a vote of 209 to 188) a measure that would have required a national referendum to declare war. A majority of Americans favored complete withdrawal from China, according to a poll taken a few months later.[3] Even after America had joined the fight and was on the verge of winning, the vast majority of Americans (80 percent) thought that Roosevelt should have been trying to keep the United States out of the war when Japan attacked Pearl Harbor.[4]

---

2. Hadley Cantril, ed., *Public Opinion* (Princeton: Princeton University Press, 1951), p. 807. Cited in Thomas M. Bailey, *A Diplomatic History of the American People*, 7th ed. (New York: Appleton-Century-Crofts, 1964), p. 702.

3. Bailey, *Diplomatic History*, p. 706. The poll was taken by *Fortune* magazine and published in the April 1938 issue, p. 109.

4. National Opinion Research Center, *Opinion News*, April 3, 1945, p. 1.

The hard-core isolationists (the Irreconcilables) in Congress were thus good followers rather than great leaders. They generally represented midwestern or Rocky Mountain states that were deeply conservative, insular in mentality, and sparsely populated. Thus, isolationism was overrepresented in the Senate, and the isolationist mood of the electorate was actually magnified when viewed through the looking glass of Congress as a whole.

THE END OF ISOLATIONISM

The Japanese made one of the biggest strategic miscalculations in the history of modern warfare at Pearl Harbor. Japan's high command was not stupid. It was an error of hubris, perhaps, and ignorance, certainly. In 1941 the Japanese did not—could not possibly—understand the intricate workings of a democratic polity. They could not conceive of a political system in which public opinion or something called Congress had the power to trump executive authority. The idea that domestic politics or special interests could tie an American president's hands made no sense in the context of Japan's authoritarian political culture. The attack in itself was a huge success: 2,343 Americans dead; 9 American naval vessels, including 5 battleships and 3 cruisers, sunk or severely damaged; 177 aircraft destroyed. In addition, more than 2,000 were missing in action (MIAs) or injured, bringing the total number of casualties to nearly 4,500. In the eyes of the American people, this "sneak attack" was unprovoked and therefore proof of the perfidious nature of the enemy. In the words of one noted historian:

> With the cataclysmic attack on Pearl Harbor, the nation that had only the day before been paralyzed by division found itself united in a determination to strike down the aggressors and crush them into the ground. . . . As always in wartime, the great abstractions now took possession of the national mind. In place of Japanese, German, or Italian men, women, and children, there arose an apparition called "The Enemy," a beast whose inborn nature fulfilled itself only in aggression.[5]

Shock, anger, and outrage served to unite the nation and steel its resolve. God was on our side. The enemy would be defeated utterly. Nothing short of unconditional surrender would suffice to satisfy the vengeance of an aroused and righteous America.[6]

Whereas FDR's hands had been tied prior to Pearl Harbor, now a tidal wave of patriotism swept away moral and political constraints. At the beginning of America's war against fascism some 120,000 Japanese living in San Francisco, Los Angeles, and other communities along the Pacific Coast were rounded up and

---

5. Louis J. Halle, *The Cold War as History* (New York: Harper and Row, 1967), pp. 34–35.
6. Ibid.

sent to "relocation" camps, many in the interior states of Arizona, Arkansas, Colorado, Idaho, and Utah.[7] By the time the United States dropped two atomic bombs on civilian Japanese populations in two large cities, Hiroshima and Nagasaki, killing an estimated 115,000 men, women, and children, isolationist policy in the country had vanished.

THE ARSENAL OF DEMOCRACY: AN EMERGING SUPERPOWER

The extent of Japan's folly in attacking the American "sleeping giant" can also be measured and expressed in statistics. Although the United States pointedly did not participate in the great-power arms race in the interwar period, America's war *potential* still dwarfed that of Japan and was roughly double that of Japan, Germany, and Italy combined.[8] For good reason, Winston Churchill rejoiced at the news of America's declaration of war against Germany and Italy, as well as Japan. As Churchill later put it, "Hitler's fate was sealed. Mussolini's fate was sealed. As for the Japanese, they would be ground to powder. All the rest was merely the proper application of overwhelming force."[9] Whether or not the United States and the Allies properly applied force against the common enemy is debatable, but there is no doubt that the superior economic power and especially the prodigious industrial capacity of the United States was decisive.[10]

What the numbers reveal, according to the exhaustive research and analysis of one noted scholar, is that "even after the expansion of the German and Japanese empires, the economic and productive forces ranged upon each were *much more disproportionate* than in the First World War."[11] According to this expert:

---

7. FDR signed Executive Order 9102 establishing the War Relocation Authority in March 1942 and named Milton Eisenhower, the brother of Gen. (and later President) Dwight David Eisenhower, as its first head. For more information, go to http://www.oz.net/~cyu/internment/main.html and http://historymatters.gmu.edu/d/51531. Also see Geoffrey S. Smith, "Racial Nativism and the Origins of Japanese American Relocation," in *Japanese Americans, from Relocation to Redress*, ed. Roger Daniels, Sandra Taylor, and Harry Kitano (Salt Lake City: University of Utah Press, 1986), pp. 79–85.

8. Paul Kennedy, *The Rise and Fall of the Great Powers* (New York: Vintage Books, 1989), p. 332. Kennedy relies heavily on Roger Hilsman, "Comparative Strength of the Powers," in *The World in 1939*, ed. A. J. Toynbee and F. T. Ashton-Gwatkin (London: Oxford University Press, 1952).

9. Quoted by Ronald H. Spector in *Eagle against the Sun: The American War with Japan* (New York: Random House, 1985), p. 123.

10. Aircraft production of the United States alone went from 5,856 annually in 1939 to a high of 96,318 in 1944, dwarfing at its peak the combined Axis powers' production, which went from 14,562 in 1939 to 67,987 in 1944. Likewise, the United States went from spending an estimated $1.5 billion in armaments production in 1940 to $37.5 billion in 1943, whereas the total Axis spending on armaments production went from an estimated $7.75 billion to $18.3 billion. Kennedy, *Rise and Fall*, pp. 354–355.

11. Ibid., p. 354.

[T]he decisive events of December 1941 entirely altered these [existing] balances: the Russian counterattack at Moscow showed that it would not fall to Blitzkrieg warfare and the entry of Japan and the United States into what was now a global conflict brought together a "Grand Alliance" of enormous industrial-productive staying power. . . . The Allies possessed *twice* the manufacturing strength . . . *three* times the "war potential," and *three* times the national income of the Axis powers, even when the French shares are added to Germany's total. By 1942 and 1943, these figures of potential power were being exchanged into the hard currency of aircraft, guns, tanks and ships; indeed, by 1943–1944 the United States alone was producing one ship a day and one aircraft every five minutes![12]

In hindsight, the outcome of World War II was a foregone conclusion once the United States threw its weight behind Great Britain and the Soviet Union. The British and the Russians suffered the greatest losses in human and economic terms, endured the greatest hardships, fought valiantly for six long years, and thus deserve full credit for contributing to the crushing victory of the Allies in 1945. But the war altered the landscape of international politics fundamentally by accelerating the appearance of (if it did not exactly create) a single "superpower"—a state head-and-shoulders above the other powers. The war-ravaged Soviet Union would challenge American supremacy after 1945 and even attain superpower status a decade or so later, but it would have to strain its economic and political capacities to the limits to do so and would eventually collapse as a consequence. In the aftermath of World War II, there would be no basis for a multilateral balance-of-power system because the former Great Powers emerged from the war battered, weakened, and exhausted—with one exception: the United States.

Germany would be forced to surrender unconditionally, militarily occupied, and divided into two antagonistic rival states each dependent on an external patron for political and military cover. The United States knocked Japan out of the war and off its feet with the dropping of the two atomic bombs. Like Germany, Japan would be occupied and its government reinvented under the watchful eye of the American military commander on the scene (the redoubtable Gen. Douglas MacArthur). In the case of Japan, however, the United States would have no occupation partners, so Japan would not be divided into zones or separate jurisdictions. Indeed, the island of Okinawa would become a virtual American territory for the indefinite future. It would also become the home to one of the most important overseas military-base complexes in the world.

As for the other former Great Powers, France had fallen to new depths as a result of the occupation and the collaboration of the Vichy regime. Its economy was in shambles. The French nation was demoralized and dispirited. Great Britain had suffered severe damage to its economy as well. British cities, factories, and infrastructure were left badly battered by German bombing, and the British

---

12. Ibid., p. 355.

people psychologically traumatized and drained. The war had unleashed forces of nationalism in the colonial territories of the European powers as well. The historic upshot was an end to the glory days of the British Empire, despite Winston Churchill's gallant efforts to stave off the inevitable. Of the empires that were still in existence at the start of the twentieth century, only one—that of Russia, which had become the Union of Soviet Socialist Republics (USSR)—had survived and remained intact by the middle of the century. Astonishingly, Soviet Russia under the iron dictatorship of Joseph Stalin would emerge from the ashes of World War II, like the phoenix of Egyptian mythology. The Soviet "phoenix" was actually stronger, relatively speaking, than ever before in its long history of struggle against invasion by aggressive neighbors on three flanks (eastern, southern, and western)—stronger, but not necessarily more secure militarily or psychologically.

Looking back, it is clear that the Soviet Union was never a complete superpower, never the military equal of the United States, and certainly never in the same league economically. Militarily, the Soviet Union was a formidable adversary—a nuclear power with the capability to inflict enormous damage directly on strategic targets in the United States. That fact, alone, was enough to justify elevating Moscow to "superpower" status in the minds of most observers during the heyday of the cold war, but it diverted attention from the underlying economic weaknesses of the Soviet system, weaknesses for which the Soviet leadership never found a "fix." This Achilles' heel meant time was on the side of the West in the cold war, essentially for the same reason that it was on the side of the Allies in World War II: the sustained economic vitality of market economies linked to one another by a liberal trading regime proved to be an overwhelming advantage for the Western alliance system in the long run.[13]

The existence of a common enemy made the wartime collaboration an urgent necessity for the United States and the Soviet Union—as the saying goes, the enemy of my enemy is my friend. However, this very collaboration gave rise to a conundrum: How to lay the foundations for a postwar world order conducive to peaceful relations between the West (committed to democracy) and the Soviet Union (the antithesis of democracy)—an enterprise almost certain to accentuate differences—while trying to make common cause against the Axis?

Stalin met with Roosevelt and Churchill for the first time at Tehran, the capital of Iran, in late 1943.[14] The meeting was a diplomatic success, as Roosevelt

---

13. By the same token, the breakdown of this system in the interwar years—and especially after 1929—had set the stage for the dictatorships of the Rome-Berlin-Tokyo axis to challenge the system.

14. Roosevelt and Churchill met several times without Stalin between August 1941 and June 1942. They invited Stalin to meet with them at Casablanca in January 1943, but the Soviet leader declined, apparently in order to stay in Moscow and direct the Soviet counterattacks that were then turning the tide against the invaders. The seeds of mistrust were sown well before the war's end.

and Churchill pledged to invade German-occupied France and Stalin promised to launch a simultaneous offensive from the east. The Big Three did not meet again until February 1945 at Yalta in the Crimea. The Yalta Conference was arguably the most important of all the wartime summit meetings. The Big Three worked out postwar plans for the unconditional surrender of Germany at Yalta, including the decisions to divide the defeated Third Reich into four zones of occupation (American, British, French, and Soviet), to disarm Germany, to punish Nazi war criminals, and to impose reparations. The victorious Allies set the stage at Yalta for a conference in San Francisco to draft a United Nations Charter, as well.

Roosevelt, Churchill, and Stalin also cut secret deals in the Crimea, which became public knowledge only months (or in some cases years) later. Roosevelt agreed that Russia would get three votes in the embryonic United Nations General Assembly. But the secret concessions Roosevelt and Churchill made to Stalin in the Far East in return for his pledge to join the fight against Japan were to have a far more explosive effect on domestic politics in the United States. These concessions, giving Moscow Outer Mongolia, the southern half of Sakhalin Island, and the Kurile islands, as well as special rights in Manchuria, caused an uproar in the United States when they were later made public.[15] For the rabidly anti-Communist Far Right in American politics, "Yalta" became a symbol of betrayal, much as "Munich" is a symbol of appeasement. Roosevelt died suddenly in April 1945, only weeks before the war in Europe formally ended.

The last Big Three meeting occurred in the summer of 1945 at Potsdam near Berlin. Although it came six months after Yalta, Truman, now the U.S. president, feared that Stalin might not honor his pledge to enter the war in the Far East. Under the Yalta pact, Stalin was obliged to attack Japan in early August at the latest (three months after the German surrender). The United States successfully tested the first atomic bomb in history at Los Alamos, New Mexico, in mid-July, the day before the Potsdam Conference convened. The Allies issued a formal ultimatum to Japan from Potsdam: surrender or be destroyed. The Soviet Union had not yet declared war on Japan, so Moscow was not a party to this ultimatum. But Stalin was anxious to collect the territorial prizes he had won at Yalta, so he was keen to jump into the fray before Japan surrendered.

The other big issue at Potsdam involved arrangements for control of Germany, including the precise postwar boundaries between Germany and Poland and between Poland and the Soviet Union. Stalin insisted on taking territory that

---

15. For an in-depth account of the Yalta Conference, see Herbert Feis, *Churchill, Roosevelt, Stalin: The War They Waged and the Peace They Sought* (Princeton: Princeton University Press, 1957). Feis defends Roosevelt's wartime diplomacy, arguing that FDR did not "sell out" to Stalin at Yalta and that unconditional surrender probably did not prolong the war as some of FDR's detractors have claimed.

belonged to Poland before the war and compensating Poland with territory that belonged to Germany. This is where relations among the Big Three stood on August 6, 1945, when the United States dropped an atomic bomb on Hiroshima.

CONTAINMENT: BIG IDEA, BIG PRICE TAG

The policy of containment was America's response to the perceived Soviet threat to Western Europe in particular and democracy in general after World War II. The policy as it evolved was not the brainchild of a single individual but rather the precipitate of a lively debate, a kind of political-philosophical power struggle, that went on within the ranks of the government's top policy thinkers and planners. But the *concept* of containment and the theoretical rationale for the policies it inspired was the product of the fertile mind and facile pen of a career foreign service officer named George F. Kennan.[16]

Lest the reader get the wrong impression, the containment doctrine, like America's long romance with isolationism, was always controversial, always had its detractors, and never had a fixed and generally agreed-upon meaning or content. But it could be and was embraced by both sides in the great debates that gripped the nation at different times during the cold war (and, oddly, failed to gather any real momentum or draw much public attention in the 1990s). Indeed, many of the same issues raised at the inception of the cold war were simply resurrected and updated throughout its duration.

The Theory of Containment

In that original cold war debate, Kennan stands out as a major figure. Although popularly identified as one of the principal architects of the cold war "containment" policy, he has long since disavowed the policy itself and re-thought the "X Article" (see below), which remains synonymous with that policy. Kennan's disillusionment with the direction of American diplomacy at the half-century mark is a matter of record. "Never before," he wrote, "has there been such utter confusion in the public mind with respect to U.S. foreign policy." The president, the Congress, the public, and the press "all wander around in a labyrinth of ignorance. . . ."[17] To succeed, Kennan realized, the White House would have to earn "public confidence and respect" and carry "the public up to a clear and comprehensive view of the occurrences of these recent years."[18]

---

16. This section draws heavily on my article entitled "George F. Kennan's Memoirs" in *Political Science Reviewer* 15 (fall 1985): 295–336. The author wishes to thank the publisher, the Intercollegiate Studies Institute, for permission to reprint portions of the article here.
17. George F. Kennan, *Memoirs: 1925–1950* (Boston: Atlantic–Little, Brown, 1967), p. 500.
18. Ibid.

Based on his personal experiences as a career diplomat in the 1930s and 1940s, Kennan decried "one of the most consistent and incurable traits of American statesmanship—namely its neurotic self-consciousness and introversion, the tendency to make statements and take actions with regard not to their effect on the international scene to which they are ostensibly addressed but rather to their effect on those echelons of American opinion, congressional opinion first and foremost, to which the respective statesmen are anxious to appeal."[19] In particular, Kennan believed FDR had given too little weight to the brutal nature of Soviet totalitarianism and consequently misjudged the treacherous character of Joseph Stalin when the United States recognized the USSR in 1933. Even after the German attack in June 1941, Kennan held firm to his belief that the USSR was not a suitable ally of the Western democracies. "Such a view," he wrote, "would not preclude the extension of material aid whenever called for by our own self interest. I would, however, preclude anything which might identify us politically or ideologically with the Russian war effort."[20]

Before he published his famous "X Article" in *Foreign Affairs*, Kennan had set about writing several other pieces on Soviet motives, intentions, and behavior. The "Long Telegram," as one piece written at the Moscow embassy came to be known, catapulted Kennan into the Washington limelight. Kennan's transmission had five main parts. The first section was a straightforward recapitulation of Soviet official dogma based on the jaded formulations of Marx and Lenin. In the second section Kennan demonstrated a striking insight into why Marxism first found a territorial home, of all places, in Russia. "It was no coincidence," Kennan asserted. Marxist dogma was "a perfect vehicle for the sense of insecurity with which Bolsheviks . . . were afflicted." Moreover, it provided "justification for their instinctive fear of the outside world." He continued:

> [The West is portrayed as] evil, hostile, and menacing, but destined . . . to be wracked with growing internal convulsions. . . . This thesis provides justification for that increase of military and police power . . . that isolation of the Russian population from the outside world . . . and that fluid and constant pressure to extend the limits of Russian police power which are together the natural and instinctive urges of Russian rulers. Basically this is . . . a centuries-old movement in which conceptions of offense and defense are inextricably confused. . . . [I]n [its] new guise of international Marxism, it is more dangerous and insidious than ever before.[21]

Kennan argued persuasively that Soviet propaganda provided an illuminating glimpse into the dark recesses of the totalitarian mind: "The very disrespect

19. Ibid., p. 53.
20. Ibid., p. 133.
21. Ibid., p. 550–551.

of Russians for objective truth . . . leads them to view all stated facts as instruments for furtherance of one ulterior purpose or another."[22]

The third section, dealing with official Soviet policy, was a base Kennan had to cover at the time but is now passé; the fourth part, treating the issue of Soviet "unofficial, or subterranean" (that is, subversive) policy was a real blockbuster. This section laid out—in terms that could hardly have been better calculated to alarm policymakers—the lurid details of a worldwide network of clandestine organs and cover operations directed from the Kremlin. Here Kennan spoke of such ominous things as "an underground operation directorate of world communism, a concealed Comintern tightly coordinated and directed by Moscow" using "front organizations" and a "far-flung apparatus"; he predicted "particularly violent efforts . . . to weaken . . . influence of Western powers over colonial . . . peoples" and warned that "no holds will be barred." "Communists," he said, "will work toward destruction of all forms of personal independence." Soviet strategy will be designed "to set the major Western powers against each other." Simultaneously, "Soviet-dominated puppet political machines will be undergoing preparation to take over domestic power in . . . colonial areas." Finally, "all Soviet efforts on an unofficial international plane will be negative and destructive in character." The United States was dealing with "a police regime par excellence, reared in the dim half-world of Tsarist police intrigue."[23]

Having thus sounded the alarm, Kennan soothingly asserted that "the problem is within our power to solve . . . without recourse to any general military conflict." His reasoning foreshadowed the "X Article": (1) the Soviets understand the "logic of force" and can "easily withdraw . . . when strong resistance is encountered at any point"; (2) they "are still by far the weaker force"; (3) the success of the Soviet system "is not yet finally proven" and may not survive the "supreme test of successive transfer of power from one individual or group to another"; and, finally, all Soviet propaganda is "basically negative and destructive" and therefore should be easily combated by "any intelligent and really constructive program."[24]

To defeat the Soviet adversary the West would have to grasp the nature of the world Communist movement. Not only government leaders but also the public would have to be educated: "I cannot overemphasize the importance of this point," he admonished. In the final analysis, "the health and vigor of our society" is the best defense against subversion and revolution. Indeed, "Every courageous and incisive measure to solve internal problems of our own society . . . is a diplomatic victory over Moscow worth a thousand . . . joint communiqués." But to take advantage of this insight, we would have to put forward "a much more positive and constructive picture of the sort of world we would like to see than we

---

22. Ibid., p. 551.
23. Ibid., pp. 555–557.
24. Ibid., pp. 557–558.

have put forward in the past." In the process, "we must . . . cling to our own methods and conceptions of human society . . . because the greatest danger that can befall us in coping with this problem of Soviet communism is that we shall allow ourselves to become like those with whom we are coping."[25] Here was great wisdom flowing from the pen of a career diplomat, a "cog" in the government's foreign policy bureaucracy.

The parallels between this period (1944–1947) and the three-year period after the fall of communism (1989–1992) are easily overdrawn. Similarly, the use of cold war analogies to formulate or explain U.S. foreign policy since September 11, 2001, is more likely to confuse than to clarify. But the *principles* lodged in the lines and logic of the Long Telegram are arguably as valid today as they were when Kennan first put pen to paper.

The "X Article" itself must be viewed in the context of Kennan's convictions about the need for public education if the new policy of "containment" being launched was to bear fruit. His *Foreign Affairs* article, published anonymously, was the vehicle in the vanguard of this effort. Kennan introduced the word "containment" in this article and elaborated it into a compelling concept suitable for mass consumption. "It is clear," Kennan wrote, "that the main element of any United States policy toward the Soviet Union must be that of a long-term, patient but firm and vigilant containment of Russian expansive tendencies. . . . Soviet pressure against free institutions of the Western world is something that can be contained by adroit and vigilant application of counter-force at a series of constantly shifting geographical and political points."[26] Kennan elucidated the strategy behind containment in a passage that appeared amazingly far-sighted four decades later. The United States, he said, "has it in its power to increase enormously the strains under which Soviet policy must operate, to force upon the Kremlin a far greater degree of moderation and circumspection than it has had to observe in recent years, and in this way to promote tendencies which must eventually find their outlet in either the breakup or the gradual mellowing of Soviet power."[27]

Kennan's analysis represents the art and science of policymaking at its finest. Never in the history of American diplomacy has a new idea made a bigger difference. The strategy of containment redefined American foreign policy overnight, giving it a new rationale, a clear purpose, manageable aims and objectives, and a blueprint for achieving the prize without provoking another war. At the end of World War II, the United States faced the same question that had confronted the nation after World War I: how to build a new world order based on

25. Ibid., pp. 558–559.

26. George F. Kennan, "The Sources of Soviet Conduct," *Foreign Affairs,* July 1947; reprinted in George F. Kennan, *American Diplomacy 1900–1950* (Chicago: University of Chicago Press, 1951). In the Mentor Book edition (New York, 1951), see pp. 89–106; the quotation is found on p. 99.

27. Ibid., pp. 105–106.

freedom on the ruins of the old order that had been destroyed by tyranny. America failed in the wake of World War I, but after World War II, thanks in no small part to Kennan, America finally had a roadmap.

Putting Containment to the Test

With the National Security Act of 1947, the entire machinery of foreign policy underwent a massive overhaul. The new law brought the army, navy, and air force under a single umbrella in a newly created Department of Defense (the Pentagon). It also created a National Security Council within the Executive Office of the President. The function of the NSC was (is) to advise the president and facilitate the coordination of domestic, foreign, and military policies relating to national security. The assistant to the president for national security affairs, who directs the NSC staff, is also known as the president's national security adviser. The person occupying this position would in time become the natural rival of the secretary of state. In the late 1940s, however, the new foreign policy machinery was untested, roles in the new system were still ill defined, and new power relationships had not yet hardened in place.

As director of the Policy Planning Staff in the State Department, Kennan played a major role in the formulation of the European Recovery Act, popularly known as the Marshall Plan, an early cornerstone of containment devised in 1947. In particular, he argued forcefully for the rehabilitation of Germany and for inclusion of *all* Europe as possible participants, not just the former Allies or West European democracies. Any other course, he insisted, would place the onus of responsibility for dividing Europe—and thus, in effect, starting the cold war—on America's shoulders.[28]

To put the Marshall Plan into perspective, shortly before its formulation there had been a major crisis over the future of Greece and Turkey. In particular, the fear of a Communist takeover in Greece and the fact that the British had bowed out led President Truman to make a breathtaking new commitment in March 1947: "I believe it must be the policy of the United States to support free people who are resisting attempted subjugation by armed minorities or by outside pressures."[29] The Truman Doctrine was nothing short of a revolution in

---

28. The best account of the policy process that culminated in the Marshall Plan is Joseph Marion Jones, *The Fifteen Weeks: An Inside Account of the Genesis of the Marshall Plan* (New York: Harbinger Books, 1964), p. 253. Kennan's own detailed account is found in his *Memoirs: 1925–1950*, pp. 325–353.

29. The internal situations in Greece and Turkey were very different. In Greece, a Communist insurgency backed by the Soviet Union posed a threat to the existing pro-Western government. In Turkey, no such internal threat existed, but if Greece went Communist, Turkey would be increasingly vulnerable to Communist subversion and diplomatic pressures orchestrated by the Kremlin.

American foreign policy.[30] In asking Congress to approve a $400 million aid package for Greece and Turkey, the president stressed "that our help should be primarily through economic and financial aid which is essential to economic stability and orderly political processes." This is the part of the Truman Doctrine that is often overlooked by historians and was largely forgotten by Truman's successors.

The first Soviet-American confrontation of the postwar era erupted in 1948, the first time the two military titans of the cold war would go to the brink of war, stare each other down, and then step back. The focal point in 1948 was Berlin, the old German capital that had been divided into four zones of occupation since 1945. The idea had been to create temporary arrangements there pending final agreement among the Allies concerning peace terms, including the precise form of government, to be imposed on the Germans. The first Berlin Crisis was a test case for both sides. Stalin had no intention of relinquishing his foothold in Germany, Russia's great nemesis. The Truman foreign policy team was committed to reintegrating a politically and economically rehabilitated Germany into a democratic Europe.[31] Obviously, these two visions of Europe's future put the United States and the Soviet Union on a collision course that ran right through the center of Berlin.

The denouement of the crisis reads like a fast-paced work of fiction, the sort of thing a Hollywood filmmaker might turn into an "action-thriller." It started with a blockade.[32] At the London Conference in February 1948, the United States, Great Britain, France, and the Benelux countries reached a consensus on several European issues of momentous importance. First, Washington, London, and Paris would coordinate economic policies in the Western occupation zones; second, Germany would be included in the Marshall Plan; third, a German federal government would be established in the parts of Germany not under Soviet control. The Soviet Union, notably absent from the London meeting, bitterly opposed all these moves.[33]

Stalin answered this challenge by cutting off Western access to Berlin. A geopolitical anomaly made this ploy possible: Berlin was located 110 miles *inside*

---

30. The full text of the Truman Doctrine is reprinted in Jones, *Fifteen Weeks*, pp. 269–274.

31. The most prominent members of President Truman's distinguished foreign policy cabinet were Secretary of State George C. Marshall, Undersecretary (later Secretary) of State Dean Acheson, Ambassador Charles ("Chip") Bohlen, and George Kennan.

32. A fascinating account by the American ambassador to the USSR at the time of the Berlin blockade can be found in Walter Bedell Smith's memoirs entitled *My Three Years in Moscow* (New York: Lippincott, 1950), esp. pp. 230–260. See also W. Phillips Davison, *The Berlin Blockade* (Princeton: Princeton University Press, 1958).

33. Thomas Magstadt, "The Berlin Crisis of 1948: A Case Study," paper prepared for the National Security Strategy course, Air War College, Maxwell Air Force Base, Montgomery, Ala., Spring 1992, p. 9.

the Soviet-controlled zone. As an "island" in a hostile sea, the divided city became a powerful symbol, a microcosm of the cold war. West Berlin was a surrogate for Western-style democracy; East Berlin was a satellite of the totalitarian Soviet state. As an astute student of Machiavellian power politics, Stalin believed he had the upper hand: Berlin was exposed and the Soviet military had an enormous numerical advantage in local and theater forces. The United States and Great Britain had demobilized rapidly after the war; the Soviet Union had not. Moscow also had geography on its side: Soviet troops could march en masse and unimpeded right across territory under the Kremlin's political control. The United States would have to cross an ocean. But first it would have to demonstrate the political will—would a war-weary America, a "soft" bourgeois society if ever there was one, rise to the occasion again, without resistance, so soon? By making the first move, a move that was aggressive but nonlethal, he would force Truman to start the next war or back down.

Thus, Stalin no doubt thought the dice he was rolling were loaded. He was wrong. He made the mistake of "doing the math" in the old-fashioned way, putting too much stock in raw military power on the ground and too little in economic and technological factors.

Truman's reply was two-pronged: a counterblockade of East Berlin and an airlift. The latter—the Berlin airlift—was arguably the most spectacular demonstration of nonlethal power in world history. The United States won the first battle in the war on communism without firing a shot. The Berlin airlift illustrates the essence of early containment, namely, stopping Soviet expansion without going to war. Second, it demonstrated America's airlift capabilities at a time when the Soviets could not begin to match us—it thus put Stalin on notice that we could move forces to the European theater quickly and on a large scale. Third, it affirmed America's commitment to the defense of Western Europe at a time when the European democracies were still vulnerable to a Soviet land invasion.

Institutionalizing Containment

The crisis over Berlin gave impetus to the idea of creating a permanent military alliance linking the democratic states of North America and Western Europe. The idea became a reality with the launching of the North Atlantic Treaty Organization (NATO) in 1949.[34]

---

34. In addition to the United States, the charter members of NATO included Belgium, Canada, Denmark, France, Iceland, Italy, Luxembourg, the Netherlands, Norway, Portugal, and the United Kingdom. Other members include Greece (1952), Turkey (1952), the Federal Republic of Germany (1955), and Spain (1982); the Czech Republic, Hungary, and Poland joined in 1999.

The birth of NATO represents a landmark in the history of American foreign policy, the first time Uncle Sam had joined a military alliance in peacetimes in 150 years. The North Atlantic Treaty Organization created a joint military command structure headed by an American "supreme commander." It created "joint and combined" military forces and a permanent bureaucracy with headquarters in Paris (later moved to Brussels).[35] At NATO's core was the pledge in Article 5. Invoked only once in the history of the organization—in response to September 11—it stated "that an armed attack against one or more of them [the signatories] in Europe or North America shall be considered an attack against them all." The contrast to post–World War I, when America turned its back on Europe, could hardly have been more striking: This time the United States not only breathed new life into the idea of a world organization, but as reinsurance also kept military forces there that would be permanently stationed on European soil under the roof of a regional security organization.[36]

In Washington, "bipartisanship" was a popular buzzword and eventually became a foreign policy icon. It was formed in the crucible of the cold war when Republicans, led by Sen. Arthur H. Vandenberg, supported the Truman Doctrine, the Marshall Plan, and the entire "containment" package of foreign policy initiatives. The famous Vandenberg Resolution called for a united front in the fight against communism. The rallying cry of the resolution's supporters was that politics ends at the water's edge. It made sense in the prevailing climate of fear and uncertainty, but it was (and is) a two-edged sword in a society that takes the virtues of democracy seriously. Patriotism, as Samuel Johnson (1709–1784) said, is that last refuge of a scoundrel. When the idea of bipartisanship becomes a kind of political commandment and questioning its value is by definition unpatriotic, there is a danger that debate will cease or be severely constricted. The chilling effect on the public discourse is one of the results. Ill-considered policy and presidential immunity to criticism are others. History shows that war and peace are too important to be left to one or a few—especially one who is immune to criticism and shielded from the consequences of his or her actions.

Thus, by mid-century the die was cast. The United States had accepted the Soviet challenge, taking on the self-appointed role as "leader of the Free World." For the next four decades a cold war would pit "democracy" against "totalitarianism," "freedom" against "communism," an epic battle between the forces of good

35. For an authoritative account of NATO's origins, aims, and strategy, as well as issues of common defense in the first decade or so of its existence, see Robert E. Osgood, *NATO: The Entangling Alliance* (Chicago: University of Chicago Press, 1962).

36. Article 51 of the UN Charter allows for "individual or collective self-defense" on the part of its members. As such "it constituted an acknowledgment that the founders of the United Nations had devised no plan for dealing with the threat of great power aggression; it represented a decision for indefinite postponement of this issue." Inis Claude Jr., *Power and International Relations* (New York: Random House, 1962), p. 165.

and evil. It would be a war fought with all available means, a war of ideologies and words, threats and brinkmanship. It would involve an arms race that would give new meaning to the word "irony," an arms race so competitive and terrifying in its implications that neither side would dare to use any of the weapons in its arsenal, from rifles to rockets, against the other for fear of unleashing a nuclear holocaust. It was this irony that soon gave rise to the military-strategic concept of deterrence.

Who Will Contain Containment?

At odds with his boss, Secretary of State Dean Acheson, George Kennan left Washington in 1950, taking a leave of absence without pay.[37] Kennan and Acheson did not see eye-to-eye. The issues over which they differed—NATO, Germany, and the future of Europe—were big and basic.[38] How the government decided these issues would determine the shape of things to come in the second half of the twentieth century and beyond.

Underlying the policy struggles within the Truman administration was an even more fundamental issue: how best to deal with the Soviet Union. What was the nature of Soviet Russia? What motivated Stalin? What were Moscow's true aims and intentions? Finally, was Marxist-Leninist ideology primarily a propaganda tool or did it actually guide Soviet behavior?

Kennan's position can be briefly summarized. First, he was opposed to the idea of a North Atlantic military alliance from the outset because it would aggravate tensions with Moscow unnecessarily, give rise to an open-ended American military commitment to Europe's defense, and lead to future military confrontations rather than a search for political-diplomatic solutions. Second, he was opposed to the hasty creation of a separate and self-governing West German state because it would solidify the division of Germany and consequently the whole of Europe. Third, he was opposed to the creation of a Western Europe dependent psychologically, economically, and militarily on the United States. Such a state of affairs would have baleful effects, he argued, not the least of which was the loss of any possibility that an actual *European* balance of power—one obviating the need for an American military presence—might in time be restored.

It is noteworthy that Kennan's policy preferences echoed Washington's Farewell Address and Jefferson's caution about "entangling alliances." In that sense, Kennan was in accord with traditionalists who emphasize "soft power,"

---

37. Kennan returned to active duty in the Foreign Service briefly in 1951 when President Truman appointed him ambassador to Moscow. The Soviets declared him persona non grata the following year, however, after which he retired to a life of contemplation and scholarship—but not exactly a quiet life. For a time, he became the most prominent critic of U.S. foreign policy in America and the center of much controversy.

38. Kennan, *Memoirs: 1925–1950*, pp. 397–470.

favor cautious commitment, and preach foreign policy parsimony. But Kennan was by no means an isolationist. It would be more accurate to say that Kennan's position was that of an internationalist who opposed militarism and interventionism—and something called "massive retaliation."

Nuclear weapons also became the subject of a great debate in the 1950s. The issues surrounding these weapons were inseparable from the German question, NATO, and the American role in Europe. In 1957 Kennan caused something of a furor with a series of six high-profile radio lectures he delivered at the invitation of the British Broadcasting Corporation (BBC).[39] The fourth lecture in the series—dealing with nuclear weapons—turned out to be the most controversial and remains the most relevant to this day. Kennan denounced reliance on such weapons as an instrument of foreign policy. The gist of Kennan's message to his radio audience was, in his own words, that "the weapon of mass destruction was, in any form, sterile and useless. It might serve for a time as an answer to itself, as a shield against utter cataclysm. But it could not serve the purposes of a constructive and hopeful foreign policy."[40]

He specifically decried the idea that was gathering momentum in Washington to base the defenses of Western Europe on tactical nuclear weapons within the framework of NATO. Creating a common pool of mass-destruction weapons, Kennan argued, would impede future disarmament talks by elevating the status of *all* NATO members, including West Germany, to the nuclear level. Moreover, it would greatly complicate any future effort to limit the proliferation of nuclear weapons, in effect turning every NATO member-state into a nuclear power.[41] Thus, Kennan adamantly opposed the strategy of "massive retaliation," which was so attractive to the Eisenhower administration's "New Look" and to Secretary of State John Foster Dulles.[42]

We turn next to the strategy of deterrence implicit in massive retaliation and the fascinating debate it sparked over the limitability of nuclear war in the 1950s. Readers are invited to consider the relevance of this old and all-but-forgotten debate to the current scene at a time when weapons of mass destruction and the attempt to isolate the so-called "axis of evil" (Iraq, Iran, and North Korea) are at the very heart of Washington's war on terrorism.

---

39. These were the prestigious Reith Lectures. George F. Kennan, *Memoirs: 1950–1963* (New York: Pantheon Books, 1972), pp. 229–266.

40. Ibid., p. 244.

41. Ibid., pp. 244–246. The United States hoped to preempt any possible move by other NATO members, especially France, to acquire independent nuclear capabilities, as well as off-set the Soviet advantage in conventional forces with tactical weapons of mass destruction (WMD). To Secretary of State John Foster Dulles and other hawks in the Eisenhower administration, creating a multilateral nuclear force (MLN) seemed like a relatively low-cost quick fix.

42. On Dulles's romance with "massive retaliation," see esp. Townsend Hoopes, *The Devil and John Foster Dulles* (Boston: Little, Brown, 1973), pp. 191–201.

CONTAINMENT GOES TO WAR: KOREA

The undeclared Korean War (officially called the "Korean conflict") followed closely on the heels of another shattering event: the Communist takeover of China. After World War II the Korean peninsula was divided, with a pro-Soviet government in the north and a pro-Western government in the south. With Moscow's backing, North Korea attacked South Korea in 1950 and was close to claiming victory when the United States intervened (with the imprimatur of the United Nations) under the command of Douglas MacArthur. The United Nations forces (mostly Americans) suffered reversals but eventually pushed the North Korean forces back to the thirty-eighth parallel (the original north-south dividing line). The United States then made a crucial decision: to cross the thirty-eighth parallel into North Korean territory. The tide turned dramatically as MacArthur's army drove nearly all the way to the Chinese border. But there was one more surprise in store: Chinese troops came streaming down in a ferocious counterattack that put the invading UN (American) forces on the defensive. Retreating back across the thirty-eighth parallel, the UN (American) forces barely managed to stave off utter defeat, eventually battling back to the original line. There the conflict finally ended in 1953, with the signing of a truce that settled nothing.

The scale and unsatisfying outcome of the Korean conflict fueled a great debate over the whole question of limited war. Korea had been extremely costly for the United States in blood and treasure, but despite the high cost it ended in a draw.[43] For Americans, unaccustomed to losing (or not winning) wars, the outcome of the Korean conflict was profoundly unsettling. The United States had weapons it no longer dared to use; instead, it settled for a limited objective (preserving South Korea's "independence") after having failed to achieve an unlimited objective (crushing North Korea and reuniting the Korean peninsula under a pro-American government). Clearly, Americans did not want a repeat of Korea anywhere else in the world. But the U.S. government faced a dilemma: it was committed to containment of communism abroad, but as a liberal democracy it was disinclined to ask or call for the sustained economic sacrifices required for a protracted struggle.

CONTAINMENT AND DETERRENCE

In 1953 President Eisenhower inherited a sizeable defense budget of about $42 billion from the outgoing Truman administration (compared with a paltry $13 billion in 1949). The Republicans also inherited a large budget deficit (nearly $10 billion, a sizeable sum at that time). About three-quarters of the last Truman

---

43. For an excellent account, see David Rees, *Korea: The Limited War* (New York: St. Martin's, 1964).

budget was for "national security programs" (roughly 60 percent for the armed services).

Rearming America: NSC-68

In 1950, following the first Soviet atomic test, the Departments of Defense and State had undertaken a joint study of America's national security needs. The study known as NSC-68 warned that by 1954 the Soviet Union would probably have the capability of launching a devastating nuclear attack directly against targets in the United States. This nuclear capability would neutralize the American deterrent and leave the Soviet Union with an overwhelming superiority in conventional forces. Thus, 1954 would be a "crisis year" unless the United States moved decisively to redress the balance in conventional forces. In 1950 the Korean War prompted a rapid remobilization and incurred large war-related expenditures and budget deficits.

When President Eisenhower came into office he promptly cut $7.5 billion from the defense budget and rejected the "crisis year" concept: "Defense is not a matter of maximum strength for a single date," he admonished, but rather a matter for the "long haul." Eisenhower's desire to cut military spending even further spurred Admiral Arthor W. Radford, Chairman of the Joint Chiefs of Staff, to suggest that one way to economize would be to allow the Pentagon's military chiefs to build reliance on nuclear weapons into war plans rather than having to prepare for a broad range of wars (all-out nuclear war, general conventional war, limited nuclear war, and limited conventional war).

Massive Retaliation: Who's Containing Whom?

Containment was a self-liquidating concept: if it succeeded, it would become irrelevant. Deterrence is just the opposite: if it fails, nothing else matters.

The theory of deterrence is a product of the nuclear age, pure and simple: the world had war long before it had nuclear physics, but in prenuclear times military science was all about war-fighting strategies, all about offense or defense. In the middle of the twentieth century, the language and logic of war changed fundamentally. When modern science first smashed the atom it also smashed all pre-existing limits on organized violence.

The story of the atomic bomb does not need retelling in these pages. Suffice it to say that joint British-American scientific experiments during World War II succeeded. President Truman's decision to drop radioactive bombs on civilian populations has been the subject of controversy and academic debate, but Truman himself expressed no regret then or later.[44] So-called "revisionist"

---

44. See, for example, Merle Miller, *Plain Speaking: An Oral Autobiography* (New York: Berkeley Medallion Books, 1974), p. 244.

historians, however, have questioned everything, including the military necessity of this action, Truman's motives, and, in particular, the morality of dropping the *second* bomb. Was the first "demonstration" not enough, they ask? A scholar who delved in detail into this decision in an imaginative "history" of the cold war written in the 1960s, had these thoughts: "I have given this much account of the circumstances that led to the actual employment of the atomic bomb in action because, in ways that defy definition, this terminal resort to its use created the psychological atmosphere of the postwar world upon which the nations now looked out as the smoke cleared away from the ruins. This was a somber victory."[45] This "somber victory" set the stage for the "brave, new world" of push-button nuclear peril that stands as the terrible legacy of World War II—a legacy that, like it or not, bears the stamp "made in America."

The American debate over nuclear weapons goes back to the earliest days of the cold war. At that time the United States, of course, enjoyed a nuclear monopoly. No one knew how long this advantageous state of affairs would last, but there was no doubt that it was temporary. Few expected the beginning of the end to come as early as 1949, which it did, when the Soviet Union built and detonated an atom bomb at a test site. From this test stage to the production and stockpiling of mass-destruction bombs was only a matter of time, a few years at most. So, too, was the step-up from fission to fusion bombs.[46]

The Soviet Union kept a multi-million-man army on active duty throughout the cold war. As a Communist dictatorship, the Kremlin leadership could conscript as many young men as it chose, keep them in military service indefinitely, and pay them a pittance. The cost of maintaining equivalent *peacetime* standing forces in a democratic society was politically and economically prohibitive. Moreover, standing astride two continents, one of which was Europe, the Soviet Union enjoyed natural geostrategic advantages over the United States in that part of the world. In these circumstances, the temptation for military-strategic thinkers and planners in Washington to look around for a quick fix was irresistible. To Secretary of State John Foster Dulles, the American lead in nuclear weapons in the early 1950s appeared to be the answer. To be more specific, the now-notorious strategy of "massive retaliation" was the answer.

Dulles set out the rationale for massive retaliation in a speech to the Council on Foreign Relations, a foreign policy think tank, in January 1954. In the past, he

45. Louis J. Halle, *The Cold War as History* (New York: Harper and Row, 1967), p. 96.

46. The explosive power of the first atomic bombs was the result of a chain-reaction of splitting atoms (fission). The bomb dropped on Hiroshima was a fission bomb with an explosive charge equivalent to about 12.5 kilotons of TNT. Subsequent advances in nuclear science led to the discovery of a process called nuclear fusion involving hydrogen as the basic element. Today's bombs are thus "H bombs" of far greater yield (up to one megaton or 1,000 kilotons). The United States and Russia both possess weapons of this size. After a series of strategic arms reduction agreements, both countries retain thousands of both strategic and tactical (or "battlefield") nuclear weapons.

said, "what we did was in the main emergency action, imposed on us by our enemies." That means, he explained, "the enemy has the initiative." The aim of the new strategy was to get better results and save the taxpayers money "by placing more reliance on deterrent power, and less dependence on local defensive power." The latter must be reinforced by "the further deterrent of massive retaliatory power." He explained that the president had made a decision "to depend primarily upon a great capacity to retaliate, instantly, by means and at places of our choosing." Such a strategy, Dulles told his audience, "permits of a selection of military means instead of a multiplication of means."[47]

This electrifying new stance raised a lot of questions and even more eyebrows.[48] It caused a furor in the press and confusion in the public mind. Did Dulles mean that the United States would use nuclear weapons in any future skirmish or border incident? Or was it all a bluff? In poker, bluffing is risky and the player who bluffs all the time soon loses credibility—not to mention money. Dulles subsequently wrote an article in *Foreign Affairs* explaining the new policy in terms clearly intended to defuse the uproar by ratcheting down the rhetoric of deterrence. Inverting Kennan's "X Article" thesis, Dulles stressed the *economic* dimension of the policy but argued that if the West tries to "match the potential [of the] Communist forces, man for man and tank for tank . . . it could bankrupt itself and not achieve security over a sustained period."[49]

Without renouncing the policy of containment, Dulles stood Kennan on his head. Apart from the alarm bells Dulles set off in the United States and Europe (on *both* sides of the East and West divide), apart from the bluster and absence of finesse, and the lack of military or political or diplomatic logic, there was a fundamental contradiction between the world according to Dulles and the worldview implicit in Kennan's idea of containment. Where Kennan was optimistic, Dulles was pessimistic. Where Kennan put his faith in the natural moral and economic superiority of liberal democracy to prevail over the stultifying effects of "totalitarian" tyranny in the long run, Dulles believed the West would "bankrupt itself" without heavy reliance on nuclear weapons. And where Kennan emphasized "soft power"—the kind of power that flows from economic, political, and cultural

---

47. "Evolution of Foreign Policy," speech to Council on Foreign Relations, Jan. 1954 (Department of State Press Release no. 8). Quoted in Hoopes, *Devil*, p. 198.

48. In an interview with Turner Catledge published in the *New York Times* on May 10, 1957, Nikita Khrushchev pointedly referred to Dulles's saber-rattling foreign policy without mentioning his name: "It is one thing when a skilled acrobat balances on a tightrope. If he loses his balance and falls off only one person perishes. Even that is a pity. But if a statesman who is conducting a policy of 'the brink of war' falls, then his mistake can lead to the death of millions of people. This must not be forgotten." Quoted in Herbert S. Dinerstein, *War and the Soviet Union* (New York: Praeger, 1962), pp. 84–85.

49. John Foster Dulles, "Policy for Security and Peace," *Foreign Affairs*, Apr. 1954, pp. 357–358. Quoted in Hoopes, *Devil*, p. 200.

affinity rather than military dependency and the kind that flows from attractive rather than coercive attributes—Dulles emphasized military force (or "hard power") in its most lethal and terrifying form.

Ironically, when Stalin's successor, Nikita Khrushchev, boasted that "we will bury you" in 1957, he was playing upon fears that Dulles himself had done a great deal to engender. As we know now, Dulles was wrong and Kennan was right. Time was not on the side of Communist tyranny, nor did the Soviet Union's rigid centrally planned economy have a snowball's chance against the dynamic market economies of the West (and later Asia).

Nonetheless, the die was cast: the heavy American reliance on an ever-growing arsenal of nuclear weapons would continue, precluding any serious efforts at strategic arms limitation, as we shall see, until the early 1970s. By that time, it would be too late to halt the proliferation of nuclear weapons and way too late for the United States to set a positive example or assert any moral leadership on this all-important issue.

Thinking about the Unthinkable: Limited War

By 1957 a great debate was bubbling in both academic and policy circles over the political and military implications of nuclear weapons.[50] Was limited war possible between two nuclear powers or would a conventional war inevitably escalate into an "all-out" thermonuclear war? Would (or should) the United States risk the use of nuclear weapons to defend Paris if it meant provoking Moscow to retaliate directly against Washington or New York?[51] In *Nuclear Weapons and Foreign Policy*, Henry Kissinger rejected overreliance on strategic nuclear weapons and derided "the secret dream of American military thought: that there exists a final answer to our military problem, that it is possible to defeat the enemy utterly, and that war has its own rationale independent of policy."[52]

Kissinger advocated a return to the limited wars fought in Europe before and after the time of Napoleon. The kind of warfare he had in mind involved "an attempt to affect the opponent's will, not to crush it, to make the conditions to be imposed seem more attractive than continued resistance."[53] But the notion that two implacable enemies with unlimited means could fight a war for limited ends,

---

50. In 1957 two scholarly books on nuclear weapons and foreign policy appeared in the United States, one by Henry Kissinger, *Nuclear Weapons and Foreign Policy* (New York: Harper 1957) and the other by Robert E. Osgood, *Limited War: The Challenge to American Strategy* (Chicago: University of Chicago Press, 1957). The appearance of these two books was symptomatic of the escalating controversy over questions of war and peace in the nuclear age.

51. This was the famous question France's President Charles De Gaulle was to ask in defense of his decision to build an independent French nuclear strike force in the 1960s.

52. Kissinger, *Nuclear Weapons and Foreign Policy*, p. 25.

53. Ibid., p. 140.

observing saintly self-restraint and disdaining to cross the nuclear threshold even when losing, stretches the credulity of all but the most naive observers. Others less nostalgic for the past rejected the ideas of both Dulles and Kissinger as naive or dangerous or both.[54]

Kissinger's basic argument—that war must be subordinate to policy rather than a substitute for it—was and is valid, although not original.[55] What explains the considerable attention it received was its obvious relevance to the debate over nuclear weapons and the possibility of fighting limited wars in the future. Kissinger rejected the idea that nuclear weapons were a magic bullet, an all-purpose solution to America's national security needs. He rejected the Dulles penchant for nuclear "brinkmanship" and criticized a strategy that put all our eggs in one basket. Survival in the nuclear age necessitated the avoidance of "all-out war" and "unconditional surrender," associated with the two great wars of the twentieth century. The United States would have to learn to live in a world in which limited wars were fought for limited objectives—a world not unlike Europe before World War I, a world, in other words, in which the United States had never been comfortable, and one it had emphatically rejected.

The last thing most Americans ever wanted was to live in an armed camp where national security takes precedence over personal freedom and vigilance trumps prosperity. The inauguration of Dwight Eisenhower in 1953 brought conservative business-minded officials into decision-making roles. In the fifties, Republicans were still opposed to deficit spending and Big Government. Translated, this meant tax cuts and balanced budgets—but how, given U.S. commitments and responsibilities in the world, could public spending be curtailed? The answer for the party of Big Business (the Republicans controlled both the White House and Congress from 1953 to 1955) was reliance on nuclear deterrence rather than conventional defense—what came to be called "A bigger bang for a buck."

But despite the "new look" rhetoric, despite the dalliance with big-bang deterrence, President Eisenhower, unsurprisingly, did not find a way to cut defense spending while simultaneously upholding America's worldwide commitments, nor, in fairness, did any other president, irrespective of political party or the best intentions, during the entire run of the cold war.

---

54. Perhaps the most vehement were to be found in the Kremlin. Soviet military thinkers generally rejected the idea that limited (conventional) wars could be fought between nuclear powers without risk of escalation or, indeed, that the nuclear threshold (involving tactical nuclear weapons) could be crossed without ending up in a catastrophic mutually suicidal exchange.

55. Kissinger was merely restating Gen. Karl von Clausewitz's dictum, "War is a continuation of politics by other means."

The Berlin Crisis: Act II

The Korean conflict was one of two big events that bracketed the great debate over limited war during the Eisenhower administration; the other was the second Berlin Crisis. It was a foreshadowing of the future, a pattern that would be repeated throughout the cold war, in which the superpowers would often intervene directly in local conflicts, but only one at a time, never going head-to-head. This pattern of mutually avoiding direct confrontation, however, was most severely tested in Germany, the likely battlefield if a war between the nuclear titans broke out. In 1958–1959 East-West tensions once again turned Berlin into a tinderbox. If Berlin became the "tripwire" for a Soviet-American clash of arms, could or would the level of violence or the scope or the duration be limited? Would one side accept defeat on the ground rather than use tactical nuclear weapons? If Washington used tactical "nukes" to offset Moscow's conventional superiority, would that not provoke a Soviet nuclear strike against NATO countries, American military bases, or even New York City, Washington, D.C., Omaha (home of the Strategic Air Command), and other population centers in the United States?

To put the danger of this cold war moment into perspective, we have to recall that in 1957 the Soviet Union launched Sputnik, the first orbital satellite in history, thus beating the United States into outer space. The rocket technology required for this feat could also be used to create an intercontinental ballistic missile (ICBM) force capable of obliterating targets in North America. Khrushchev, in fact, began using Soviet missile technology to blackmail the West, making extravagant claims and veiled threats, even before the Kremlin actually had a credible long-range missile system.[56]

If this interpretation is correct, then clearly Khrushchev's primary objective was to resolve the festering issue of Berlin. It was "festering" because Berlin had become a major political problem—an embarrassment and a propaganda disaster—for Moscow. East Europeans who wanted to defect to the West had only to make their way to Berlin, where they could quite easily slip across the line dividing the city. By the late 1950s, Berlin had become the major escape hatch for the "captive nations" of Eastern Europe. The flow of refugees was a veritable hemorrhage in the eyes of the Communist regimes behind the iron curtain, whose leaders were alarmed about a "brain drain"—losing their "best and brightest" scientists, engineers, writers, musicians, and the like. This, then, is the backdrop to the crisis that flared up in 1959.

---

56. An excellent account of Khrushchev's ill-starred nuclear diplomacy can be found in Arnold L. Horelick and Myron Rush, *Strategic Power and Soviet Foreign Policy* (Chicago: University of Chicago Press, 1966). Khrushchev's bluster gave rise to the so-called "missile gap myth"—the prevalent but short-lived notion in the United States in the late 1950s that the Soviet Union had taken a giant leap ahead in strategic rocket forces.

The crisis, sparked by the Soviet Union's demand that the four-power occupation of Berlin be terminated, lasted until August 1961, when the Soviet Union built the Berlin Wall, a wide booby-trapped no-man's-land protected by attack dogs and guard towers, in addition to a high concrete barrier topped with barbed wire. The ultimate result of this joint Soviet–East German action was to defuse the Berlin time bomb; the immediate result, however, was to intensify the crisis. A few days after the wall started going up, Moscow announced that "to cool the hotheads in the capitals of certain NATO powers" it was resuming nuclear testing (suspended since 1958). The following day, the Russians began a series of fifty nuclear tests culminating in a fifty-megaton explosion on October 30.

If the Kremlin's intent was to intimidate the young American president, John F. Kennedy, it failed. Instead, it set the stage the very next year for a nuclear showdown over Cuba that brought the two superpowers much closer to the brink than the one over Berlin. It also sparked off a renewed strategic nuclear arms race that the Soviet Union was destined to lose. (See Table 5-1.)

THE NIFTY FIFTIES: CALM BEFORE THE STORM

The 1950s are sometimes called "the American decade" because it was a time of domestic economic prosperity, political consensus, and social peace (compared with what was coming). The contrast between the 1950s and the two decades that followed would serve only to reinforce this tendency toward nostalgia for the fifties.

Middle-class Americans had good reason to feel optimistic about the future. Under America's leadership, world trade soared. The United States balanced its trade and payments surpluses with overseas investments and carefully dispensed foreign aid. Business and construction were booming, and good jobs were open to the able-bodied willing to work. Most people were not rich, but they were earning decent money and there was an abundance of consumer goods thanks to the booming economy. In 1955 alone, Americans purchased between 9 million and 10 million new automobiles. Tom Brokaw, the NBC news anchor, writes about how "the sounds of construction created a welcome cacophony across America" after World War II. Brokaw notes, "In 1940, there were slightly more than 23.7 million single-family homes in America; by 1950 another 5.5 million had been constructed and by 1960 the total had jumped to more than 40 million."[57]

There is more than a hint of nostalgia in Brokaw's account of his boyhood in the "American heartland"—and for good reason. There has likely never been a better time to be young, white, Protestant, middle-class, and male in America.

---

57. Tom Brokaw, *A Long Way from Home: Growing Up in the American Heartland* (New York: Random House, 2002), p. 66. The Eisenhower administration also launched a mammoth series of federally funded public works projects, including the interstate highway system and construction of two huge dams on the Missouri River.

Table 5-1	Crises and Conflicts, 1946–1962		
Year	Place	Event	Policy
1946	Iran	Soviet troops	Demand removal
1947	Greece	Insurgency	Truman Doctrine
1948	Czechoslovakia	Coup	Denounce from sidelines
	Germany	Berlin Crisis	Airlift
1949	China	Revolution	Back Nationalists from sidelines
1950–53	Korea	War	Military invasion
1955	Taiwan	Shelling of islands	Warn People's Republic of China; show the flag
1956	Egypt	Suez Crisis	Oppose allies; back UN force
1958	Lebanon	Instability	Send troops
1958–61	Germany	Berlin Crisis	Stand firm; hike arms spending
1960	Congo	Independence	Use UN peacekeeping force
1961	Cuba	Invasion	Back proxy anti-Castro forces
	Vietnam	Insurgency	Send military "advisers"
1962	Cuba	Missile Crisis	Naval blockade of Cuba

The optimism and values of millions of middle-class Americans like the Brokaw family were depicted in popular TV situation comedies such as *Leave It to Beaver* and *Ozzie and Harriet*. But this optimism masked a wide array of domestic social issues that could not be deferred indefinitely. It also ignored the war dangers at our doorstep.

The optimism of the fifties coexisted with a growing sense of vulnerability as the American nuclear monopoly gave way to what Churchill called the "balance of terror." On one side of the debate over nuclear weapons were idealists, who argued that weapons of mass destruction were simply too terrible ever to be used and that the only moral solution was to freeze existing arsenals or abolish them altogether. On the other side were realists, who argued that now that the nuclear genie was out of the bottle there was no way to put it back in. Faced with the threat from "totalitarian" communism, the only *realistic* moral solution for "the leader of the Free World," therefore, was to have an effective deterrent, according to this view. Seldom has the tension between power and principle been more sharply drawn or did the outcome of a debate have more profound implications for the future of the nation and the world than in the 1950s.

From Missile Crisis to Mutual Deterrence

Four decades after the fact, the Cuban Missile Crisis is still recalled vividly by anyone who is old enough to remember it. At the time, it created a kind of suspense that was at once novel and terrifying: the imminent possibility of an all-out nuclear war.

The facts can be quickly recounted. Fidel Castro rode a revolutionary wave to power in 1959, overthrowing a corrupt and dictatorial (but pro-American) government. Castro had Marxist leanings, but his popularity was based on nationalism and resentment against "yanqui imperialism." (Throughout Latin America, the epithet "imperialism" is often used as a general all-purpose term to describe U.S. foreign policy.) Upon seizing power, one of Castro's first moves was to nationalize the property of wealthy Cubans and to expropriate foreign (mostly American) assets. American business owned the vast majority of Cuba's utilities, mines, and cattle ranches, virtually all its oil, and almost half of its sugar. Cuba's dependence on the United States was also reflected in its sugar quota equal to 25 percent of the huge American market. Basically, Americans owned Cuba.

The Eisenhower administration did not look kindly on Castro, and American business interests had close ties to the Republicans in control of the Washington foreign policy establishment. Nor was Castro inclined to yield to American diplomatic or economic pressures. The result was a standoff that could only lead to a downward spiral in relations. The United States placed a crippling economic boycott on Cuban sugar and began preparations for a proxy invasion (using Cuban fighters) to oust the Castro regime. Although President Eisenhower ordered the planning, recruiting, and training for this operation, it fell to his successor, John F. Kennedy, to decide whether or not to give the go-ahead. Given a loaded "gun" before he was even settled into office, presented with a fait accompli as far as mission preparations were concerned, hearing soothing assurances from his star-studded advisory group, JFK pulled the trigger. It was "a perfect failure," the kind of fiasco that ruins a president, and it happened only a few months into Kennedy's first term at a time of great tension between the superpowers over Berlin. It probably emboldened Khrushchev to test the youthful new American commander in chief in ways he might not have tested Eisenhower, the four-star general who had commanded all U.S. forces in Europe at the end of World War II.[58]

In any event, Khrushchev made the fateful decision to place medium-range ballistic missiles in Cuba. Just as the Eisenhower administration had hoped to use nuclear weapons ("massive retaliation") as a quick fix, now the Kremlin sought a quick fix in an accelerating strategic arms race with the United States. If this gambit had succeeded, Moscow would have had a nuclear deterrent on the cheap, one that would have been all the more politically effective because of the psychological impact its very proximity to U.S. territory would have had on the American peo-

---

58. For a fascinating study of the decision-making process leading up to the Bay of Pigs ("a perfect failure"), see Irving L. Janis, *Groupthink,* 2nd ed. (Boston: Houghton Mifflin, 1972), pp. 14–47. On JFK's foreign policy, including an account of the Bay of Pigs by two insiders, see Arthur M. Schlesinger Jr., *A Thousand Days* (Boston: Houghton Mifflin, 1965), and Roger Hilsman, *To Move a Nation* (New York: Doubleday, 1967).

ple: population centers within range of those Soviet missiles included Washington, D.C., and New York City. In the era after September 11 there is no denying the importance of those two cities in the making of American foreign policy.

The denouement of the missile crisis is a fascinating story in itself. Photo-intelligence obtained by U-2 spy planes flying over Cuba indicated clearly that the Soviets were up to no good. Following a dramatic presentation of the evidence at the United Nations by Ambassador Adlai Stevenson, JFK issued an ultimatum and imposed a naval quarantine on Cuba. Now Khrushchev was faced with an excruciating choice—either challenge the U.S. Navy far from the Soviet motherland or back down. He backed down.

The Cuban Missile Crisis taught both sides sobering lessons. Apart from the obvious lesson that nothing is worth fighting a nuclear war over, there was this: even if neither side intended to be the first to use nuclear weapons, in the confusion and turmoil of a crisis the Armageddon that was everyone's nightmare might come by accident. The scenarios for accidental war were numerous, ranging from a technical malfunction to human error to an act of God. If a meteor were to land precisely where it once did in Siberia with precisely the same impact (a massive explosion), would Moscow not launch its long-range nuclear weapons thinking America had started a preemptive strike? Far more likely would be a scenario involving an accidental launch from land or sea or an "early warning" system (radar) picking up a rapidly moving object that could be (but is not) a bomber or a long-range rocket. Would the United States wait until the bomb(s) hit (possibly wiping out critical "pieces" of America's national-security architecture) or would the president "launch on warning"—in effect, shoot first and ask questions later?

Apart from the fact that there might not be a "later," nuclear weapons are a poor foundation on which to build a sound and constructive foreign policy. In 1958, back in private life, Kennan wrote:

> The beginning of understanding rests . . . with the recognition that the weapon of mass destruction is a sterile and hopeless weapon which may for a time serve as an answer of sorts to itself and as an uncertain sort of shield against utter cataclysm, but which cannot in any way serve the purposes of a constructive and hopeful foreign policy. The true end of political action is, after all, to affect the deeper convictions of men; this the atomic weapons cannot do.[59]

> In sum, the American nuclear monopoly was long gone. The age of "mutual deterrence" was dawning. It now fell to the Kennedy administration to sort out the national security implications of this terrible truth and to devise a new set of foreign and defense policies for dealing with the Soviet threat.

---

59. George Kennan, *The Nuclear Delusion* (New York: Pantheon Books, 1983), pp. 6–7. Kennan originally penned the words quoted here in 1958 under the title "A Sterile and Hopeless Weapon."

Flexible Response: A Bigger Military Toolbox

Kennan joined Kissinger and other critics of the Eisenhower-Dulles policy outlined earlier in this chapter in advocating a more flexible approach to the use of military force as an instrument of foreign policy. Kennan argued that the "suicidal nature" of the ultimate weapon made it an ineffective instrument of diplomacy and not "one with which one readily springs to the defense of one's friends." Indeed, "[t]here can be no coherent relations between such a weapon and the normal objects of national policy. A defensive posture built around a weapon suicidal in its implications can serve in the long run only to paralyze national policy, to undermine alliance, and to drive everyone deeper and deeper into the hopeless exertions of the weapons race."[60]

President Kennedy apparently admired Kennan, so much so that he brought Kennan back into the government as ambassador to Yugoslavia.[61] Bringing Kennan back into an active role in the Foreign Service was symbolic of the new president's intent to conduct a wide-ranging, no-holds-barred review of the nation's foreign policy.

JFK launched the Alliance for Progress in Latin America, the Peace Corps, and the Food for Peace program in an effort to improve U.S. ties in developing countries—three bold initiatives that highlighted the role of principle in American foreign policy. In the aftermath of the Cuban Missile Crisis, he also moved to reduce nuclear tensions by signing a "test ban" treaty with Moscow (the first ever nuclear accord) and to forestall an accidental war by creating a direct communications link between the White House and the Kremlin (the famous "Hot Line"). All these steps were visionary and welcome in a world learning to live on the edge of instant extinction.

So it seemed was one other policy initiative forever associated with JFK—the doctrine of *flexible response.*[62] This new doctrine was intended as an alternative to massive retaliation. In stark contrast to the New Look of Eisenhower-Dulles, the Kennedy New Frontier defense policy emphasized conventional forces and the development of war-fighting capabilities along a wide spectrum. At the "low-intensity" end of this spectrum was the possibility of counterinsurgency engagements that would require specialized troops trained and equipped

---

60. Ibid.
61. Shortly before taking office, JFK wrote a note to Kennan prompted by a 1958 BBC talk Kennan had given. "It impressed me," Kennedy wrote, "as does everything you say, with its dispassionate good sense." JFK had also written Kennan a note after the 1957 Reith Lectures saying he (JFK) was glad to know "that there is at least one member of the 'opposition' who is not only performing his critical duty but also providing a carefully formulated, comprehensive and brilliantly written set of alternative proposals and perspectives." Kennan, *Memoirs: 1950–1963*, pp. 266–267.
62. Schlesinger, *Thousand Days*, pp. 851–856.

to fight in all types of environments against an enemy that did not "play" by the traditional rules of war.

The doctrine of flexible response must be seen in the context of Vietnam, where the perceived threat took the form of a guerrilla war leading to a Communist takeover. The Vietcong did not fight positional warfare using tanks and heavy artillery. They were guerrillas wearing "pajamas" and sandals, they moved at night, knew how to survive in the jungle, and required astonishingly little in the way of logistics and supplies. The United States would need "special forces" to fight an unconventional war of this kind. Whether or not it would ever be necessary to fight such a war remained to be seen, but JFK and his military advisers were convinced that the United States needed to have the option.

Vietnam: Failing the First Test

In Vietnam, deterrence failed utterly. Likewise, conventional war strategies and tactics (naval blockade, aerial bombardment, and the like) were surprisingly ineffective. Worse still, the disconnection between military means and political ends was near total. In the mid-1950s, when the United States enjoyed a clear nuclear superiority, diplomacy was put on the back burner. Nor did the Kennedy or Johnson administrations seek a political solution. Not until the presidential campaign of 1972, when an articulate antiwar candidate (Senator George McGovern) sought to spoil President Richard Nixon's bid for reelection, was a serious effort made to find a diplomatic way out. By that time, the antiwar movement was in full swing and most of America's closest allies had jumped ship. Containment was still the watchword, but it had mutated into a strategy and set of policies very different from what George Kennan had had in mind back in 1947. It worked in Europe and in the Western Hemisphere (where it was an extension of the Monroe Doctrine). It did not work in Asia.

Vietnam, like Germany and Korea, was a "frontier" during the cold war, a place where the United States had drawn a line that Moscow or its proxies dared not cross. Unlike Germany, however, Vietnam was a remote and unfamiliar frontier not easily accessible to American military forces. Unlike Korea, the climate and vegetation were also very different from Europe or North America—monsoons, jungles, and rice paddies. Unlike either Germany or Korea, Vietnam had not been divided at the end of World War II, but only after the French defeat in 1954.[63]

---

63. The Vietnam War spawned many books in many languages. Among the best-known studies in English is David Halberstam's bestseller, *The Best and the Brightest* (New York: Random House, 1969; reprinted in paperback, Greenwich, Conn.: Fawcett, 1973). See also *The Pentagon Papers*, published by the New York Times and reprinted in paperback by arrangement with Bantam Books in 1971. Another very useful volume on Vietnam is Marcus G. Raskin and Bernard B. Fall, eds., *The Viet-Nam Reader* (New York: Random House, 1965).

The two states of Vietnam came into existence in 1954 as a result of diplomatic efforts at the Geneva conference, where the principals agreed to an armistice line along the seventeenth parallel, temporarily dividing the country into northern and southern sections.[64] The United States and South Vietnam did not sign the Geneva Accords. President Eisenhower declared that the United States would not be bound by nor interfere with the terms of the armistice. The Geneva Accords called for nationwide elections in Vietnam to take place by July 20, 1956. No such elections occurred, but there is little doubt that Ho Chi Minh would have won. Instead, the line between North and South hardened. The United States and France backed South Vietnam; the People's Republic of China and the Soviet Union backed North Vietnam. "Bipolarity" was about to descend on Southeast Asia with a vengeance.

The superpowers sought to divide the world into two camps, forcing every country to choose sides in the cold war that split Europe first, then Asia. Many former colonies that became independent in 1945 preferred to be neutral or nonaligned. For these nations, anti-imperialism was a more meaningful ideology than either socialism or capitalism and recompense for the injustices of colonialism was more important than idealistic abstractions such as liberty or equality.

The process of "national liberation" for developing countries varied greatly from place to place, as did the experience of colonialism itself. The desire to break the yoke of colonialism was universal, however. In some instances, independence came without a struggle. In Vietnam (as well as Algeria), however, France fought to stay in control and suffered a resounding military defeat sealed by the Vietminh's successful assault on the French fortress at Dienbienphu in 1954.

Vietnam's independence drive was a struggle of mythical proportions. Ho Chi Minh led the fight against French colonial rule. Ho was a kind of living legend among the illiterate masses that comprised the vast majority of the Vietnamese people. In the eyes of U.S. policymakers, however, Ho was a Communist and a revolutionary.

Marx's writings were tailored to societies in the throes of rapid urbanization and industrialization. Vietnam was (and still is) largely an agrarian society populated by villagers and peasants rather than factory and office workers living in big cities. The idea of a "proletarian revolution" never really caught on even in the advanced industrial countries; in Vietnam it was an absurdity. But these facts were largely lost on American leaders who viewed Ho as a puppet of Moscow and Vietnam as a "domino" that, should it fall, would trigger a chain-reaction of Communist takeovers in Southeast Asia.

---

64. "Final Declaration of Geneva Conference, July 21, 1954" in Raskin and Fall, *Vietnam Reader,* pp. 96–98.

The Eisenhower administration, projecting a hawkish foreign policy couched in the bellicose language of "massive retaliation," "rollback," and "liberation," now faced a dilemma: the president was not about to accept a Communist Vietnam, but as commander in chief with a professional soldier's understanding of military strategy and tactics he was loath to send American soldiers to fight there. Eisenhower's half-in, half-out solution was to pledge direct U.S. economic and military assistance, while demanding reforms.[65]

Eisenhower's caution notwithstanding, Vietnam was a presidential war from start to finish. At no time did any American president ask Congress for a declaration of war, because, in contrast to World War II, there was no Pearl Harbor to galvanize Congress and the country into action. Moreover, memories of World War II were still fresh when the Korean conflict broke out, and the American public was weary of war. The United States sank deeper and deeper into the quagmire of Indochina, gradually displacing the Army of the Republic of Viet-Nam (ARVN), as a result of decisions made by five presidents over a period of more than two decades.[66] This "incrementalism" was a poor substitute for a consistent and coherent policy. Eisenhower had decided to give aid directly to the government of South Vietnam rather than channeling it through France as Truman had done. He had also directed the Military Assistance Advisory Group to take over the training of the South Vietnamese army. Clearly, America's postwar obsession with "national security" had fueled a growth spurt in the powers of the president, but few in the 1950s imagined just how far these powers could or would be extended in the decades to come.

Washington and Saigon blocked national elections, dashing Hanoi's hopes of gaining power in the South by peaceful means. Denied certain victory at the ballot box, ironically, by the Americans and the very government (Saigon) Eisenhower had lectured on the need for "reforms" in 1954, Ho Chi Minh turned once again to armed struggle in 1959. By that time, the United States was deeply involved in propping up South Vietnam. In Indochina, power and principle collided head-on.

Vietnam was not Washington's highest priority in the 1950s, but if Saigon were to fall to the Communists, it would make the United States look weak and indecisive. Allies and client states alike would question America's commitments, and adversaries would take heart. Guerrilla wars would sprout like mushrooms,

---

65. Don R. Larson and Arthur Larson, "What Is Our Commitment in Viet-Nam?" reprinted in Raskin and Fall, *Viet-Nam Reader,* p. 100. The authors quote President Eisenhower's letter of Oct. 23, 1954, to President Diem as proof that Eisenhower never intended to make an open-ended commitment to the government of South Vietnam.
66. For a detailed chronology of the Vietnam War, see Raskin and Fall, *Viet-Nam Reader,* pp. 377–402.

so the thinking went. No, the president and his top advisers reasoned, the United States must hold the line in Vietnam and, further, must be prepared to fight unconventional (counterinsurgency) wars.[67]

Fast forward to 1963. The United States had not yet openly committed combat troops to Vietnam nor had the U.S. Air Force bombed the North. JFK ruled out combat missions in Vietnam but increased the number of "military advisers" there from less than 800 in 1960 to 16,500.[68] ARVN (the South Vietnamese army) and the Vietcong were doing most of the fighting, if not quite all of it.[69] But the war was not going well for the South, the Saigon regime was fractious and despised by the people it claimed to represent, and the United States had, at the very least, acquiesced in a military coup in early November 1963 in which Diem was assassinated. Only weeks later the same fate befell JFK himself.

How the United States came to be involved in a protracted guerrilla war (a "quagmire") in a remote corner of the world remains something of a mystery despite the volumes that have been written about it.[70] Kennedy's Vietnam policy "is a veritable case study of how the military submerged the political in action, if not always in intention and thinking."[71] In retrospect, Vietnam started out as a low-intensity effort and ended up becoming a high-intensity unconventional war—seemingly an oxymoron. What was initially a test—dipping a toe in the water—turned into a contest from which there was no easy escape. The water was deeper than we imagined, and the vortex that sucked in more than 58,000 American lives (and countless Vietnamese) was invisible to the decision makers in Washington.

American foreign policy was moving into a new phase in which military intervention—either direct or by proxy—would become the norm for the two nuclear superpowers. Vietnam was the first test of these new low-intensity tools.

---

67. Among Kennedy's advisers several stand out in connection with the Vietnam War, including Gen. Maxwell Taylor, Robert McNamara, McGeorge Bundy, and W. W. Rostow. Rostow's address, "Guerrilla Warfare in the Underdeveloped Areas," to the graduating class at the U.S. Army Special Warfare School at Fort Bragg in June 1961 is particularly revealing in light of subsequent events in Vietnam. For a complete text of this address, see Raskin and Fall, *Viet-Nam Reader*, pp. 108–116.

68. The Truman administration backed the French in Indochina but avoided any direct involvement. After the French withdrew in defeat (1954), President Eisenhower backed the South Vietnamese government with economic and military aid but stressed "self-help."

69. See Douglas Pike, *Viet Cong: The Organization and Technique of the National Liberation Front of South Vietnam* (Cambridge, Mass.: MIT Press, 1966).

70. See, for example, Halberstam, *Best and Brightest*; Theodore Draper, *Abuse of Power* (New York: Viking Press, 1967); Leslie Gelb and Richard K. Betts, *The Irony of Vietnam* (Washington, D.C.: Brookings Institution, 1979); see also Janis, *Groupthink*, pp. 97–130, and *The Pentagon Papers*, the Defense Department's own internal study of this question leaked to the press by Daniel Ellsberg, one of its authors.

71. Draper, *Abuse of Power*, p. 50.

But increasingly, America would use "special forces" in place of regular army units to deal with "unconventional" threats and enemies. These threats would often take the form of guerrilla-style insurgencies (Vietnam and Central America) or terrorism (Somalia and Afghanistan). The war against Iraq (1990–1991) would be fought with "smart" weapons and "stand-off" weapons. These new "high-tech" weapons would also be used in Afghanistan, along with drones or so-called UAVs (unmanned aerial vehicles) such as the Predator and Global Hawk. But no miracle of modern technology would arrive in time to avert disaster in Vietnam. Nor would military invincibility guarantee the desired political outcomes in the post-Vietnam era.

CONCLUSION

America changed on the day Japan attacked Pearl Harbor. December 7, 1941, was a turning point not only in the war but also in the history of American foreign policy. We know in hindsight that one general war fought in the second decade of the twentieth century was not enough to jolt the United States (either Congress or the public) out of its isolationist dream-state. Regrettably, ignorance and self-delusion triumphed over reason in the aftermath of World War I, despite the enormous carnage, unprecedented scale, first-time use of air power and chemical weapons (poison gas), and the best efforts of a visionary president who, unlike ordinary politicians, dared to imagine a better world.

Today, few remember that Franklin Delano Roosevelt was a high-ranking official in Woodrow Wilson's administration or that he was the running mate of James Cox, a presidential candidate in 1920. Some two decades after the demise of Wilson's dream for a new world order, formalized in the League of Nations, and in the throes of a second general war worse than the first, FDR revived the dream. The United Nations as he envisioned it would be a new and improved version of the League. Far from discrediting Wilson's idea of "collective security," the interwar period had vindicated Wilson in FDR's view. FDR believed Wilson had been right to insist that America take its place among the great powers and accept the moral responsibilities that accompany rank and privilege in the world. Second, like Wilson, FDR sought an alternative to traditional alliances and arms races in a set of rules (international law). Finally, FDR imitated Wilson in attempting to codify norms of acceptable behavior (the UN Charter replaced the League Covenant) and create an institutional framework through which to encourage respect for these norms and punish violators.

To say that Wilson was on the "right track," however, is not to say that the League was perfect in FDR's eyes—far from it. But some of the League's flaws were not Wilson's fault—above all, the failure of the United States to join. The principle of universality was never realized in the League; as a consequence the League was never a fully established fact. But the way the League functioned was a problem in any event. Every member state was equal under the League Covenant. Any member state could veto League action. Obviously, in the real world, there is a rank order among the powers. In the real world, some states have far greater weight than others on the power scales. The United Nations envisioned by FDR would reflect the real world. Every sovereign state would be represented in the General Assembly, where the principle of equality would govern voting procedures. But the use of force—the collective security function—would not be decided in the General Assembly. Instead, there would be a smaller body, the Security Council, with a rotating membership except for the five permanent members—the United States, the Soviet Union, Great Britain, France, and China. Decisions of the Security Council would be taken by majority vote but would be approved only if and when all five permanent members concurred. In other words, the "Big Five" at the UN would have a veto. It was an admirable attempt to mix idealism and realism. Clearly, something had to be done to break the cycle of war or at the very least limit its scope and consequences.

This time, in contrast to Wilson's fate, the White House would have the full support of Congress. This time, Republicans in the Senate, following Arthur Vandenberg's lead, would not oppose the United Nations or reject the idea of "collective security" as they had, following John Cabot Lodge, after World War I.[72] This time, it would not be the Senate or public opinion that dashed hopes for a new world order.

FDR, like Wilson, dared to dream of a world governed by rules rather than raw power and random acts. He did not live to see the dream shattered only moments after World War II ended. Once the die was cast and the cold war was on, there was no possibility that the United Nations would or could function as the main facilitator of peace and stability. Some other "system" or "model" would have to be found or else the world would again be plunged into general war. This time, however, it would truly be a "war to end wars"—not a third world war but an end-of-the-world war.

Enter containment. The United States would take upon itself the burden of defending freedom and defeating tyranny in the world.[73] The coming struggle was a call to arms in a moral as well as a military sense, a matter of principle as well as

---

72. Senator Vandenberg's support for the United Nations in 1945 was unequivocal. "We must have collective security," he said, "to stop the next war, if possible, before it starts; and we must have collective action to crush it swiftly if it starts in spite of our organized precautions." Arthur H. Vandenberg Jr., *The Private Papers of Senator Vandenberg* (Boston: Houghton Mifflin, 1952), p. 217. Quoted in Claude, *Power and International Relations,* p. 119.

73. John F. Kennedy did not invent but merely echoed this sweeping new American commitment when he intoned, "we shall pay any price, bear any burden, meet any hardship, support any friend, oppose any foe to assure the survival and success of liberty." Quoted in Schlesinger, *Thousand Days,* p. 689.

power. For a time, power and principle were fused in a common, righteous purpose. We would not do it alone, but we would lead the "Free World." The strategy of containment would necessitate a long-term commitment of resources—foreign economic assistance—as exemplified by the Marshall Plan. It would also mean pledging to stand with friends and allies militarily if need be—something the United States had never done before in peacetime. This was the rationale for creating NATO in 1949.

What else containment meant, that it would evolve into a "doctrine" involving massive retaliation and armed intervention, that it would, in a word, be militarized over time and come to bear little resemblance to George Kennan's original conception—all this was unclear in 1950. Half a century later, the United States would be the archetype of an "armed camp," with military forces far exceeding those of any potential rival and a defense budget larger than the combined military expenditures of the next fifteen to twenty powers ranked below it. This focus on threats and the phenomenal growth in military might led to the coining of a new term for American democracy—the "national security state."[74] After the September 11 attacks in 2001, President George W. Bush would ask Congress to pass the Homeland Security Act as part of a "war on terrorism." The full and final outlines of the new "homeland security state" were still a matter of conjecture at the end of 2003, as were the implications of the current "homeland security" mindset for American democracy.

By this time, the metamorphosis of containment from a strategy involving primarily economic and political instruments to one involving primarily military means, ironically, had severely eroded the role of diplomacy (and the secretary of state) in America's foreign relations. Moreover, American military intervention would be very closely associated with repression in the eyes of the world. Astonishingly, the American people would be largely oblivious to this problem, and the Bush administration would act as though it did not matter. The fact that this situation came to pass only thirty years after Vietnam—the most humiliating and costly foreign policy failure in American history—made these developments all the more inexplicable.

---

74. See especially Daniel Yergin, *Shattered Peace: The Origins of the Cold War and the Rise of the National Security State* (Boston: Houghton Mifflin, 1977).

6

Intervention against Communism:
From Kennedy to Reagan

OVERVIEW

This chapter begins with a study of the Vietnam War. The causes, course, and consequences of that war are reviewed and its lessons examined. I then turn to the Nixon-Kissinger policy of détente with the Soviet Union and the simultaneous opening of a new era in Sino-American relations and consider the major post-Vietnam diplomatic reversals that occurred under President Jimmy Carter toward the end of the 1970s. I discuss what Americans might have learned from the Carter legacy about the limits of idealism in foreign policy. Next, an exploration of the Reagan presidency (1981– 1988) focuses first on the Reagan administration's offensive approach to containment in general and then on the Reagan Doctrine and its abuses (the Iran-Contra affair). The chapter ends with some reflections on the apparent triumph of the containment policy signaled by the collapse of communism at the end of the 1980s.

The decade of the 1960s opened with a superpower confrontation over Berlin and Cuba and ended with half a million American soldiers fighting a guerrilla war in the jungles of Southeast Asia. In the crises over Berlin and Cuba, the United States prevented the Soviet Union from achieving its aims without firing a shot. Containment worked.

President Kennedy's finest hour—the face-off over Cuba—was also the most dangerous because the two superpowers had gone to the very brink of nuclear war. JFK's prestige soared in the wake of the crisis. The president that Lee Harvey Oswald assassinated on a bright, sunny day in Dallas, November 22, 1963, was extremely popular. The man who replaced him, Vice President Lyndon Baines Johnson, was not.

Nonetheless, LBJ was elected in his own right in a landslide against the arch-conservative Republican candidate, Barry Goldwater, in 1964. Goldwater had campaigned on a saber-rattling foreign policy personified by his running mate Gen. Curtis Lemay, who is most often remembered for his solution to the Vietnam War—"We should bomb them into the Stone Age."[1] There were muted voices

---

1. Quoted in David Halberstam, *The Best and the Brightest* (New York: Random House, 1969; reprinted in paperback, Greenwich, Conn.: Fawcett, 1973), p. 560.

1964   Congress approves Gulf of Tonkin Resolution

1967   Six-Day War fought between Israel and Egypt

1968   Tet Offensive launched in South Vietnam; Nuclear Non-Proliferation Treaty signed

1969   America puts man on moon

1970   United States invades Cambodia; massive student protests in United States escalate after National Guard kills four students at Kent State University

1971   War fought between India and Pakistan over secession of Bangladesh (formerly East Pakistan); the People's Republic of China joins the United Nations

1972   Watergate affair triggered when police arrest members of secret White House "plumbers" unit

1973   Vietnamese peace agreement signed; OPEC embargoes oil to United States because of American support for Israel; Congress passes War Powers Resolution over Nixon veto

1974   Nixon resigns; Gerald Ford becomes first president not on ticket

1976   Jimmy Carter elected president

1977   United States hands full control of Panama Canal to Panama

1978   Soviet-engineered coup in Afghanistan succeeds; President Carter mediates Egyptian-Israeli peace "framework" at Camp David

1979   Shah of Iran is overthrown; Ayatolla Khomeini establishes Islamic republic; hostage crisis in Iran

1980   Carter Doctrine commits United States to security of Persian Gulf region; Ronald Reagan is elected president

1982   Reagan backs anti-Communist regimes in El Salvador and Nicaragua

1983   United States invades Grenada, deposes Marxist government

1984   Latin America slides into debt crisis

1985   First Reagan-Gorbachev face-to-face meeting (in Geneva)

1986   Chernobyl nuclear accident in Ukraine, USSR, called worst in history; Iran-Contra scandal revealed

1987   Palestinian *intifada* (uprising) begins in December

1988   Soviet Baltic republics assert desire for independence from USSR

within the Johnson administration expressing doubts about the effectiveness of bombing a country like Vietnam (the morality of doing so was apparently not an issue). Would air power work against guerrilla fighters who scorned modern technology? Setting aside any such questions, and given blanket authority by Congress to do as he saw fit in Vietnam, President Johnson ordered the bombing of the North on February 7, 1965, and began a military buildup that would soon put hundreds of thousands of American troops on the ground.[2] Even after half a million soldiers had taken over the ground war, American strategists continued to place primary reliance on air power, believing that it would, in time, bring North Vietnam to its knees. They were wrong.

The bombing campaign was brutal by any reckoning, using incendiary bombs (napalm) and defoliants (Agent Orange), as well as conventional explosives. The extreme violence of the war, coupled with the difficulty of sparing (or even identifying) civilians, helped to fuel a growing antiwar movement in the late 1960s. Television cameras for the first time brought the battlefield into American homes. Images of bombed villages, burned children, and broken lives flashed across the TV screens and gave faces to the innocent victims of the war. For the first time in the nation's history, the mass media—which Presidents Johnson and Nixon both, rightly or wrongly, viewed as an ally of the antiwar movement—played a major role in foreign policy. Whether or not it was deliberate, there can be little doubt that journalists and television news anchors helped to mobilize college students and eventually voters of all ages against the war.

The scale and length and moral ambiguity of the war, brought to public awareness by the exploding media coverage, caused President Johnson's popularity to plummet and induced him not to seek reelection. Critics said there was "no light at the end of the tunnel." The Tet Offensive launched at the end of January 1968 demonstrated to an increasingly skeptical public that the war in Indochina was not going well. With the presidential primary season about to get under way, it was a knockout blow for the incumbent in the White House. Lyndon Johnson was a lame duck president from then on. Stuck in a quagmire of his own making, he left office in disgrace and died soon thereafter.

President Johnson's successor, Richard Nixon, came into office saying he had a plan to end the war. "Peace with honor" became the watchword of the Nixon administration's Vietnam policy. President Nixon and his national security adviser, Henry Kissinger, appeared to embrace diplomacy. It was a welcome change, but unfortunately the change did not extend to Vietnam. The Nixon-Kissinger plan stressed "Vietnamization" of the war and gradual withdrawal of American forces. An early plan—the so-called strategic hamlet program—had

---

2. The authorization, know as the Gulf of Tonkin Resolution, was passed on August 7, 1964, by a vote of 88–2 in the Senate and 416–0 in the House.

failed miserably, causing American military planners to turn to air power. When the massive bombing campaign against the North failed to produce the desired results—as air power alone nearly always does—there were no good options left. This was the predicament facing Richard Nixon in 1969.

The cost of the Vietnam War is most often measured in social and economic terms, deaths and dollars. By these measures it was extremely high. Politically, the costs were also high. In 1972, with the antiwar movement in full swing and an election right around the corner, Nixon needed a face-saving way out of Vietnam. One month before the presidential election, Hanoi made peace overtures, and Washington responded.

Nixon won the 1972 election by a landslide. But the Paris peace talks failed and in December, with a new mandate in hand, he ordered a massive punitive bombing campaign against the North. The so-called "Christmas bombings" were a ferocious aerial assault meant to soften the enemy and demonstrate the president's resolve. This decision made Nixon appear duplicitous to antiwar activists and sympathizers. A majority of Americans as well as the outside world saw the war in Vietnam as utterly at odds with America's principles, a shameful example of the "arrogance of power."[3]

Then came the revelations about the Watergate break-in and charges that the Nixon White House had conspired to steal the election and subvert the Constitution. In June 1974, facing impeachment and a Senate trial, Nixon resigned—himself a victim of his obsession with communism and military victory in the Vietnam War.

American foreign policy was also a casualty of the Vietnam War. The war had preoccupied the United States for a decade, draining the treasury, straining relations with allies, dividing the country, and fueling anti-American sentiment throughout the world. It was an astonishing turn-around. Uncle Sam's reputation in the world had soared to new heights after World War II. This huge reservoir of good will was a priceless foreign policy asset, but it was intangible and easily taken for granted. Perhaps that is why it was so easily squandered.

American prestige fell to an all-time postwar low in the mid-1970s, and in the great game of world politics, prestige is power. America went through a period of soul-searching and self-doubt, setting the stage for a major setback—the fall of the shah in Iran—and opening the door to Soviet adventurism. Within a few short years, Moscow would, for the first and only time during the cold war, invade a neighboring state that was not a member of the Warsaw Pact—Afghanistan.

---

3. In 1967, with the Americanization of the war in full swing, Senator William J. Fulbright, chairman of the Senate Foreign Relations Committee, memorialized the phrase "arrogance of power" in an influential book that was highly critical of American military intervention. See William J. Fulbright, *The Arrogance of Power* (New York: Vintage Books, 1967).

Vietnam also demonstrated the limits of technology. Gen. Maxwell Taylor was not alone in advocating air power as a kind of magic bullet, but air power by itself was not enough.[4] Wars are still won or lost on the ground. For democracies, the home turf can become a battleground as well. Vietnam illustrated the importance of domestic consensus when "American boys" are sent abroad to fight and die. American decision makers had the "illusion of invincibility," and neither the Pentagon nor the people could imagine losing a war to a "Third World" country like North Vietnam.[5] After all, the United States had not lost a war since the British sailed up the Potomac in 1812. In the twentieth century, America had twice defeated Germany; in World War II, we had fought Germany and Japan simultaneously and emerged victorious. True, America did not win in Korea, but neither did it lose, despite the fact that Communist China joined the fight. By comparison, Vietnam was a Lilliputian power on paper. Unfortunately, wars are not fought on paper.

FOREIGN POLICY ON HOLD (1964–1971)

Not surprisingly, there were few foreign policy initiatives coming out of Washington during the major escalation phase of the Vietnam War. It was as if the self-styled leader of the Free World had taken an extended holiday. This holiday, however, was more like open-heart surgery.

If one tries to track American diplomacy in the 1960s, the trail goes cold between the partial nuclear test ban treaty and the "hot line" agreement (both in 1963) and the Nuclear Non-Proliferation Treaty (NPT) signed in 1968. The United States has opposed the spread of nuclear weapons to nonnuclear states since 1945. There was a short-lived "great debate" within the government over whether or not to back a total ban on nuclear weapons, but advocates of disarmament lost out. Instead, the United States sought to create disincentives for nonnuclear states while controlling the flow of weapons-grade nuclear materials. The United Kingdom was the exception in large part because the Manhattan Project (creating the atom bomb) was in actuality a joint British-American research and development program conducted at Los Alamos, Nevada, during World War II.[6] But the Soviet Union had other ideas, of course, and, later, France

---

4. There was a consensus on bombing the North in Johnson's inner circle; near the end of 1967, Johnson replaced Secretary of Defense Robert McNamara, apparently over the bombing issue. McNamara advocated de-escalation before LBJ was willing to consider it. See Irving L. Janis, *Groupthink,* 2nd ed. (Boston: Houghton Mifflin, 1972), pp. 117–120.

5. The phrase "illusion of invincibility" is found in Janis, *Groupthink,* pp. 35–37 and 121–125.

6. See, for example, Carl B. Feldbaum and Ronald J. Bee, *Looking the Tiger in the Eye: Confronting the Nuclear Threat* (New York: Harper and Row, 1988), esp. pp. 60–71.

under President Charles de Gaulle also decided to create a nuclear strike force of its own.

Thus, by the mid-1960s there were four nuclear powers, and other countries, including China, India, Israel, Pakistan, and South Africa, had nuclear ambitions. The NPT prohibited nuclear states from transferring nuclear weapons and nonnuclear states from acquiring them. That the two superpowers and the United Kingdom were able to induce fifty-nine states to sign the treaty is hardly surprising. France did not sign it. Neither did China, India, nor several other threshold states sign it. It did not prevent nuclear proliferation. Instead, it indicated just how far out of touch America was with the rest of the world.[7] The superpowers sought to dissuade other states from acquiring weapons they themselves were amassing at a breakneck pace, engaging in a nuclear arms race while demanding that weaker states renounce such arms. The hypocrisy of this stance made America's appeal to principle (that is, using nuclear science only for peaceful purposes) appear to be nothing but a transparent cover for power politics.

Progress toward nuclear arms control—modest but not insignificant during the Johnson administration—included a treaty banning nuclear weapons in outer space. Here again, however, the treaty was inherently flawed because both superpowers possessed large numbers of intercontinental ballistic missiles (ICBMs) that, if launched, would go into "outer space" before reentering the earth's atmosphere and homing in on a target. In addition, orbital satellites— platforms in outer space—would come to be a vital link in the guidance systems for weapons of all kinds. Nonetheless, the signatories to the treaty pledged not to deploy nuclear weapons in outer space.

Behind these modest steps, the White House was able to launch few positive domestic *or* diplomatic undertakings until the 1970s, and even then the circumstances were unfavorable and the consequences unsatisfactory. At home and abroad, both the Johnson and Nixon administrations faced turbulent seas in a leaky boat. The turbulence had much to do with Vietnam; the leak had everything to do with it. A rising chorus of opposition weakened the president while it gave Vietnam and its strategic allies—Beijing and Moscow—every reason to believe that time was on their side. Presidents were engaged in constant damage control as bad news from the war front went hand in hand with an accelerating antiwar protest movement and falling popularity—the reason for Johnson's political downfall. One would have to believe in fairytales to imagine that adversaries would not try to take advantage of this situation. In Chile, for example, where American business had a huge stake, a political figure with avowedly Marxist sympathies was elected president in 1970. The Nixon administration's

---

7. Some 135 nations signed the NPT prior to the breakup of the Soviet Union; during the 1990s that number increased to 187. France and China signed it in 1992. By that time, however, India, Israel, Pakistan, and probably North Korea had joined the ranks of nuclear powers.

response appeared to have been taken right out of a page in the Soviet KGB's operational handbook.

WHEN DEMOCRACY IS BAD FOR AMERICA: CHILE

The election of Salvador Allende, a Marxist, caused alarm bells to go off in the United States, notably at the corporate headquarters of International Telephone and Telegraph (ITT) and the White House. Allende came to power with a narrow victory (36 percent of the popular vote) in a three-way contest followed by a run-off vote in the Chilean Congress, which he also won. He had campaigned on a promise to break the power of Chile's large landowners and stand up to American multinational corporations. Both of these themes resonated with the masses, not only in Chile but throughout Latin America, where "anti-imperialism" had become synonymous with anti–United States sentiment. Upon taking office, Allende nationalized about $1 billion worth of American corporate assets. This act reminded the right-wing Republicans and the American business community of Castro's policies in Cuba in the late 1950s. ITT (and possibly others) urged the Nixon administration to do something.[8]

Do what? That was the question. What could the United States do? Sending in the Marines without provocation (shades of Vietnam) would create a furor in Latin America, where memories of U.S. military intervention were all too fresh. Besides, the United States was already bogged down in a nasty guerrilla war on the other side of the world. But doing nothing would make America look weak and risked allowing the infection of socialist revolution to spread throughout the region.

Ruling out direct military action left only one "good" option: subversion. Undermining a freely elected president thus became the task of the Central Intelligence Agency (CIA), a part of the government presumably capable of carrying out such clandestine operations but not necessarily designed to do so. Indeed, the CIA's mandate was primarily to collect and analyze foreign intelligence, as well as coordinate all the intelligence efforts of the federal government. Critics argued that covert action—especially action designed to overthrow an elected government—was not only immoral but also illegal.

Nonetheless, the Nixon administration set about systematically undermining the Allende government. Exactly what happened remains shrouded in secrecy, but in 1973 the Chilean military led by Gen. Augusto Pinochet seized control and Allende was killed. Did the United States kill him or arrange to have him killed? No. Was he the answer to Chile's problems? No. In fact, Allende was a divisive

---

8. American corporations owned and operated copper mines, banks, and other industries in Chile.

figure whose rhetoric and policies polarized a society already ripe for revolt because of the enormous economic inequality and widespread poverty common in Latin America. Still, he *was* duly elected, and the appropriate constitutional means for removing him did exist. But he had greatly antagonized the professional middle class and the military. Moreover, when he did not get his way he circumvented the Chilean Congress and the courts, thus creating a split between the executive branch and the legislative and judicial branches.

At first the Chilean military dutifully served Allende, but the generals became increasingly alienated. The appearance of leftist paramilitary elements calling for armed struggle against "reactionaries" alarmed the military. Allende's personal involvement is unclear, but there can be little doubt that tensions in Chilean society were running high when the military intervened in 1973.

Chile under Pinochet became the poster child for mass violations of human rights. Unfortunately, the stigma extended to the United States. America's reputation would be one of Pinochet's victims, but it could have been otherwise: "Had Nixon abstained from meddling, responsibility for the Chilean coup would probably have fallen on Allende. Instead, the United States was condemned for its covert intervention, and Chile became for many critics a symbol of American imperialism."[9]

In Chile as in Vietnam, America seemed to lose its way, deserting its principles and practicing a crude form of power politics that demoted diplomacy while elevating military force as the instrument of choice in foreign policy. Instead of a last resort, coercion in all its variants (economic and psychological, as well as military) was becoming the norm—or so it appeared.

DÉTENTE AND DECLINE (1972–1980)

In the wake of Watergate and Vietnam, American foreign policy—measured in prestige and power broadly defined—went into a steep decline.[10] The failure of containment (specifically, the American military's counterinsurgency doctrine) in Southeast Asia set the stage for a dramatic shift in superpower relations during the Nixon-Ford administration (1968–1976) from confrontation to "détente" (relaxation of tensions). The new version of containment, so-called super-containment or containment-plus, unveiled by Richard Nixon and his chief foreign policy adviser Henry Kissinger in the early 1970s, reflected the changed realities of international politics—above all, the emergence full-blown of a Soviet counterweight

---

9. Steven W. Hook and John Spanier, *American Foreign Policy since World War II*, 16th ed. (Washington, D.C.: CQ Press, 2004), pp. 155–156.

10. See, for example, Robert W. Tucker, *The Purposes of American Power: An Essay on National Security* (New York: Praeger, 1981), esp. pp. 7–37.

to American power: by 1972, when the first strategic arms limitation agreement (SALT I) was signed, the Soviet Union appeared to have achieved "nuclear parity" with the United States.[11]

In reality, the United States was negotiating from a position of weakness, politically speaking. Not surprisingly, therefore, the results were singularly unsatisfactory, although the Nixon administration hailed the SALT I accords as a history-making achievement.

It is generally acknowledged that the SALT I agreement had glaring defects, including the fact that, far from reducing nuclear weapons, it actually legitimatized increases in these weapons. Rather than strategic arms limitation, it was a strategic arms *legitimation* agreement because it limited only delivery vehicles or launchers, not warheads. It did not curb multiple-warhead strategic missiles (MIRVs) in any way.[12] More significant was the antiballistic missile (ABM) treaty that was the other half of the SALT package. Under the terms of the ABM treaty, the superpowers pledged not to build missile defense systems, a step of major significance in perpetuating a stable nuclear balance.[13] In addition, the first SALT summit was an important confidence-building step for the superpowers, one that could (and would) in time lead to bigger and more meaningful steps. But the basic insolvency of American foreign policy would later become evident even in arms control, one of the few areas of diplomacy in which Washington made any real progress at all in the 1970s. China was one other area.

In 1972 President Nixon traveled to Beijing to meet with Chairman Mao and Premier Chou En-lai to finalize the terms of a new relationship between the two longtime rivals. The two countries did not have formal diplomatic ties in 1972. Since 1949, when the Chinese Communists defeated the Kuomintang (Nationalists), forcing Generalissimo Chiang Kai-shek to flee the country, the United States had recognized the government that Chiang and his Kuomintang (KMT) party set up on the island of Formosa (Taiwan). In 1972 the United States finally agreed to exchange ambassadors with the People's Republic of China

---

11. "SALT is short-hand for Strategic Arms Limitation Talks. The SALT process [begun] ... in 1972 produced its first fruits in the form of the ABM Treaty and the Interim Agreement on Strategic Offensive Arms. The most significant achievement of SALT I was the virtual ban on ABM (anti-ballistic missile) systems. In the topsy-turvy calculus of mutual deterrence, limitations on defensive weapons take on an importance once reserved exclusively for offensive weapons." Thomas Magstadt, "SALT II: A Wedge towards Real Arms Control," *Argus-Leader*, Aug. 26, 1979, p. 5A.

12. Ibid. "MIRV" stands for multiple independently targetable reentry vehicle.

13. In the strange logic of nuclear deterrence, this mutual vulnerability is the flipside of mutual assured destruction—if either side can knock down the other side's incoming missiles it would ipso facto no longer be deterred from attacking. By the same token, if one side had reason to believe the other side was about to deploy such a system it would have a strong incentive to strike while it still could (preemptively).

(PRC), but this meant de-recognizing Taiwan because Beijing has always insisted that there is only one China. The U.S. decision to embrace the concept of "one China" as official policy was a major diplomatic triumph for Communist China.

Clearly, the Nixon-Kissinger strategy was to put pressure on Moscow by repairing its ties with Beijing. By this time the two Communist giants were bitter rivals. The idea of playing off one side against the other is a time-honored ploy. No policy comes with any guarantees, however, and the chances of success depend on the "big picture." The old threadbare policy of nonrecognition made little sense. The Chinese Communists were in control of the mainland whether Washington liked it or not. In this sense, the Nixon-Kissinger gambit in China was logical and overdue. But to the extent that it was an attempt to gain leverage over the Soviet Union, the policy was a spectacular failure.

First, neither Moscow nor Beijing subsequently helped the United States save face in Vietnam. Second, neither Soviet-American détente nor the Sino-American rapprochement prevented the Soviet Union from ramping up its strategic nuclear capabilities in the 1970s. Third, détente and its policy spin-offs did not deter the Russians from intervening forcibly in Angola in 1975, buttressing a brutal Marxist dictatorship in Ethiopia in 1977, or invading Afghanistan in 1978.

No foreign policy gambit will work unless the balance—the big picture—is favorable. In the 1970s it did not favor the United States. In addition to the breakdown of domestic consensus caused by Vietnam and Watergate, there was the crippling effect of the 1973–1974 OPEC oil embargo on the United States, Western Europe, and Japan. The passive American response to this crisis suggested weakness or indecision or political-moral paralysis—anything but a self-confident and proactive America prepared to face new challenges and "bear any burden." One close observer argued, "The Nixon policy reformulation called for a new modesty in thought and action; it emphasized the inherent limits to any nation's wisdom, understanding, and energy."[14] It can be argued that by the early 1970s a scaling down of America's commitments was good for the country or even *necessary*. But that apparently is not what Nixon and Kissinger had in mind. Indeed, the Nixon administration was "not prepared to accept a significant change in role and interests," despite the radical redefinition of "containment" implicit in the very concept of détente.[15] The specter of insolvency loomed large *before* Jimmy Carter moved into the White House.

The one-term Carter presidency (1977–1981) witnessed a series of foreign policy disasters. The Carter administration intended to change the thrust of American foreign policy, rejecting the idea that might makes right and placing more emphasis on moral than on military power. America had placed too much

---

14. Tucker, *Purposes of American Power*, p. 9.
15. Ibid.

faith in military power, forsaking its principles in pursuit of an elusive victory in an unnecessary war—that was the real lesson of Vietnam. Only by going back to the basics—first principles (freedom, democracy, and respect for human dignity)—would it be possible to heal the wounds left by that terrible war and restore America's self-respect in its own eyes and the eyes of the world. Accordingly, Carter made respect for human rights rather than containment (anticommunism) the cornerstone of his foreign policy. He did not renounce containment, but neither did he take steps to reinforce it in the wake of America's defeat in Vietnam.

On the contrary, declaring America free of "that inordinate fear of Communism which once led us to embrace any dictator who joined us in that fear," President Carter set out to reassure the Soviet leadership of his good will and set the stage for a follow-on SALT agreement, while admonishing the dictatorships of the world (including Moscow) on human rights.[16] The Carter administration quickly put a new face on American foreign policy, reversing U.S. policy toward Vietnam by extending diplomatic recognition to Hanoi, lowering the U.S. profile in Asia generally (planned withdrawal from South Korea; closer cooperation with Beijing at the expense of Taipei), staying on the sidelines in the Horn of Africa conflict despite an active Soviet role, canceling the neutron bomb and the B-1 bomber programs, and backing the Panama Canal treaties (granting control of the canal to Panama).

All these diplomatic overtures were overshadowed by the biggest foreign policy achievement of his presidency: the 1978 Camp David summit that produced the first (and last) real breakthrough in the Middle East "peace process"—a framework for the laying down of arms. In brief, Israel agreed to return the Sinai to Egypt, and Egypt agreed to recognize Israel's right to exist. The other Arab states bitterly denounced the treaty, but elsewhere it was hailed as a moment of "historic" importance. It was Jimmy Carter's finest hour. The Egyptian president, Anwar Sadat, and the Israeli prime minister, Menachim Begin, were awarded the Nobel Peace Prize. The whole world knew that President Carter was no less deserving.[17]

This exultant moment preceded the overthrow of the shah in Iran and the Soviet invasion of Afghanistan in 1979. These two developments, punctuated by the 444-day hostage crisis in Iran, proved to be President Carter's undoing and set the stage for the election of Ronald Reagan, an ex-movie-star and former governor of California with strong backing from the Far Right. In 1980, an election year, Carter showed a different face to the American people and the world—a

---

16. Norman Graebner, *The Age of Global Power: The United States since 1939* (New York: Wiley, 1979), p. 295.

17. Jimmy Carter did win the Nobel Peace Prize in 2002. Officially it was for his work as a former president, but the award also signified that his efforts as president to bring about a lasting peace in the Middle East have not been forgotten.

scowl rather than the familiar toothy smile so often captured on camera and depicted in cartoons.

When the attempt to de-emphasize the East-West conflict and give more attention to North-South issues foundered in the late 1970s, the Carter administration reversed engines, sending Congress a request for steep increases in military spending in 1980. President Carter reacted to the Soviet invasion of Afghanistan by imposing a grain embargo, banning high-technology sales, boycotting the Moscow Olympic Games, and "temporarily" withdrawing the SALT II treaty from the Senate. He ordered a commando-type operation to rescue the hostages in Iran, but it failed. Eight Americans died and five were injured when one of the helicopters collided on the ground with the refueling aircraft for the extraction-and-exit phase of the operation. Ironically, this most dramatic evidence of a new get-tough policy backfired. When the helicopter crashed in the desert, President Carter's reelection hopes crashed with it.[18]

In his anger and anguish for the fate of the hostages, Jimmy Carter enunciated a policy that came to be known as the Carter Doctrine, committing the United States to the security of the Persian Gulf states if they were threatened by external aggression. Cynics would say the issue for America was not one of principle (peace, justice, or freedom) but interest (oil). Later events would only deepen this controversy and, in 2003, once again, point to the peculiar tendency of American foreign policy to lapse into insolvency.

THE LIMITS OF IDEALISM: THE CARTER LEGACY

The thesis of this book grows out of the tension between morality and power in American foreign policy and in the never-ending search for the proper mix of principles and interests. Striking the balance is the essence of diplomacy; in the context of America's self-image as the world's first and foremost constitutional democracy, it is the difference between a foreign policy that commands respect and one that does not.

Jimmy Carter is not the first president to be blamed for the errors of his predecessors, nor will he be the last. Was he a victim of circumstances or was there a fatal flaw in his whole approach to foreign policy?

> It was not the Carter Administration that concluded the first SALT agreements, within the terms of which the Soviet Union was able by 1977 to [catch up and possibly surpass the U.S.] counterforce capability. Nor was it the Carter Administration that inaugurated détente in 1972 and claimed that in doing so it had laid the foundation of a stable and lasting structure of peace. And it was not the Carter Administration that remained

---

18. The Iranians released the American hostages on January 20, 1981, the day after Jimmy Carter left office.

passive before the first great challenge mounted by the OPEC states in 1973–74. . . . The Carter Administration had to contend with the consequences.[19]

It is obviously unfair to blame Carter for the "diminished legacy" he received upon taking the oath of office any more than to blame Hoover for the 1929 stock market crash or Roosevelt for the Great Depression or Eisenhower for the outcome of the "wrong war" in Korea. But FDR responded to the domestic crisis creatively, and the economy was on the road to recovery even before the inoculating effects of World War II. Carter's "cure" for the post-Vietnam crisis of American diplomacy was not lacking in creativity, but it did not work. In foreign policy, as in politics generally, nothing succeeds like success, whereas failure often proves fatal.

More than any other president in American history, certainly more than Washington or Jefferson, more than Lincoln, more even than Woodrow Wilson, Jimmy Carter was and is an idealist. Many American presidents, indeed most, have exhibited a streak of idealism. John F. Kennedy, for example, characterized himself as "an idealist without illusions." Kennedy thus put his finger on the main danger inherent in idealism, namely, a tendency to fall prey to illusions about the world, to believe that human beings are basically good, that peace and progress are the norm, that war is an aberration.

As a born-again Christian, Carter tried to put his principles into practice and continued doing so after he left office. Based on his moral activism and humanitarian efforts, many Americans would probably agree that he is the best ex-president we have ever had.

There is no way of knowing if things would have turned out better had Carter engaged in Dulles-style anti-Communist rhetoric rather than soft-pedaling the East-West conflict. His principal innovation was to make human rights the centerpiece of American foreign policy. Ironically, that campaign, however well intentioned, was met with hostility, if not alarm, by many governments in many parts of world. The human rights campaign cut both ways: it was an indictment of Stalinist dictatorship, but it could just as easily be used to condemn anti-Communist military dictatorships in developing countries and the absolute monarchies of the Middle East. Indeed, some of America's staunchest non-European allies—including Egypt, Iran, Nigeria, Saudi Arabia, South Korea, Taiwan, and Turkey—were by no means above reproach. Nor, as America's critics at home and abroad delighted in pointing out, was the United States. Wielding human rights as a big stick rather than treading softly and using it as a carrot opened the United States up to charges of hypocrisy when, inevitably, we were not consistent: for example, when we loudly denounced the Kremlin's human-rights violations but muted our criticism of Beijing's.

---

19. Tucker, *Purposes of American Power*, p. 8.

Carter was idealistic but not dovish. It is naive to think that ideas are less threatening than guns. For a police state, any police state, inciting the population to demand political and civil rights is by definition a provocation. Had Carter launched a military buildup in 1977 rather than a moral crusade, it would probably have been less alarming to the Soviets. Whether it would have deterred them from meddling in Angola and Ethiopia or invading Afghanistan, however, is pure conjecture.

By the same token, defense expenditures did rise modestly during the Carter presidency in contrast to the preceding period of military retrenchment associated with the American withdrawal from Southeast Asia.[20] In retrospect, the Carter administration "stood between the reductions of the Nixon/Ford period and the substantial increases initiated by the Reagan administration in an effort to narrow the wide gap between U.S. commitments and capabilities"—a gap owing much to Carter's late-inning decision to commit the United States to a police role in the Persian Gulf.[21] Thus, the Carter foreign policy can be criticized from both the Right and the Left for trying to do too much and for actually doing too little. But the fairest criticism is the most familiar to students of American diplomacy: President Carter, like so many of his predecessors, paid too little heed to the problem of solvency: he made commitments that exceeded America's existing political and military capabilities.

The chief lesson of the Carter years is not that ideals have no place in foreign policy or that principles and interests always collide but rather that ideals are hostage to circumstances beyond mortal control. Carter's campaign slogan was "Why not the best?" His presidency demonstrated anew that in foreign policy as in all politics (and life in general) the best can become the enemy of the good— and sometimes less is more.

BOUNCING BACK: THE REAGAN PRESIDENCY (1981–1989)

The election in 1980 of a conservative Republican with no previous experience in Washington opened an extraordinary chapter in American diplomatic history. At the beginning of the 1980s, an aging dictator ruled the Soviet Union, the Soviet army was battling the U.S.-backed *mujahidin* (Afghan guerrillas), and the superpower arms race was again shifting into high gear. As the decade drew to a close,

---

20. James E. Dougherty and Robert L. Pfaltzgraff Jr., *American Foreign Policy: FDR to Reagan* (New York: Harper and Row, 1986), pp. 331–332. Comparisons between defense spending at the beginning of the Carter administration in 1977 and 1981 (Carter's last year in office) "illustrate the essentially static quality of the defense capabilities of the US," according to the authors, but the trend nonetheless differed from the Nixon/Ford administration, "when there was a sharp decline in most of these indicators."

21. Ibid.

the Soviet empire in Eastern Europe cracked, crumbled, and at the end of 1989 collapsed. During this time, the so-called Reagan Revolution dominated the American political scene; oddly enough, its impact was greater abroad than at home. Nowhere was it followed with more rapt attention than inside the Kremlin.

We will never know whether the Gorbachev phenomenon, the spell-binding but ill-fated reform campaign memorialized in catchy concepts like *glasnost* (openness) and *perestroika* (restructuring), would have happened at all without the phenomenon of Ronald Reagan. Given the profoundly dysfunctional nature of the Soviet economy, far-reaching reforms had to be instituted in the USSR sooner or later. But the *sequence* of events—Reagan's election followed by Gorbachev's rise to power, Reagan's arms buildup followed by Gorbachev's charm offensive—suggests that these developments were closely related.

The "collapse of communism" can be interpreted as (1) a foreign policy success for Ronald Reagan; (2) a vindication of Kennan's long-term "containment" strategy; or (3) an outgrowth of specific historical circumstances within the Soviet Union having little or nothing to do with the United States. Perhaps "all of the above" is the best answer.

The rhetoric of the early Reagan administration was truculent—more so than at any time since the days of John Foster Dulles. President Reagan's style stood in stark contrast to the substance of his foreign policy. He spoke softly and without a trace of the arrogance that would one day characterize the presidency of his vice president's first son, George W. Bush. And yet he was vitriolic in his denunciation of Soviet tyranny. Before we draw any firm conclusions, however, let us take a closer look at the actual performance of the Reagan White House.

Offensive Containment

As chief executive, Ronald Reagan was extremely adept at sensing the mood of the public and playing to it. He assumed the presidency after a prolonged period of national soul-searching and self-doubt. Détente had yielded disappointing results; the Soviet Union appeared to have manipulated and outmaneuvered the United States for nearly a decade. The disillusionment was palpable, but memories of Vietnam lingered, producing a kind of malaise in Washington—until Ronald Reagan came to town.

Exuding an optimism and self-assurance not seen in Washington since the days of John Kennedy, Reagan excoriated Soviet communism as "the focus of evil in the modern world" and asserted that Soviet leaders would "lie, steal, cheat, and do anything else" to get what they wanted.[22] Reagan spoke in the language of

---

22. First phrase quoted from Reagan's address to the National Association of Evangelicals, Mar. 8, 1983, in Strobe Talbott, ed., *The Russians and Reagan* (New York: Vintage Books, 1984), p. 113; second phrase quoted in *New York Times,* Jan. 30, 1981.

evangelical Protestantism at times. He predicted the apocalyptic end of Communist tyranny in the terms Karl Marx had once used to forecast the demise of capitalism: freedom and democracy would leave "Marxism-Leninism on the ashheap of history." At the same time, Reagan hinted at a proactive approach to containment of a kind for which there was no precedent. The United States would not abide the "permanent subjugation of the people of Eastern Europe."[23]

Cold wars differ from hot wars in that they are fought primarily with words rather than swords while mutual mistrust and the ever-present possibility of armed conflict preclude any meaningful efforts to replace swords with plowshares. Even during the heyday of "massive retaliation" in the 1950s, both the White House and the Kremlin interlaced rhetorical flourishes and strategic bluster with cautious policies.

Why did it matter whether the Soviet Union was outspending the United States on strategic nuclear weapons? After all, the United States had a huge arsenal of these weapons, surely enough to deter an attack or retaliate if deterrence failed. But here is where the theory of deterrence gets complicated. In fact, deterrence has more to do with diplomacy than with war, more to do with the political and psychological value than the military uses of nuclear weapons. Imagine a future situation similar to the Cuban Missile Crisis. At the time of that crisis, the United States enjoyed both nuclear strategic superiority and local conventional superiority (in the Caribbean) over the Soviet Union. In that crisis, Kennedy induced Khrushchev to back down without a shot being fired. It was the most dangerous moment in the cold war and would likely not have turned out so well had the "correlation of forces" (to use the old Soviet term) favored Moscow, as many alarmists feared it would during the "missile gap" scare.[24]

Two decades later, the situation was different. The Soviet Union was producing and deploying mobile SS-20 intermediate-range rockets at the rate of one new system every six days.[25] To make matters worse, Soviet adventurism in developing countries (backing North Vietnam in Cambodia, using Cuban proxies in Africa, invading Afghanistan) had accompanied the Kremlin's nuclear-strategic buildup. President Carter had initiated programs for beefing up America's military capabilities at the tail end of his term in office. But it was Ronald Reagan who

---

23. Quoted in Talbott, *Russians and Reagan*, pp. 89–104, from Reagan's speech to the British Parliament, June 8, 1982.

24. This fear persisted long after the missile gap episode was forgotten. The possibility that the Soviet Union would break out as a result of some new scientific or technological discovery was a big factor in fueling America's determination to stay ahead in the nuclear arms race. The alternative—falling behind—might be fatal. This kind of reasoning gave hawks (enthusiasts of big defense spending) and the defense contractors who benefited from America's Communist phobia a huge advantage in annual congressional debates over budget priorities.

25. Each SS-20 missile was armed with three nuclear warheads.

launched a massive rearmament program that rocked the Kremlin's geriatric leadership back on its heels.

At the center of Reagan's defense plans were two new U.S.-based strategic delivery systems—the MX missile with ten warheads each and the B-1 (stealth) bomber—and two theater missile systems—the Pershing II and ground-launched cruise missile (GLCM)—to be deployed in West Germany. All told, this buildup would cost one trillion dollars. (Actually, the price tag over Reagan's two terms came to nearly twice that amount.) For Moscow, the handwriting was on the wall: There was no way the Soviet Union, given the deplorable state of its decrepit economy, could hope to keep up.[26]

The rhetoric of the Reagan administration matched or exceeded its deeds. Secretary of State (and former general) Alexander Haig talked openly and ominously about "prevailing" in a nuclear war and about nuclear "war fighting" capabilities. Not since the 1950s (Dulles) had the head of America's corps of diplomats sounded so undiplomatic, so unabashedly belligerent. All this tough talk alarmed rather than reassured Western Europe (and especially West Germany). U.S. deployment of intermediate-range nuclear forces (INF) in 1983 sparked widespread antiwar protests and demonstrations across Europe. (France was one of the few exceptions within the NATO alliance.) To be sure, the demonstrators represented a minority, but there was no question that most Europeans opposed the escalating nuclear arms race and did not want Europe to be the arena for a contest of wills between the superpower gladiators. This rift between the United States and Western Europe would heal, but it was a presentiment of changing relations within the North Atlantic alliance. The end of the cold war would raise questions about NATO's continued relevance, as we shall see in a later chapter, but residual fear of the Soviet Union still kept strains between the United States and Western Europe within fairly narrow limits in the late 1980s.

Paradoxically, in international politics the adage "If you want peace, prepare for war" is all too true. By the mid-1980s, with a new leader and a new look in the Kremlin, Moscow was eager to engage in a new round of nuclear arms control talks. The fact that the Soviet army was bogged down in a bloody and costly war of attrition in Afghanistan only added to the Soviets' sense of urgency.

---

26. Thomas M. Magstadt, "Communism between Marx and the Marketplace: Implications for U.S. Foreign Policy," Policy Analysis 87, Cato Institute, Washington, D.C., June 2, 1987, and "Gorbachev and Glasnost—A New Soviet Order?" Policy Analysis 117, Cato Institute, Washington, D.C., Mar. 20, 1989. See also the excellent study comparing the performance of centrally planned and market economies by William U. Chandler, "The Changing Role of the Market in National Economies," Worldwatch Institute, Washington, D.C., Sept. 1986.

For its part, the Reagan White House denounced past efforts at arms control, particularly the so-called "SALT process." As noted, the red-hot rhetoric of the early Reagan years fueled antinuclear protest movements in the United States and Western Europe, which, in turn, prompted the president to throw down the gauntlet: if you want disarmament, he retorted, let us have the real thing, let us *reduce* nuclear arsenals, not simply "limit" them. This was a masterful political stroke: it both challenged Moscow to "build down" the strategic forces Washington found objectionable and at the same time appeared to go left-leaning critics at home and abroad one better. Let us replace SALT, Reagan declared, with START (strategic arms reduction talks). By this time, there could have been no doubt in the minds of the Kremlin's chief propagandists that in Ronald Reagan they had met their match.

But actions speak louder than words, and the president who once played cowboy roles on the silver screen now faced off for a showdown with Moscow. The weapon he chose was not a nuclear Colt 45 but rather a "gun" capable of shooting nuclear "bullets" out of the air. It was called "Star Wars."

It would have been difficult to imagine a greater inducement for the Soviet Union to seek serious arms reduction with the United States than "Star Wars"— the popular name given to the Strategic Defense Initiative (SDI) that was to become the centerpiece of a new plan to protect the land and people of the United States from nuclear attack. The SDI concept called for research and development of a missile defense system capable of intercepting and destroying incoming enemy ICBMs. Although defensive in nature, it set off alarm bells in the Kremlin. Why?

The answer takes us back to the theory of mutual deterrence or mutual assured destruction (MAD). The one irreducible condition of nuclear deterrence, according to this theory, is that it must be mutual, meaning both sides must have the capability of destroying the other. If either side lacks the means to attack or one side possesses the means to defend itself and the other does not, the resulting "asymmetric" relationship is destabilizing. In a worst-case scenario for Moscow, Washington might launch a first strike in hopes of destroying much of the Soviet nuclear arsenal on the ground and then using its missile defense system to defeat a Soviet second strike. That would tempt the Kremlin to make a "use or lose" decision to launch first in a crisis. So goes the theory.

Moscow faced the prospect of a return to the 1950s, when the United States enjoyed a nuclear monopoly. The problem was not so much that the United States might actually launch a nuclear attack as that it would be in a position to play the nuclear card to telling effect in a crisis or simply to gain a diplomatic advantage. Thus, SDI was the wedge that opened the first superpower talks aimed at reducing the size of existing nuclear arsenals.

In the Kremlin the elevation of Mikhail Gorbachev to the position of supreme leader in 1985 signaled a new day in Soviet and world history. The succession of the amiable and energetic Gorbachev (the fourth change at the top in three years) represented a welcome change. Strangely, the revitalization of American politics under Reagan had coincided almost perfectly with the ossification of Soviet politics, as one top party boss after another (Brezhnev, Andropov, and Chernenko) fell ill and died. By the 1980s, the pace of economic, technological, and political change had accelerated to a point where neither superpower could afford to have its policy- and decision-making machinery put on hold for several years without incurring serious risks. Now it fell to Gorbachev, faced with a faltering economy and a resurgent adversary, to shake things up, get the country moving again, and find a way to derail—or at least slow—the freight train called "Star Wars."

The Reagan Doctrine and Its Abuses

To put the Soviet sea change into more complete perspective, it is necessary to recall that President Reagan also launched a broad counteroffensive in developing countries, thus turning the tables in the cold war. In the past the pattern had been one of U.S. military intervention in defense of anti-Communist regimes (including right-wing dictatorships) and Soviet support for left-wing insurgents. Taking a page out of the Soviet Union's playbook, the Reagan administration actively backed "freedom fighters" (guerrilla insurgencies) in Central America and elsewhere. Basically, anybody seeking to overthrow a "Marxist dictatorship"—that is, a regime linked to Moscow and Cuba—qualified as a freedom fighter under the Reagan definition. Known as the Reagan Doctrine, this was the basis for U.S. foreign policy in the Caribbean (the 1982 invasion of Grenada) and Central America, where the U.S. supplied economic and military aid to the Contras in Nicaragua and to President José Napoleón Duarte in El Salvador.[27]

In 1986, during Reagan's second term, this rationale for U.S. interventionism would be broadened in response to popular uprisings against dictators in Haiti (Jean-Claude "Baby Doc" Duvalier) and in the Philippines (Ferdinand Marcos). The Reagan administration was now moved to declare: "The American people believe in human rights and oppose tyranny in whatever form, whether of the left or the right."[28]

However, the Reagan administration, unbeknownst to the American people or the U.S. Congress, was engaged in a covert operation involving Iran and Nicaragua. The scheme was designed to circumvent a 1984 congressional ban on

27. Duarte was a moderate who was walking a fine line between right-wing security forces blamed for widespread human rights violations on the one side and left-wing insurgents hardly less brutal on the other.
28. From President Reagan's message to Congress, Mar. 14, 1986, in the *New York Times*, Mar. 15, 1986.

funding for the Contras, who were fighting the Sandinista (Marxist) government of Daniel Ortega. Run by a U.S. Marine lieutenant colonel named Oliver North from a small room in the Old Executive Office building adjacent to the White House, the operation entailed an under-the-table (and illegal) sale of arms to Iran (officially branded a sponsor of international terrorism) intended to "buy" Tehran's help in freeing American hostages held by pro-Iranian terrorists in Lebanon. North then funneled the money to the Contras. But arms sales to Iran were only the tip of the iceberg: North and his superiors on the National Security Council were secretly tapping tax-exempt organizations, wealthy Americans, and even foreign governments for invisible cash, as well as directing an impressive network of arms dealers, ships, and airplanes supplying the anti-Sandinista guerrillas in Nicaragua.

Although the Iran-Contra affair tarnished the Reagan presidency, it did not lead to impeachment proceedings as the Watergate break-in had, despite the scandal that surrounded it. But the episode nonetheless violated the public's trust in a president the vast majority of Americans liked and, until the scandal broke, supported. It also left the country in a daze, creating confusion as to how it could have happened. President Reagan claimed to know little or nothing about it. Polls showed that the public thought he was lying. The alternative explanation was even worse: American foreign policy had been hijacked by a handful of appointed officials in defiance of Congress and behind the president's back.

CONCLUSION

Vietnam was a costly war for America, but costs that can be measured (wealth squandered and lives lost) are only part of the picture. There are also hidden costs. These costs can be imagined but not measured. For example, how would events have evolved in Asia and elsewhere had the United States not gotten bogged down in a losing war in Vietnam for more than a decade? For example, would the Soviet Union have invaded Czechoslovakia in 1968, right next door to West Germany, if the United States had not been stuck in Vietnam and if President Johnson had not been fighting for his political life after the Tet Offensive?[29]

The Vietnam debacle is a standing rebuke to power without principle or purpose. Like the imperial powers of old, the United States arrogated to itself the

---

29. According to one noted scholar of American foreign policy: "The Tet Offensive of early 1968 against the cities of South Vietnam was scarcely a Vietcong triumph, but its momentary successes stalled the President's carefully sustained illusion of victory and sent his popularity into a sharp decline." Shortly thereafter, LBJ announced he would not seek reelection. Graebner, *Age of Global Power*, p. 248.

right to decide the fate of a people Americans knew little, and cared less, about. Unfortunately, pacifists and critics on the Left who are opposed to the use of force across the board often invoke Vietnam as "proof" that military intervention is always a bad idea. But critics and policymakers alike often fail to make the proper use of historical lessons.

Thus, it is all too easy for critics to invoke Vietnam whenever the United States confronts a troublesome adversary. However, in Iraq, to cite one recent example, it was too easy for policymakers to dismiss the Vietnam analogy because Iraq and Vietnam are so different in climate, terrain, culture, ethnicity, and geography. In fact, the relevant lessons from Vietnam in this case have more to do with politics and diplomacy than with the problems of nation building or war fighting:

1. Having no idea how or when to get out.
2. Not knowing whom you can trust once you are there.
3. Not understanding the local language or customs.
4. Being increasingly perceived as occupiers.
5. Having soldiers getting killed on a daily basis by an invisible enemy.
6. Watching the American public gradually turn against the president who "got us into this mess" in the first place.
7. Facing condemnation abroad, including by one's own allies.
8. Fostering obsessive secrecy in government on "national security" grounds.
9. Eroding civil liberties at home while claiming to intervene on behalf of liberty abroad.

The list goes on but the reader can take it from here.

Three decades later, Vietnam was a fading memory at home, but it had not faded overseas, as the war against Iraq (despised virtually everywhere but in America) clearly demonstrated. The possibility that a preemptive war against Iraq would revive the stigma of Vietnam apparently did not occur to the Bush administration.

Vietnam is a textbook case of how not to make foreign policy, how not to fight a war, and how not to end it. When the last Americans evacuated Saigon in 1975 it was in a hail of bullets. There are few more ignominious moments in American history.

President Ronald Reagan led the country out of self-imposed exile—a kind of banishment that was moral and psychological, not geographic. As such, it affected the political will of the nation rather than its military capabilities, which were unsurpassed despite America's slumping self-confidence after the debacle in Vietnam. All this changed under Reagan. Not even the Iran-Contra scandal could obliterate the gains of the eighties or obscure the contrast between the way the world looked to Americans in 1989 and the way it had looked in 1979. In

1989—the year Reagan left office—the Soviet satellite empire in Eastern Europe collapsed. The Soviet Union would follow suit in just a few years.

George Kennan had predicted the implosion of the Soviet Union, with its repressive political controls and rigid planned economy, in 1947 when he unveiled the strategy of containment in his famous *Foreign Affairs* article. Slightly more than four decades later, that remarkable prediction came true. The fact that it happened at the end of the 1980s, a decade dominated by the personality and political philosophy of Ronald Reagan, a staunch anti-Communist who decisively reasserted the role of military force in foreign policy, does not prove cause and effect. It does, however, strongly suggest a correlation.

Even before the Communist regimes in Eastern Europe began falling like so many dominoes, Reagan's hard-line approach had started to pay big dividends when, in 1987, Gorbachev agreed to mutual elimination of all intermediate-range nuclear missiles—the so-called "double zero" solution to the long-standing INF controversy. The INF treaty remains one of the signal achievements in nuclear arms control to this day.

This success came at a heavy cost to the taxpayer. The Reagan administration ran up the largest budget deficits in American history.[30] The trade-off between "national security" and Social Security would become a major issue in the 1990s and beyond, due in no small part to the massive growth in the national debt on Reagan's watch. Nevertheless, in regard to relations with the world outside, President Reagan left the country in better shape than he found it.

There is a lot of irony in the fact that we associate good things with Reagan's foreign policy and bad things with Jimmy Carter's. After all, Jimmy Carter was a born-again Christian who was guided by principle in both his public and private life. This is not to say that Ronald Reagan was unprincipled—he was not. However, Reagan made no secret of his belief in hard power—superior military might—as the only thing that would ensure America's victory in the cold war. At the same time, everything we know about Reagan's personality tells us that in his basic beliefs he was naive and childlike: he truly believed in the myth of America as the Promised Land and that the Soviet Union was the Evil Empire. The world according to Reagan was divided into good guys and bad guys; the former fight for the right, and the latter believe that might makes right. Yet, Reagan never ruled out making a deal with the devil (be it the Soviet Union or Iran), as long as it was a good deal for the United States. This judicious marriage of power and principle puts Reagan in the front ranks of American presidents who deserve to be remembered as ardent idealists.

---

30. The national debt skyrocketed from $907 billion in 1980 to $2.6 trillion in 1988, roughly a fourfold increase in just eight years. During that time, the per capita debt increased from slightly under $4,000 to $10,534, while the interest on the debt climbed from 12.7 percent of federal outlays to over 20 percent.

I predict that Reagan will also be remembered as a successful president by future generations, less because he made the United States stronger (in fact, it was plenty strong under his predecessors) than because he rekindled pride in America. I believe that newfound pride had at least as much to do with principle as it did with power.

Democracy and Anarchy
America in the New World Order

O V E R V I E W

This chapter covers the period from 1989 to 1997. As the beginning of the post–cold war era, it was an especially crucial time. First I consider the foreign policy of President George H.W. Bush, who was faced with the challenge of defining America's role in a world without a Communist threat or serious rival. I stress that President Bush lacked a "vision" or concept to redefine America's role in the world, which, in the wake of the cold war, included a radically changed Europe, intensified regional conflicts, and the lingering threat of a nuclear Armageddon. Next, I discuss the diplomacy of the Clinton administration, including its push for ratification of the North American Free Trade Agreement (NAFTA), a Palestinian state with security guarantees for Israel, and an end to the fighting in Northern Ireland, while seeking international cooperation on global warming and the environment. I then take a critical look at President Clinton's decisions to intervene militarily (including deployment of ground forces) in Bosnia and at his decision not to intervene in Rwanda. In a concluding section I reflect on America's post–cold war policy.

The end of the cold war paralleled the end of World War II in its impact on world politics and implications for American foreign policy. Throughout this book I have noted the historic tension between power and principle in American foreign policy. The cold war's passing once again brought this tension to a crisis point and energized the quest for a new balance between these two competing elements.

The search for a foreign policy paradigm congruent with the new world order occurred in the context of a unipolar international system. The ironies of the contemporary period are difficult to overlook: a nation that was once a pawn on the chessboard of European imperialism is now not only the sole regional hegemon in the world but also the only great power capable of fighting and winning wars in all regions of the globe. More than a half-century after World War II, Europe's former Great Powers were still not strong enough—either individually or collectively—to break the bonds of military-strategic dependence on the United States.

We can debate the precise point when the cold war ended, whether it was the end of 1989, when jubilant Germans tore the Berlin Wall down, or the end of 1991, when President Gorbachev resigned, having survived a bizarre political

163

CHRONOLOGY, 1989-1997

1989   George H. W. Bush inaugurated as forty-first president of the United States; Mikhail Gorbachev becomes first "elected" president of the USSR; Communist regimes fall in Eastern Europe; Chinese Communist leaders brutally crush pro-democracy uprising in Beijing; Berlin Wall falls; United States invades Panama

1990   Iraq invades Kuwait

1991   U.S.-led coalition evicts Iraqi forces from Kuwait and defeats Iraq in short war; Warsaw Treaty Organization dissolves; Soviet Union dissolves

1992   UN peacekeeping force intervenes in Balkans crisis

1993   European Community initiates single market and moves toward full union; Islamic terrorists bomb World Trade Center; North Korea withdraws from Non-Proliferation Treaty (NPT); end of apartheid in South Africa; William Jefferson Clinton is inaugurated as forty-second president

1994   Civil war breaks out in Rwanda; Republicans gain control of U.S. Congress in midterm elections

1995   Peso devaluation puts Mexican economy in crisis; Dayton Accords lead to Balkans cease-fire

1996   President Clinton signs Comprehensive Test Ban Treaty; Clinton seeks NATO expansion by 1999

1997   President Clinton inaugurated into second term

kidnapping episode. Certainly, after the collapse of the Soviet political system there could no longer be any doubt that the cold war was history.

The tenure of George Herbert Walker Bush, the nation's forty-first president (1989–1993), coincides with the collapse of communism in Eastern Europe. This period is especially important to students of foreign policy because it represents a transition from one era to another. As noted in previous chapters, among the ideas and policy issues that dominated the past era were the strategy of containment (anticommunism), the iron curtain (East-West bifurcation of Europe), military intervention against revolution (often in support of right-wing dictatorships) in developing countries, mutual assured destruction (MAD), a bipolar global distribution of power (the "balance of terror"), and efforts to reduce the danger of nuclear war (above all, the SALT and START treaties).

What idea or doctrine, if any, would replace containment as the cornerstone of U.S. foreign policy? Surely some cold war issues would vanish, but others would remain. Besides old unsettled disputes and unresolved issues, there would just as surely be new foreign policy problems calling for new solutions and even a whole new way of thinking about the world.

In this chapter, then, we will look at two presidential administrations—the one-term presidency of George H. W. Bush and the first term of President William Jefferson Clinton (1993–1997). The first had the good fortune to be at the helm when the policies of the past four decades bore the sweet fruits of victory, but the economy turned sour; the second had the good fortune to be president when the economy was vibrant, but the world turned sour.

POLICY WITHOUT VISION (1989–1993)

President George H. W. Bush did not pretend to be a visionary interested in big ideas. He was criticized and even ridiculed for having little or no imagination. He responded to such criticism with good-natured aplomb, dismissing what he called "the vision thing" with a wave of the hand. He was, above all, a pragmatist who displayed sober judgment both in and out of office. Indeed, his political résumé told the story. He had served briefly in the U.S. House of Representatives before embarking on an illustrious career in the executive branch, first as a diplomat, then as CIA director, and after that as vice president in the Reagan administration.

Fate decreed that at the very moment in history when the cold war ended and a new day was dawning, the United States would have a president without a vision. Pundits proclaimed the advent of a new world order and suggested that America was adrift in the world. What we needed, according to the president's critics on both the Left and the Right, was a new vision or cause that could serve as the moral and political equivalent of anticommunism. But George H. W. Bush was the wrong man to devise a grand strategy based on a big new idea.

To say the earlier Bush administration lacked a "vision" is tantamount to saying American foreign policy, for the first time in nearly half a century, was not guided by a doctrine. Most nations conduct foreign affairs without doctrines. The United States after World War II became one of the rare exceptions. Framing a foreign policy in terms of a doctrine or formula or ideology is fraught with risks and problems, as the United States learned during the cold war. Nevertheless, the idea of "containment" did have the advantage of lending a certain clarity and coherence to the new "national security" strategy. It also helped to mobilize the population for a protracted struggle against a formidable adversary.

Although George H. W. Bush did not enunciate a new grand strategy, he did manage foreign policy with a firm hand. He adopted a no-nonsense approach to dealing with problems one by one, as they arose—an approach that was reactive rather than preemptive, pragmatic but not phlegmatic. During his four years in office, he faced three "legacy" problems pushed to the fore by the fading away of the cold war, two humanitarian crises resulting from a descent into anarchy in failed or failing states, and one big war triggered by an act of naked aggression in a region long deemed to be of vital interest to the United States. We will look at these problems, crises, and the first Gulf War (1990–1991) in the following sections.

Legacy Number 1: Europe's Cold War Hangover

As the fog and friction of the cold war faded, several new issues came clearly into view. First, how might a Europe without the iron curtain look, and what new challenges and opportunities would such a Europe present for American foreign policy? One big question was what to do about NATO in the absence of a Soviet threat. An even more immediate policy matter was how to deal with the German question that resurfaced with a vengeance the day the Berlin Wall came down. Then, too, throughout Eastern Europe new democracies were replacing the old Communist dictatorships and, in the process, giving rise to a host of new policy questions.

Ever since the end of World War II, Germany had been divided into two separate states, one under Communist rule (and Soviet tutelage) and the other governed democratically (and under American protection). This anomaly of a divided Berlin and divided Germany ended in 1989–1990 after the collapse of the East German state left no doubt that the popular revolt against communism could and would not be contained in Berlin—or, for that matter, anywhere else in Eastern Europe. The demise of communism in Germany was a victory for containment and cause for great celebration in Germany and the United States, but it was greeted with a degree of ambivalence in Europe. Europeans on both sides of the disappearing East-West divide had good reason to fear a united Germany.

Historically, Germany (or its precursor, Prussia) had launched wars of aggression too many times, including both "world wars" fought in the twentieth century. Geographically, Germany was located bang in the middle of Europe, at the very fulcrum of power. Economically, Germany was easily the most powerful and robust country in Europe. At least the German nation had not been so imposing physically when Germany's territory and population were divided; but a reunified German state would have a far larger population than France or the United Kingdom, by far the largest in the European Union, exceeded in size only by a post-Soviet Russia (an economic basket-case).[1]

---

1. The territory of France is still substantially larger than that of Germany, however. The new Germany has a population of 82 million to 83 million; by comparison, France and the United Kingdom each have a population that has stabilized at about 58 million. Russia's population is 147 million to 148 million, but this figure includes non-Russian nations that in some cases have secessionist yearnings (for example, Chechnya).

But the United States had always considered the division of Germany a temporary expedient pending a final settlement of World War II. For more than a decade after the outbreak of the cold war, the United States made German "reunification" a high priority in its declaratory policy. Germans on both sides of the barbed wire barrier that separated them from each other naturally wanted the German Humpty-Dumpty put back together again. One big question, however, was how Germany's neighbors—Austria, Belgium, Czechoslovakia, Denmark, France, Luxembourg, the Netherlands, Poland, and Switzerland— would feel about having a single German state next door again. A still bigger question was how the Soviet Union (and later Russia) would react to the idea. The Soviet Union still had a sizeable military presence in Czechoslovakia, East Germany, and Poland in 1990 (after the Communist regimes in these places had collapsed).

Moreover, if Europe were ever to become one geopolitical expression rather than two, something would have to be done to bring the long-stagnant economies of Eastern Europe closer to the norm in Western Europe. A microcosm of this problem existed in Germany, but there it would be up to West Germans to finance the cost of East Germany's reconstruction. In Eastern Europe, including Russia, money would have to come from outside sources.

At first, Soviet president Gorbachev declared that membership in NATO for a reunited Germany was "absolutely out of the question." He soon bowed to the inevitable, however, and on July 16, 1990, Gorbachev acquiesced on this issue of enormous symbolic and political importance for Europe and the world. In a real sense, the cold war officially ended on this date.

But Soviet acquiescence (for a price) did not settle all accounts. There was also the question of whether, when, and how to bring the other East European countries, especially the fastest to institute democratic and market reforms, into the structures that had evolved in the West during the cold war. NATO, a creature of the cold war, had started out in 1949 as an alliance of twelve West European states (Belgium, Canada, Denmark, France, Great Britain, Iceland, Italy, Luxembourg, the Netherlands, Norway, Portugal, and the United States). In the four decades between NATO's inception and the collapse of Soviet power, NATO membership grew to sixteen with the admission of Greece and Turkey in 1952, West Germany in 1954, and Spain in 1982 (see Table 7-1). If NATO were to remain relevant after the cold war was over it would have to change in many ways. It would have to change its strategic focus and force levels, its function, and its raison d'être (justification). It would also have to consider opening its ranks to new members, as it had done several times in the past. But this time would be different; this time NATO would be mulling the admission of countries that were formerly on the opposite side of the battle lines, countries that only yesterday were ruled by Communists and that were unproven either as democracies or as market economies or, above all, as useful military allies.

Table 7-1 The North Atlantic Treaty Organization, 1949–Present		
Member state (date of membership)	Population (millions, 2001)	Armed forces (active duty, 2000)
Belgium (1949)	10.1	42,000
Canada (1949)	30.6	59,000
Czech Republic (1998)	10.3	52,900
Denmark (1949)	5.3	25,000
France (1949)	58.7	420,800
Germany (1954)	82.1	333,500
Greece (1952)	10.6	204,800
Hungary (1998)	10.1	60,000
Iceland	< 0.3	—
Italy (1949)	57.4	390,900
Luxembourg (1949)	< 0.5	1,400
Netherlands (1949)	15.7	55,500
Norway (1949)	4.5	32,600
Poland (1998)	38.7	187,500
Portugal (1949)	9.9	71,700
Spain (1982)	39.6	155,200
Turkey (1952)	64.5	797,300
United Kingdom (1949)	58.7	217,600
United States (1949)	274.0	1,489,000

In this radically changed environment, some experts questioned whether NATO itself served any useful purpose and suggested that it simply be dissolved (like the Warsaw Pact, its cold war counterpart). There is no evidence than any U.S. president has ever seriously considered dissolving NATO. Therefore, George H. W. Bush, ever mindful that a hibernating Russian bear could stir at any time, gave a high priority to Europe in general and the question of how to reconfigure and redirect NATO in the "new world order" in particular. The importance Washington assigned to Europe as a region would not decline noticeably throughout the decade of the nineties. However, when events finally prompted a reappraisal—as a direct result of the split in NATO prompted by America's decision to invade Iraq in 2003—the decline was so abrupt that NATO itself appeared for a time to be in jeopardy.

Legacy Number 2: Beyond Europe—Regional Conflicts

The East-West conflict quickly faded after 1989, but another legacy of the cold war—namely, regional conflicts fueled by the superpower rivalry—did not.

Except for the Berlin crises, which ended with the building of the Wall in 1961, the cold war battlegrounds were generally located in the so-called third world—in the Middle East, Africa, Asia, and Latin America. As we know, one of these zones of conflict, namely Southeast Asia, had turned into a calamity for the United States (not to mention the Vietnamese people). Yet another, in Central Asia, had become the Soviet Union's "Vietnam."

Like U.S. policymakers in Vietnam, the leaders of the Kremlin had no idea what they were getting into when they decided to invade Afghanistan at the end of 1979. When the Soviet forces finally withdrew roughly a decade later, thousands of Soviet soldiers had been killed and an estimated 2 million Afghans had died in the war; in addition, some 6 million Afghans had fled, mostly to neighboring states that could ill-afford an influx of war refugees. Meanwhile, the United States was actively supporting the Afghan *mujahidin* (Islamic "freedom fighters," or guerrillas). Under these circumstances, Soviet president Mikhail Gorbachev was eager to find an excuse to get out and cut Soviet losses. Ending the cold war was the perfect excuse. Thus, two regional conflicts, both in Asia, not only preceded the superpowers' decision to abandon the cold war but also helped to precipitate that decision. The first one, Vietnam, damaged the United States at home and abroad; the second, Afghanistan, did the same (and worse) to the Soviet Union.

Gorbachev also helped end regional conflicts fed by superpower rivalry in southern Africa and Southeast Asia. In Angola, Cuban proxy forces withdrew in return for South Africa's withdrawal from neighboring Namibia. Vietnam, a Soviet client state, withdrew from Cambodia after its invasion of that country following the brutal Pol Pot regime's campaign of mass murder against its own population ("autogenocide"). Thus, President Bush was able to achieve major foreign policy objectives during this transition period as a result of a sudden dovetailing of American and Soviet (Russian) interests: if Moscow was in a mood to cut its losses, Washington was prepared to offer rewards for doing so. The carrot was replacing the stick in America's relations with Russia.

Even in Central America, where Moscow persisted for a time with moral and economic support for the Marxist Sandinista regime in Nicaragua, and where a bloody insurgency war was still going strong in El Salvador, the conflicts died out after Nicaraguan president Daniel Ortega allowed free elections. It was ballots not bullets that ousted the Sandinistas in February 1990. Thereafter, the fighting in El Salvador also receded. That left only Castro's Cuba as a remnant of the cold war in the Western Hemisphere. As if to underscore Moscow's total renunciation of past policy, Gorbachev discontinued the generous Soviet subsidies to Havana in 1991 (including petroleum, arms, and food) and announced his intent to withdraw the Soviet military training brigade, as well.

The Middle East was one region where conflict did not abate. The seeds of violence were present in that part of the world before the outbreak of the cold war and would continue to grow like an inoperable tumor long after the cold war had passed into history. This was a problem even Gorbachev could not help the United States fix.

Legacy Number 3: Defusing the Nuclear Time Bomb

As the cold war was winding down, the question of what to do about the vast nuclear arsenals that had played such a key role in the superpower rivalry loomed large. The START negotiations were largely completed before President Reagan left office. Each side agreed to a ceiling of 1,600 delivery vehicles, 4,900 warheads, and 6,000 strategic weapons. These numbers fell short of an overall halving but did reduce land-based missiles by 50 percent.

President Reagan's commitment to the Strategic Defense Initiative was the main obstacle to the START treaty. Recall that the United States aimed at reducing the threat posed by Soviet land-based missiles. The Soviets, on the other hand, aimed at derailing the U.S. antiballistic missile program. The Reagan administration's refusal to cancel the SDI research-and-development program thus created an arms control impasse.

George H. W. Bush, however, was not wedded to SDI. Therefore, when Gorbachev offered to sign the START treaty if the United States pledged to abide by the 1972 ABM treaty, the deal was struck and SDI quietly faded away. By this time, Gorbachev had already announced major unilateral cuts in Soviet conventional forces. In addition, in 1990 Washington and Moscow mutually agreed to make deep reductions in existing levels of conventional forces in central Europe.

This movement toward arms reduction and cutbacks in military spending continued after Gorbachev's departure from the political scene in December 1991. Barely six months later, President Bush and Gorbachev's successor, Boris Yeltsin, met face-to-face and announced an agreement to cut strategic nuclear weapons to about 3,000 by 2003, if not sooner. For the moment, it appeared as though weapons of mass destruction were no longer hanging over the planet like the fabled Sword of Damocles.[2]

THE GULF WAR (1990–1991)

The Iraqi dictator Saddam Hussein ordered his army to invade Kuwait in August 1990, only two years after the bloody eight-year Iran-Iraq war had ended in a

---

2. According to Greek legend, Damocles was a courtier in ancient Syracuse whom the king invited to a feast and then seated under a sword hanging by a single hair as a lesson in the constant perils to a ruler's life.

draw, despite America's secret "tilt" toward Baghdad.[3] The war with Iran, a war Saddam himself had started, nearly bankrupted the country. His best and only hope of economic recovery was to persuade the Organization of Oil Exporting Countries (OPEC) to raise oil prices. Led by Saudi Arabia, OPEC refused. Frustrated by the Saudis, Saddam became aggressive once again. Invading the small oil-rich and defenseless Kuwait was only the first step. The real prize was the rich oil fields of Saudi Arabia that lay just across the Kuwaiti border to the south.

As Saddam amassed his forces near the border, President Bush put a war plan in motion (dubbed Operation Desert Shield), deploying some 250,000 troops to deter, prevent, or repel an Iraqi invasion of Saudi Arabia. Control of Saudi oil fields, plus Iraq's and Kuwait's, would have placed 40 percent of the world's oil supplies at the Iraqi dictator's disposal. A triumphant Saddam would also have posed a threat to moderate Arab regimes (strategic partners of the United States) and, arguably, a challenge to the post–cold war global balance of power. Thus, the stakes for Washington and the West, as well as for the Arab world, were extremely high.

President George H. W. Bush acted decisively and, no less important, with careful attention to the diplomatic (political) dimension of contemporary war. This key aspect of the first Gulf War deserves special mention in light of the very different approach taken more than a decade later by President George W. Bush in the second Gulf War. The United Nations strongly backed the United States in the first Gulf War, giving Baghdad a deadline (January 15, 1991) to withdraw from Kuwait or face the consequences (military action). The resolution containing the ultimatum and authorizing the use of force against Iraq passed unanimously in the UN Security Council. The United States also had the full support of its NATO allies and broad support in the Arab world, as well.

An unintended consequence of Iraqi aggression was to provide the first real post–cold war test of the UN's potential for "collective security"—an idea that had been on the shelf at least since the early 1950s (the Korean War). In order for collective security to work, it required at a minimum the collaboration of the five permanent members of the UN Security Council (China, France, the United Kingdom, the United States, and the USSR). At the appropriate time, the U.S.-led coalition acted with the legal authority of the United Nations and the overwhelming moral support of the world community. It is worth noting that the United Nations wavered far less than the U.S. Congress, where a vigorous debate occurred and opponents (remembering Vietnam) demanded that the administration abide by the War Powers Act.

---

3. The Reagan administration secretly supplied Iraq with supercomputers, machine tools, and biological agents (including anthrax) between 1984 and 1988.

Nonetheless, when the January 15 deadline passed, President Bush transformed Operation Desert Shield into Operation Desert Storm. The attack on Iraq's military forces and infrastructure was hard-hitting and devastating. For the first time, the U.S. military put the war-making potential of new "smart" (precision-guided) bombs, standoff weapons, computerized communications, command and control systems, and global positioning satellites (GPS), among other high-tech innovations, to the test. Although not all these capabilities were brand-new, they had never before been used in combination.

The effect was stunning, literally and figuratively. The Iraqi army and air force were wiped out in short order. The coalition forces surrounded most Iraqi army units within 100 hours—many surrendered without a fight. The war was over in just forty-three days. More than 100,000 Iraqi combatants were killed compared with fewer than 200 coalition casualties (many of whom were victims of friendly fire).[4]

Saddam was defeated, humiliated, and stigmatized, but he remained in power. The United Nations had not authorized Saddam's ouster nor would the Arab rulers have welcomed the overthrow of an Arab government (*any* Arab government) by the United States or any other Western power, given the recent history of Arab subjugation at the hands of European colonial powers. Critics would later question the wisdom of not removing Saddam "when we had the chance," but this line of reasoning totally ignores the political dimension of war: the first Bush administration (unlike the second) believed it was vitally important to achieve a consensus on the war, both at home and abroad, *and hold it together after the war.*

The first Gulf War cost $61 billion. It was short but the price tag was not sweet. Nonetheless, because President Bush had played the game of diplomacy as well as the game of war, members of the allied coalition reimbursed the United States for 88 percent of this amount, so the actual cost to the American taxpayers was about $7 billion (about the same as for the Spanish-American War), or $235 per person.

Apart from the cost of financing the war, the Bush administration quite rightly did not want to occupy Iraq or get involved in "nation building" in a society deeply divided along ethnic and religious lines. Washington was also worried that a post-Saddam Iraq would break up, possibly descending into civil war, destabilizing the region, and tempting neighboring states (including Iran, Syria, and Turkey) to carve up the rotting carcass.

The way the United States dealt with Saddam after the war occasioned a great deal of controversy. With the war won and the American public breathing

---

4. In the first Gulf War, one-fourth of the Americans killed in combat were killed by so-called friendly fire. The same thing happened in Afghanistan in 2002. CBS News, "Friendly Fire," Mar. 12, 2003. See *60 Minutes II,* online at www.CBS.com for complete text.

a collective sigh of relief, President George H. W. Bush made the fateful decision to give the task of working out the "details" of the cease-fire to a professional soldier, Gen. Norman Schwarzkopf, rather than a seasoned diplomat. Schwarzkopf made a huge concession to his Iraqi counterpart: Iraq would be allowed to fly armed helicopters in the "no-fly zones." This concession was an unmitigated disaster for the Shia population of southern Iraq, allowing Saddam to crush his opponents, nip any spontaneous uprisings in the bud, and virtually guarantee that his repressive regime would remain in power indefinitely.[5]

Saddam thus snatched political victory from the jaws of military defeat. In the ensuing years, he would bully and murder the Iraqi Shia population in the south, the Iraqi Kurdish population in the north, and anyone else who did not genuflect at his feet.

The Gulf War nonetheless changed the political-military balance in the Middle East. The United States now had military bases ringing Iraq, from Kuwait and Saudi Arabia (among others) in the south to Turkey in the north, as well as the formidable naval armada that had long been present in the Mediterranean and Persian Gulf. The United States would use "containment" to keep a defiant Saddam under military and economic pressure in the years to come. The United Nations' sanctions put in place before the war would be kept in place after the war, when Saddam refused to comply with a UN order to disarm. A UN inspections team would be sent into Iraq to verify that Saddam had disarmed (that is, destroyed his WMD). Finally, the no-fly zones would be strictly enforced in the north and south when it became clear that Saddam remained defiant and singularly untrustworthy. Thus, although Saddam was still in power, he was constrained and contained.

THE NEW INTERVENTIONISM

According to one prominent scholar, the upshot of the first Bush administration's vacillation over first principles resulted in a new foreign policy doctrine. In an article that appeared in the prestigious journal *Foreign Affairs* in late 1992, Stephen John Stedman lamented:

> [T]he end of superpower rivalry continues to entrance America with the chimera of a new world order. That illusion, alongside often violent disorder in many states, has

---

5. See, for example, PBS's *NOW* with Bill Moyers on the eve of the second Gulf War, Mar. 17, 2003 (online at www.pbs.org/now/). This special edition of *Frontline* includes an interview with the Iraqi scholar and opposition leader Kanan Makiya and reviews past *Frontline* reports on Saddam Hussein's Iraq from the first Gulf War to the "containment" policy and, finally, the failure of diplomacy in the run-up to President George W. Bush's televised ultimatum of Mar. 17, 2003.

produced a kind of "new interventionism." This outlook combines an awareness that civil war is a legitimate issue of international security with a sentiment for crusading liberal internationalism. The new interventionists wed great emphasis on the moral obligations of the international community to an eagerness for a newly available United Nations to intervene in domestic conflicts throughout the world.[6]

Stedman went so far as to suggest, "future historians may compare 1991–1992 to the years just after World War II, when the doctrine of containment evolved." The United States "may be taking upon itself a more crusading, interventionist role in world affairs," he warned. "Followed unthinkingly, the new interventionism could become increasingly expansive, until the United States and United Nations ultimately take on tasks for which they are ill-prepared, leaving themselves embroiled in numerous internal conflicts without the will or resources to bring peace to any."[7]

In retrospect, Stedman's analysis appears prescient, if not prophetic. Over the next decade, the United States would dispatch military forces to the former Yugoslavia (both Bosnia and Kosovo), Haiti, Afghanistan, the Persian Gulf (including Saudi Arabia, Kuwait, Qatar, and Oman), and the Philippines, among others. In each instance, U.S. intervention was the prelude to a long-term military presence. At the same time, the United States continued to maintain military bases in Europe (notably Germany, Italy, and the United Kingdom), Asia (the Japanese island of Okinawa, South Korea, and Thailand), and elsewhere (for example, at Incerlik in Turkey and Guantanamo in Cuba). Except for the fiasco in Somalia (see below), the only major U.S. military withdrawal in the post–cold war period occurred in the Philippines in 1992, when anti-U.S. ferment there led to the closing of the naval base at Subic Bay, but a decade later Washington was again sending combat forces to help fight Islamic insurgents operating in the chain of Philippine islands known as Sulu Archipelago.[8]

Operation Restore Hope: Somalia

Readers familiar with the Hollywood film *Black Hawk Down* will have some prior knowledge of what happened in Somalia in the early 1990s. Unfortunately, the movie does not provide enough background information. President George H. W. Bush sent 21,000 troops to Somalia, a country in the throes of civil war and anarchy. Why?

---

6. Stephen John Stedman, "The New Interventionists," *Foreign Affairs,* autumn and winter 1992–1993; reprinted in *The Future of American Foreign Policy,* ed. Eugene Wittkopf, 2nd ed. (New York: St. Martin's, 1994), p. 318. The reader will recall that *Foreign Affairs* is the same journal that published George Kennan's X article in 1947.

7. Ibid., p. 319.

8. "Back to the Jungle," *Economist,* Mar. 1, 2003, p. 41.

The United Nations authorized the use of military force on December 4, 1992, to save starving Somalis caught in the crossfire between ruthless rival warlords. For a year prior to this UN action, the Bush administration had been pressured to do something by congressional leaders from both parties, human rights organizations, and the media. Bowing to this pressure, President Bush offered to intervene on "humanitarian" grounds, and the UN Security Council agreed.

Compassion was a factor, but realism was behind the key calculations of Washington's policymakers. In this case, principle and power intersected. Somalia is strategically located south of the oil-rich Arabian Peninsula at the entrance to the Red Sea. The Horn of Africa, like virtually every region of the world, had become a playing field in the never-ending superpower contest that was the cold war. For many years when Ethiopia's Emperor Haile Selassie I was an ally of the United States, the Somali dictator Siad Barre looked to the Soviet Union for patronage. After the aging Ethiopian emperor was ousted in a military coup in the mid-1970s, the two rival states switched sides and fought a bloody war. Ethiopia's military rulers embraced Marxism and welcomed Soviet military and economic aid, as well as direct military intervention by Cuban proxy forces in Ethiopia's war with Somalia. When the cold war ended, a fragmented but widespread rebellion quickly swept the Somali ruler from power and the country descended into anarchy.

The drama of war and revolution in the Horn of Africa occurred against a backdrop of drought and mass starvation. It was going on during much of the 1980s, at the same time as the tragic war between Iran and Iraq. After 1989, things came to a head more or less simultaneously in the Balkans (Yugoslavia), Central America (Nicaragua and El Salvador), the Horn of Africa, North Africa (Sudan), the Persian Gulf, and West Africa (Liberia).

In central Asia (Afghanistan and beyond), too, the Soviet withdrawal had settled nothing, and the subsequent breakup of the Soviet state left a pall of uncertainty hanging over the entire region. In short, as the euphoria over the cold war's end swept Europe and North America, tragedies on a massive scale were playing out in nearly every other region of the world.

It is only in this larger perspective that the U.S. intervention in Somalia makes any sense at all. The UN action and the Bush administration's decision to intervene came amid several human rights calamities (including the slaughter of Kurds in northern Iraq, Muslims in Bosnia, and Nubians in southern Sudan). In each case, as in Somalia, the unfolding human tragedy occurred in the context of a failed state.

Until Operation Restore Hope in Somalia, Washington and the West, preoccupied with Europe as the East-West conflict subsided, looked the other way. Somalia would be a test case of the UN's new sense of competence now that the Security Council was no longer permanently deadlocked by the veto power of the permanent members. For the United States, it was a chance to test-drive a new foreign policy, one that married liberalism and pragmatism, old-fashioned American idealism and the American penchant for problem solving. Unfortunately, Somalia proved that the problems presented by failed states are not easily solved.

The aftermath of the Gulf War provided the precedent for Operation Restore Hope. When Saddam Hussein attacked the rebellious Kurds in northern Iraq, the UN Security Council adopted Resolution 688, establishing the principle that an act of internal aggression may be a threat to international order and thus laying the groundwork for "humanitarian" interventions in civil wars by the United Nations or a UN-authorized coalition of states. This principle appeared to be at odds with Article 2, paragraph 7, of the UN Charter, stipulating, "Nothing contained in the present Charter shall authorize the United Nations to intervene in matters which are essentially within the domestic jurisdiction of any state."

But the die was cast. The "humanitarian intervention" in northern Iraq set a precedent that was taken up in the case of Somalia and later in Bosnia and elsewhere.

What emerged after the cold war was a flawed new world order if the emphasis is on the word "order," but it was definitely new in several ways. The United States embarked on a *new* career of interventionism, this time with the active participation of other countries and the blessing of the international community. The "new interventionism" was accompanied by a *new* realism that combined humanitarian and strategic values. Finally, Washington embraced a *new* multilateralism, looking to the approval of the United Nations and NATO and world opinion as a precondition for military intervention. This desire for legitimation by the international community was one of America's guiding principles in the first decade of the post–cold war era.

Rescuing Failed States: Duty or Folly?

At the dawn of the decade, the new world order looked more like a new world disorder. There was evidence everywhere except in North America and Western Europe that the forces of anarchy were gathering momentum in the power vacuums created in part by the pullback of the two superpowers.[9] Yugoslavia in the

---

9. Robert Kaplan's article "The Coming Anarchy" (*Atlantic Monthly,* Feb. 1994) was widely read at the time and appeared in a later book. See Robert D. Kaplan, *The Coming Anarchy* (New York: Vintage Books, 2001). Kaplan argued that the optimism with which many American policymakers greeted the post–cold war era was unwarranted by the facts; instead, he painted a grim picture of exploding populations, mass deprivation, deteriorating environmental conditions, and ethnic violence in the Balkans, West Africa, and elsewhere beyond the boundaries of the affluent Western world.

early 1990s was a prime example of a failed state in the throes of a violent breakup. Unlike Somalia or Sudan or Liberia, Yugoslavia was in Europe's own backyard, outside of NATO per se but too close for NATO's members (including Greece, Italy, and Turkey) to ignore.

The 1992 U.S. presidential election intruded upon the scene of this international turbulence and itself became a major variable. The upset victory of a young governor from Arkansas (a backwater in the minds of many easterners) with no experience in national politics stunned the establishment (the elite political class with strong connections in and to Washington, D.C.). George H. W. Bush's sudden departure left a huge question mark over America's foreign policy. His own ambivalence evidenced by a tendency to vacillate between traditional realism and Wilsonian liberalism did not provide any clarification. That task would fall to his successor, William Jefferson Clinton.

The timing of Stedman's *Foreign Affairs* article (see above) could hardly have been better from the standpoint of its potential impact on the foreign policy of the incoming administration. Stedman wrote: "Many civil wars may have to be allowed to run an ugly course. Herein lies an irony that clouds the clear morality of many new interventionists: the possibility that humanitarian assistance may extend war and anarchy rather than end it. Aid to besieged populations, if it assists prolonged resistance, may only end up costing more lives. . . . [A] decisive victory is sometimes the best result, followed by a forward-looking conciliatory peace."[10] Unfortunately, there is no reason to believe that President Clinton ever read this article or that anybody close to him (who probably did) ever paid it any heed.

REINVENTING FOREIGN POLICY (1993–1997)

President Bill Clinton's public image when he was sworn into office closely resembled that of John F. Kennedy, whom Clinton greatly admired. Like JFK, Clinton was youthful in appearance, intellectual, articulate, and idealistic in a curiously disarming way. JFK's self-description as "an idealist without illusions" could also be applied to the new president. Like JFK (and unlike his immediate predecessor), Clinton was comfortable in the world of ideas and abstractions. Finally, like JFK, he could speak, with no apparent effort, without a script on the issues of the day, and he was formidable in debate.

Not surprisingly, his come-from-behind upset win over an incumbent who had recently led the nation to victory in war gave rise to great expectations on the part of the electorate. The new president, untested in national politics, was eager to prove himself up to the task, but the playing field he preferred, as

---

10. Stedman, "New Interventionists," p. 324 (in the Wittkopf reader).

the political heir of FDR's Democratic Party, was domestic not foreign. Clinton's campaign promises had focused on the need for economic revitalization and social reform (especially in the fields of health care and welfare). In office, President Clinton embraced the "reinventing government" movement that stressed downsizing, decentralization, and out-sourcing of public services to the private sector.[11] He caught the spirit of market reforms sweeping Eastern Europe and argued that entrepreneurship is no less important in government than business. President Clinton's liberal critics felt betrayed. His conservative critics labeled his advocacy of health care reform "socialist." In retrospect, he was neither. He was, above all, a survivor and a pragmatist with a gift for "communicating" unmatched by any other president in the modern era (including Ronald Reagan, "the great communicator").

As we have seen, the Bush administration had done a creditable job of managing America's foreign policy in an extraordinarily fluid environment but had bequeathed no grand strategy, no unifying theme, no central idea that tied its various policy initiatives together. Consequently, there was a conceptual vacuum in the minds of many observers accustomed to having "containment" as a kind of analytical crutch. Intellectually, President Clinton was quite capable of filling this "vacuum" but chose not to. Instead, he dealt with foreign policy issues as they arose and let a new pattern emerge from a series of ad hoc decisions. This approach to the making of foreign policy contrasted sharply with the past practice of formulating a doctrine in response to a specific problem and then automatically applying the same solution to future problems.

The New World Economy

After 1945 the United States took on the task of managing the world economy as well as managing the world. The means for accomplishing this purpose included substituting the gold-backed American dollar for the British pound sterling as the world's major convertible currency. The institutional mechanisms Washington created included the International Bank for Reconstruction and Development (IBRD, or World Bank), the International Monetary Fund (IMF), and the General Agreement on Tariffs and Trade (the GATT).[12]

---

11. President Clinton enthusiastically endorsed a book on this subject published just a month after his inauguration, asserting, "It should be read by every elected official in America. This book gives us the blueprint." See David Osborne and Ted Gaebler, *Reinventing Government: How the Entrepreneurial Spirit Is Transforming the Public Sector* (New York: Plume, 1993).

12. The latter was the framework for promoting "free trade" among member states. It excluded the Communist states during the cold war but opened its doors to most of these nations in the 1990s. It changed its name to World Trade Organization (WTO) during this time. In a historic move, the United States normalized trade relations with the People's Republic of China in 2000 and agreed to admit Beijing to the WTO.

With the receding East-West conflict, the major powers lowered the priority they had previously assigned to the nuclear arms race and elevated the priority they gave to economic issues such as fair trade and "competitiveness." In other words, economic competition in the minds of many leaders in both the public and the private sectors was becoming more important than military competition. President Bill Clinton personified this view when he took office in 1993.

Bill Clinton had campaigned on a promise to revitalize the economy. But keeping that promise, he realized, would depend on external as well as internal market forces. Clinton's foreign policy was driven to a considerable extent by a desire to foster conditions favorable to a strong world economy—liberal trade policies, market-oriented reforms in the former Communist states of Eastern Europe, regional conflict management, and a strong role for the United Nations, the World Bank, and other international institutions.

Through eight years in office, even under the cloud of impeachment, Clinton's popularity at home would be sustained by a buoyant economy. But the world beyond America's shores was a troubled one, and the contrast between prosperity at home and misery in so many foreign lands became a major challenge to the ideals President Clinton espoused so eloquently. What should America do in the face of human suffering on a mass scale? Should America intervene in local wars even when the outcome would not directly (or in some cases even remotely) affect U.S. interests? Will ethnic conflict inevitably spill over, as some argue, destabilizing adjacent states and causing repercussions for entire regions? Is regional conflict everywhere a threat to the global economy or only in certain regions such as Europe and the Middle East? These are the kinds of questions no president—especially not the president of a fabulously rich and powerful country—could easily ignore if America was to fulfill its self-appointed role as the world's archetype of democracy.

Negotiation and compromise, rather than strict adherence to abstract principles, were the defining characteristics of Clinton's pragmatic leadership style. These traits frustrated the president's critics who grumbled privately (and sometimes publicly) that Clinton was too opportunistic and risk-averse, too quick to abandon campaign promises in the face of political opposition, and too morally conflicted to be decisive under pressure. In the words of one seasoned observer, "Clinton was the best 'Republican' president this country ever had."[13] However, the same presidential attributes that often cause disillusionment over domestic policy can be conducive to success in the conduct of foreign policy.

There have been few moments since World War II when the White House has not had a cluttered foreign policy agenda. The Clinton era was no exception.

---

13. I am indebted to my good friend G. Ross Stephens, professor emeritus at the University of Missouri-Kansas City and a distinguished political scientist, for this observation.

What to do about post–Stalinist Russia, regional conflict, terrorism, arms control, nuclear nonproliferation, global warming, trade relations, the Asian economic crisis, and NATO expansion were only a few of the more pressing issues facing U.S. policymakers in the mid-1990s. Clinton's victory over the incumbent president George H.W. Bush was widely interpreted as a mandate for economic growth. To a considerable degree, the Clinton administration's foreign policy— predicated on the basic principles of international political economy—was driven by his campaign promise to improve the economy. The logic behind this policy is as follows: the U.S. economy is, in the words of Robert Reich, one of Clinton's top economic advisers, "but a region of the world economy."[14] Because the United States is the largest exporter of goods and services in the world, and also the largest importer of goods, the American economy cannot grow unless the world economy is growing. It follows that what the United States does or does not do can have a significant impact on the world economy, as well. This reciprocal relationship—variously called "interdependence" or "globalization"—is the key to understanding what makes the world go around.

Clinton's refocusing of foreign policy also raised other global issues that had long been neglected by the White House, including ecological disasters, the population explosion, AIDS and other epidemics, and the like. These "social" problems—seen in the perspective of "geoeconomics" and political economy—are impediments to economic growth. Rather than a Clinton Doctrine, here was an intellectually satisfying (although not necessarily valid) worldview tailored to the new world order and almost certain to find favor in Europe and elsewhere.

No country, not even one as powerful as the United States, could tackle these kinds of issues on its own, Clinton reasoned. A foreign policy agenda that emphasizes the global economy makes unilateral action impossible. Thus, the Clinton administration exhibited a strong preference for multilateral action and for operating as much as possible through major international organizations such as the United Nations, the World Bank, the IMF, the WTO, and NATO.

So-called neoconservatives continued to argue that the United States did not have to choose between "guns and butter" and could not afford *not* to continue modernizing its military forces, replacing old weapons with new, and infusing the latest technology into military doctrine, training, and strategic planning. But war hawks seemed like throwbacks to another time and place in the 1990s. Globalization was the buzzword in the capitals of the world. That was perhaps only natural: the more that problems of war and peace appear to recede, the more that nations and leaders can turn to the next order of business, namely, business itself. Nonetheless, Clinton was not a pacifist and certainly did not

---

14. Robert B. Reich, *The Work of Nations: Preparing Ourselves for Twenty-first-Century Capitalism* (New York: Knopf, 1991), p. 243.

undermine America's military establishment, despite the grumbling of certain hawkish critics.[15]

There was a great fascination with the notion of interdependence in the 1990s. The United States had embarked on a new venture with Mexico and Canada, the North American Free Trade Agreement, at the beginning of the decade in response to the challenge thrown up by a vibrant European Community (EC) that became a single market and changed its name to reflect this transformation. Thereafter, it would be known as the European Union (EU), and it would embark on the road to a single currency, creating a central European bank, and eventually inviting many of Europe's new democracies to join.

The new world economy of the 1990s was driven by large multinational corporations and by the new information technology, both of which transcended national boundaries. Many world economic issues—including regional and global environmental problems, resource management, debt relief, trade liberalization, copyright laws, and banking practices—necessitated a high level of routine international cooperation. It became painfully evident in the 1990s that no one, not even the president of the United States, could control the forces at work in the global marketplace. But as the anchor of the world economy, America was a natural to play the leading role, and the only country capable of doing so.

A stark reminder of this fact occurred in 1997 at a time when President Clinton's attention was dangerously divided owing to a sex scandal involving a White House intern that nearly cost him his job. In the winter of 1997–1998 several key Asian nations, including Indonesia, South Korea, and Thailand, experienced a sudden, sharp economic downturn triggered by a banking crisis and collapsing currencies. Responding to the fear of a global economic meltdown, the U.S.-led IMF sprang to the rescue with large bailout packages for several afflicted Asian countries. As a condition for making "soft" loans available to these countries, the recipients had to agree to institute certain economic reforms aimed at sound banking practices, greater transparency in handling public finances, and, where appropriate, the breakup of giant business conglomerates with tentacles reaching into many sectors of the economy, supposedly strangling free markets.

The "Asian flu" epidemic of 1997–1998 threatened to spread throughout the global economy. Quick action by the White House in concert with the IMF contained the crisis. The administration's decisiveness on this issue contrasted with its vacillation on other pressing foreign policy issues. It was symptomatic of America's dependence on world trade and investment for its own prosperity. The

---

15. Prominent among such critics were Dick Cheney, Donald Rumsfeld, Paul Wolfowitz, John Bolton, Robert Kagan, William Kristol, and Richard Perle. In February 1998, for example, a group of these "neoconservatives," calling themselves the Committee for Peace and Security in the Gulf, wrote an open letter demanding "a comprehensive political and military strategy for bringing down Saddam and his regime."

fact that during the 1980s the United States had gone from being the world's major creditor to being its biggest debtor meant that a lot of the lifeblood in the American economy was the result of transfusions from abroad—foreign investors putting money in U.S. Treasury notes and bonds, the stock market, and real estate. A sudden run on the dollar (capital outflow) could cause an economic calamity. And given the mammoth size of the American economy, if it collapsed it would take the world economy down with it.

Of course, it did not collapse; nor did the Asian economy. An old political bromide holds that "it's better to be lucky than good." President Clinton was both. Not only did he serve during a period of economic growth, when millions of Americans heavily (and happily) invested in a steadily rising stock market, but his first term started with a rare opportunity to reconcile Israelis and Palestinians.

The Palestine Impasse: No Way Out?

The 1980s had been a time of great turmoil in the Middle East. The decade had started with the Israeli invasion of Lebanon and ended with the intifada in the Occupied Territories (see box). The United States had tilted toward Israel ever since its establishment in 1948 but had also tried to play a mediating role between Israel and its hostile Arab neighbors. In 1956 the Eisenhower administration had opposed an attack on Egypt by Israel, the United Kingdom, and France. After the Six-Day War in 1967, which was launched by Egypt, the United States backed Resolution 242, calling for a complete Israeli withdrawal from the Occupied Territories. After the 1973 Yom Kippur War, Henry Kissinger carried on "shuttle diplomacy" between Israel and Egypt in a desperate effort to arrange a pullback of Israeli forces poised to march on Cairo. Finally, in 1978 Jimmy Carter brokered a peace accord between these two bitter enemies, again endorsing Resolution 242 and embracing the right of the Palestinians to a "homeland."

Despite these efforts at outside mediation, tensions between Palestinians and Israelis escalated in the 1980s. Several factors raised the level of frustration felt by Palestinians, including the "betrayal" (separate peace negotiations) by Egypt's President Sadat, the Likud government's policy of building settlements in the Occupied Territories, and the Israeli invasion of southern Lebanon and the eviction of the PLO from that country. The frustration turned into aggression as the decade drew to a close.

This stalemate continued, as did the violence, for several years. There appeared to be no light at the end of the tunnel. In 1992 President Bush judged the time right to push hard on all sides for a comprehensive settlement. The effort bore fruit, but not until September 1993. By this time, of course, Bill Clinton sat in the Oval Office.

The historic 1993 Israeli-PLO handshake did not settle everything; in fact, it did not really settle anything, but it was a start. Each side recognized the right

The Intifada

The tension that had existed for decades between Israeli settlers and Palestinians in the Israeli-occupied territories continued to deteriorate until, in December 1987, it erupted in the intifada, or uprising, in Gaza and the West Bank. Frequent clashes occurred between Israeli security forces and Palestinian youths, armed with little more than sticks and stones. Then the suicide bombings started. Israeli security forces were under orders to avoid fatalities and to resort to severe beatings instead. Outraged world opinion caused the Israeli government to abandon this policy, but Israel placed the territories off limits to the press. Israel's tactics shifted to curfews, searches, and exile, as well as economic pressures. Undercover elite commando units allegedly made hits on suspected Palestinian terrorists.

The intifada posed a dual threat to Israel. First, there was no way to protect Israeli citizens from suicide bombers. Second, Israel's support in the United States and Western Europe, where public opinion was becoming increasingly critical of Prime Minister Shamir and his Likud-led government, was in jeopardy.

In December 1988 Yasser Arafat, leader of the Palestine Liberation Organization (PLO), renounced terrorism and implicitly recognized Israel's right to exist. In return, the United States established low-level contacts with the PLO. Israel's hard-line prime minister Yitzhak Shamir placed various obstacles in the path of peace talks—Israel would talk only with non-PLO Palestinian leaders; the Arabs in Jerusalem could not take part in proposed West Bank elections; the intifada would have to stop before talks could start; and so on. Palestinian leaders were also unyielding: they would accept nothing short of an Israeli withdrawal from the Occupied Territories and a return to the pre-1967 borders (permitting the West Bank and the Gaza Strip to form a new Palestinian state).

In the early 1990s the Labour Party came back into power. The new prime minister, Yitzhak Rabin, was intent on defusing the conflict between Israelis and Palestinians. Rabin made overtures in the summer of 1992, promising to stop subsidizing "political" settlements (but not "security" settlements) in the West Bank and Gaza. This Israeli olive branch opened a new chapter in the story of war and peace in the Middle East.

of the other to exist, the PLO renounced terrorism, and Israel withdrew from the Gaza Strip and the West Bank city of Jericho (and later Hebron). In addition, Israel accepted the idea of at least limited Palestinian autonomy. The following year, Israel and Jordan agreed to recognize each other, thus normalizing relations between them. The United States again played a key role as honest broker. President Clinton's attempt to end the state of war between Israel and Syria, however, came to naught. Despite a major American push to keep the peace process going at this time, events soon overwhelmed all good intentions.

On November 4, 1995, a right-wing Jewish extremist assassinated Prime Minister Rabin in order to halt the movement toward peace. As if inspired by this heinous act, Palestinian extremists staged four suicide bombings in nine days in the spring of 1996, killing 60 Israelis and wounding more than 200. These acts were timed to coincide with an election campaign to choose a new Israeli leader. The upshot was the elevation of Benjamin Netanyahu, the head of the hawkish Likud Party. Once again, Palestinians and Israelis stared into the abyss. Another opportunity was lost.

It was not President Clinton's fault, to be sure, but there was a legitimate question as to whether he had applied adequate pressure on all parties, including the new Israeli government. There was also a disquieting glimpse of America's limits—and the limits of any foreign policy, even that of the world's only superpower.

In May 1994, as tempests raged in Asia, the Balkans, the Caribbean, and sub-Saharan Africa, President Clinton announced that the United States would not intervene in foreign conflicts unless four conditions were met: (1) the conflict was a clear threat to the United States; (2) intervention had solid public backing; (3) there was participation by other countries under UN authorization; and (4) there was an understanding going in that U.S. ground forces would not stay on the scene or assume responsibility for "nation building." But Clinton soon did an about-face in the Balkans.

Fighting Fires: America in the Balkans

As Eastern Europe turned away from communism, mounting economic problems, including hyperinflation, accelerated Yugoslavia's disintegration.[16] In July 1990, democratically elected governments in the provinces of Slovenia, Croatia, and Macedonia launched independence drives. On the same day, Serbs approved a referendum on a new constitution that made the formerly autonomous provinces of Kosovo and Vojvodina parts of Greater Serbia. Meanwhile, the

---

16. For background on the conflicts in the former Yugoslavia, see Robert D. Kaplan, *Balkan Ghosts: A Journey through History* (New York: Vintage Books, 1993); Warren Zimmerman, *Origins of a Catastrophe: Yugoslavia and Its Destroyers—America's Last Ambassador Tells What Happened and Why* (New York: Times Books, 1996); Maya Shatzmiller, ed., *Islam and Bosnia: Conflict Resolution and Foreign Policy in Multi-Ethnic States* (Montreal: McGilll-Queens University Press, 2002); Ivan T. Berend, *History Derailed: Central and Eastern Europe in the Long Nineteenth Century* (Berkeley: University of California Press, 2003); and Matthew McAllester, *Beyond the Mountains of the Damned: The War Inside Kosovo* (New York: New York University Press, 2002).

Kosovo assembly approved a measure making Kosovo a sovereign republic within Yugoslavia. Serbia replied by dissolving Kosovo's legislature. Finally, the stage was set for a tragedy of major proportions when former Communists in Bosnia-Herzegovina were decisively defeated at the polls.

A bitter civil war between Serbia and Croatia ensued. (Serbia and Slovenia do not share a border; Serbia and Croatia do. International mediation and a United Nations peacekeeping force brought a cease-fire but not a settlement. The conflict that started in Croatia could not be contained. Suppressing hostilities in Croatia only shifted the fighting to a different battleground, namely, Bosnia-Herzegovina. Like a rupturing balloon, pressing on one bulge only caused another to pop out somewhere else.

In Bosnia-Herzegovina, the tragedy was compounded by the fact that Bosnian Muslims, although numerically the largest ethnic group there, were caught in the cross fire between Serbs and Croats. After months of bloody fighting and a particularly brutal artillery assault on Sarajevo, the capital, Serbs (31 percent of Bosnia's population) controlled 65 percent of the territory, and Croats (17 percent of the population) held about 30 percent. That left the Muslim population (44 percent of the total) with only 5 percent of the territory. Some well-informed observers feared that the upshot of the war would be to divide Bosnia between Serbia and Croatia, leaving the Bosnian Muslims without a state. Worse, it was not entirely clear who was doing what to whom. The Yugoslav army made a pretense of neutrality, but it was widely reported that the army was supplying Serbian guerrillas with arms and ammunition.

The war in Bosnia worsened in 1992 and 1993. Egregious human rights violations by all three warring sides—Bosnian Muslims and Croatians, as well as Bosnian Serbs—characterized the conflict from the beginning, although UN and State Department reports indicated that Serbs committed the vast majority of those violations. Reports of ethnic cleansing—the systematic deportation or slaughter of Muslims by Bosnian Serbs, allegedly with the covert support of Belgrade—caused outrage in the West and led to calls (especially in the United States) for economic sanctions, no-fly zones, and even military intervention. As stories of atrocities (concentration camps reminiscent of the Holocaust; the systematic rape of Muslim women) piled up, pressures built for effective measures to punish the Serbs, who nonetheless remained defiant in the face of growing diplomatic isolation.

Bosnia's "dirty war" dragged on despite continuing efforts by United Nations peacekeepers, the European Union, and the United States to mediate. Nor did NATO air strikes stop it. Serbia was widely condemned for its role in aiding and abetting the Bosnian Serbs. The effects of the Yugoslav war and the international trade embargo against Serbia were devastating. Critical shortages of many food staples forced the Serbian government to introduce rationing. Inflation reached a million percent in 1993, prompting Belgrade to adopt a new currency, the "super dinar," in January 1994. In the summer of 1994, two-thirds of all working-age Serbs were unemployed, mainly because of plant closings caused by the embargo.

When the war finally ended in 1995, there was still a big question mark over Bosnia's future and, ironically, over Serbia's as well. Only the fate of the old Yugoslavia was beyond question: its existence was now nothing more than a fiction maintained solely for the self-gratification of Serbian nationalists.

In November 1995, the United States brokered the Dayton Peace Accords, which halted the fighting in Bosnia-Herzegovina. The Serbian government played a constructive role, finally accepting the principle of a separate Bosnia and Croatia. In return, the United States lifted economic sanctions against Serbia. There remained, however, a serious question of whether—or how long—conflict in the neighborhood of the former Yugoslavia could be contained. Would Albania, Bulgaria, Greece, Hungary, Romania, and Turkey stand by if Serbia attempted to incorporate more territories of the former Yugoslavia into "Greater Serbia"?[17]

Anarchy in Africa: To Intervene or Not to Intervene

The violent breakup of Yugoslavia was only one of several scenes of anarchy that threatened to destabilize various regions, including the Horn of Africa (see above), West Africa (Liberia and Sierra Leone), central Africa (Rwanda, Burundi, and the Congo), and central Asia. In addition, civil war raged in parts of the former Soviet Union, most notably in Chechnya, and violence between Catholics and Protestants still plagued Northern Ireland. In the midst of the mayhem occurring in so many scattered places around the world, President Clinton was forced to decide whether to intervene, when, and on what grounds. American national interests were not directly affected by any of these conflicts. But the United States was the unchallenged hegemonic power in the post–cold war world, and the international community looked to Washington for leadership. Perhaps because America's power was (or seemed) beyond serious challenge, there was increasing pressure on the president both at home and abroad to act out of *principle* in instances where innocent lives rather than vital national interests were at stake.

Africa was the scene of several civil wars. In Somalia, America's so-called humanitarian intervention had come to grief, and the president had wisely decided to withdraw. The wisdom of intervening was doubtful; the decision to

---

17. For example, hundreds of thousands of Hungarians live on the "wrong" side of the border (in a region of Serbia called Vojvodina), as well as in Slovakia and Romania. By the same token, some two million Albanians live in Kosovo (part of Serbia). Macedonia also has a large Albanian minority.

cut America's losses was arguably President Clinton's finest hour as commander in chief.

One of the low points of the Clinton presidency involved another episode of anarchy in Africa, in Rwanda, where a civil war between Hutus and Tutsis led to mass murder on a shocking scale.[18] In October 1993, Rwanda and Burundi erupted in bloody conflict between the Tutsi minority and the far more numerous Hutus. In 1994 a Hutu killing frenzy in Rwanda resulted in at least 800,000 deaths. Tutsi insurgents launched a war to stop the genocide, which sent about two million Hutu refugees pouring into neighboring countries. Most of these refugees landed in squalid camps in eastern Zaire. President Clinton decided not to intervene despite pressure from human rights groups and old-line liberals in his own party to do so on humanitarian grounds (the United States had no plausible strategic interests there). Some critics charged the president with hypocrisy for sending troops into Bosnia on humanitarian grounds and ignoring genocide in Rwanda.[19]

In the ensuing years, the spillover from the Hutu-Tutsi war turned into another African nightmare. In October 1996, two years after the genocide in Rwanda, the government of Zaire attempted to drive out hundreds of thousands of its own Tutsi citizens living in the same region where the Hutu refugee camps are located. The Tutsis, faced with imminent expulsion, launched a wave of armed assaults against the camps, spreading panic among the Hutu refugees and sparking fears of a bloody regional war. Zaire slid into a civil war that culminated in the long-awaited overthrow of its dictator, Mobutu Sese Seko, but not in civil peace.

Perhaps nowhere was the confusion of power, purpose, and principles at this time more evident than in the U.S. handling of regional conflicts. The Clinton administration left itself wide open to moral condemnation for pursuing policies that appeared hypocritical in the eyes of the world. It is true that policymakers are wise to avoid the "hobgoblin" of a "foolish consistency" (to quote Emerson), but it is no less important to avoid the loss of moral authority in international relations.

THE NEOCONSERVATIVE CHALLENGE

There was considerable confusion over America's role in the new world order after 1989. Nowhere was this confusion more apparent than in Washington's

---

18. For background on the Rwandan tragedy, see United Nations, *Independent Inquiry into the Actions of the United Nations during the 1994 Genocide in Rwanda* (New York: United Nations, 1999); see also Michael N. Barnett, *Eyewitness to a Genocide: The United Nations and Rwanda* (Ithaca: Cornell University Press, 2002), and Samantha Powers, *A Problem from Hell: America and the Age of Genocide* (New York: Basic Books, 2002).

19. Ted Galen Carpenter, *Peace and Freedom* (Washington, D.C.: Cato Institute, 2002), pp. 46–48.

response to the challenge of regional conflicts brought on by the disintegration of failed states in Europe, Africa, and elsewhere. Both the Republican president Bush and his Democratic successor, Bill Clinton, displayed a reluctance to get involved in these conflicts, but both in the end succumbed to domestic and international pressures.

By the mid-1990s a pattern was emerging, if not exactly a policy blueprint. The United States would not retreat into neo-isolationism, but there would be limits to America's willingness to intervene. We would not be the world's police, but we would join in the world's volunteer fire department. We would not put out fires (regional conflicts) ourselves, but we would respond, if the international community (United Nations) called. Also, we would not bear the cost of the fire-fighting equipment and the cleanup ourselves; we would pay our share, but other members of the community who in some cases benefited more than we did would have to reimburse us. We would downsize the bloated U.S. military establishment (a legacy of the cold war), cut defense spending, and use part of the savings to balance the budget. Above all, the United States would place primary reliance on diplomacy; force would be used sparingly and only as a last resort. Where we did act it would be multilaterally rather than unilaterally.

That this policy had high-powered detractors is a matter of public record. In 1992 Paul Wolfowitz, then and later a highly placed official at the Pentagon, wrote a secret memorandum advocating an aggressive, proactive foreign policy. Wolfowitz was not alone. Rather, he was part of a group of hawkish advisers (self-styled "neoconservatives") who believed that the aim of U.S. foreign policy should be to change the world, not merely manage it.[20] By "change" they meant democratization, and by "democratization" they meant regime change, not democracy per se. This new breed of foreign policy "hawks" used the language of idealism like a laser.

The neoconservatives saw no reason why American military might should not be used *preemptively* if necessary to remove threats and promote democracy anywhere and everywhere in the world. They argued forcefully that a world of democracies would be safe, secure, and peaceful—an ideal outcome for the modern world's first and foremost democracy, the United States. That it would also be ideal for the Middle East's only democracy, Israel, was also true but never mentioned in public.

---

20. Prominent neoconservatives include Robert Kagan, William Kristol, and Richard Perle. In the current Bush administration Vice President Dick Cheney, Secretary of Defense Donald Rumsfeld, National Security Adviser Condoleezza Rice, and Under Secretary of Defense Douglas Feith are also closely identified with the "neocons." See, for example, Ivo H. Daalder and James M. Lindsay, *America Unbound: The Bush Revolution in Foreign Policy* (Washington, D.C.: Brookings Institution Press, 2003).

Many neoconservatives were particularly frustrated at the failure of the United States to oust Saddam Hussein in 1991. They argued implausibly that democracy could work in Iraq; that Iraqis really wanted democracy; and that a democratic Iraq would be an inspiration to other oppressed nations in the Middle East.

Despite the impressive intellectual firepower of the neoconservative rear guard in the last year of the first Bush administration, it was more moderate voices within the administration, including Generals Colin Powell and Henry Shelton, that prevailed. Military professionals were unenthusiastic about a new strategy contemplating the preemptive use of force, unilateral action, and regime change as developed by civilian defense experts. This seeming "paradox" revealed a fact little known to the public and symptomatic of a policy problem dating back to the origins of the cold war: political policymakers have often been more hawkish than high-ranking military professionals. We will explore the reasons for this paradox and what can be done about it in the final chapter of the book. For now, suffice it to say that the hawks lost the first round, but they had not lost the fight.

CONCLUSION

President George H. W. Bush watched his popularity rocket as a result of Desert Storm's spectacular success. In general, it is fair to say that he guided the country through the transitional period during the last days of the cold war. His approach to foreign policy was that of the pragmatic manager rather than the great statesman or the history-minded visionary. Just as his pragmatism was a strength, his lack of vision was a weakness. In the world of war and diplomacy, a pragmatic leader is often more effective and successful than a visionary one. In a world of change and upheaval, a visionless leader can easily lose his (or her) way.

George H. W. Bush would be a one-term president. His surprising defeat in 1992, however, did not reflect popular dissatisfaction with the nation's foreign policy. On the contrary, it was due almost entirely to a wobbly economy. It is said, "A prophet is not honored in his own country." The 1992 election shows it can also be true of a pragmatist—especially one who understands power but equivocates on principle.

The first President Bush was a study in self-contradiction: a man of principle intellectually unsure of his own principles. The nation naturally looks to its president for guidance. The question that was never clear in the first Bush presidency was, "What guides the nation's leader?" The answer will vary from one president to another, but history, philosophy, and religion often provide the guideposts, for better or worse. In the final analysis, the nation's foreign policy is an expression of the president's innermost convictions.

So what were this president's innermost convictions? It was never clear. Apparently he himself was ambivalent on basic principles. He made a bid for the presidency in 1980 as a liberal Republican, battling the archconservative Ronald

Reagan in the primaries, only to accept a role as Reagan's running mate in the general election. As vice president in a right-wing government, he did not appear to be the least bit ideologically discomfited. Nonetheless, there is no reason to doubt his liberal instincts. The problem arose when the two sides of his political nature—liberalism and pragmatism—came into conflict.

In sum, President George H. W. Bush bequeathed a foreign policy lacking in clear definition. He sought to manage a messy new world rather than to change it. In that sense, he was generally faithful to a basic principle—first, do no harm. In Iraq, however, he allowed harm to be done, ironically, after the war was won and when the United States was in a position to prevent it. But to his great credit he resisted advice to turn the war against Iraq into a crusade against evil or tyranny or some other abstract enemy.

His successor, William Jefferson Clinton, entered the Oval Office with no experience in foreign affairs and a preference for solving domestic social and economic problems. But events beyond his control forced a somewhat reluctant President Clinton to pay attention to foreign policy. One of these events, the bombing of the World Trade Center in 1993, was the portent of a new national security threat. The true nature and extent of the threat would emerge slowly over time and against the background of continuing turmoil in nearby places, including the Balkans, the Horn of Africa, and central Asia.

Clinton would be one of only three American presidents since World War II to be reelected and serve for two full terms. Although a majority of Americans did not approve of his personal conduct (especially his illicit relations with a White House intern young enough to be his daughter), President Clinton was widely admired for his leadership qualities, intelligence, and personal charm. Above all, however, he was the beneficiary of the popular belief that perpetual peace was just around the corner thanks to the fading fear of nuclear war as the East-West conflict receded.[21]

The 1950s have been called the American Decade, but the same label could just as accurately be applied to the 1990s. The buoyancy in the American economy reflected the buoyant sense of optimism that animated the American consumer and investor. The result was a decade of steady economic growth and private wealth accumulation.

At the same time, the federal government was steadily paring perennial budget deficits; after 1998 revenues flowing into the U.S. Treasury exceeded federal outlays.[22] In 2000, Clinton's last year in office, the budget surplus was just

---

21. In the mid-1990s it was difficult to find pessimists anywhere. Even among political realists, who are normally pessimistic about the prospects for peace among the major powers, there was a newfound optimism. See, for example, Charles L. Glaser, "Realists as Optimists: Cooperation as Self-Help," *International Security* 19, no. 3 (winter 1994–1995), pp. 50–90.

under $237 billion. The surge of national vitality reflected in this historic turn-around was the real "peace dividend" after the cold war.

America's success in the 1990s contrasted starkly with the evidence of failure in many parts of the world. From Russia to the Balkans, from Africa to Asia, failed and failing states destabilized whole regions. In the Balkans, the breakup of the former Yugoslavia was proving to be extremely violent and threatening to spill over into neighboring states. Meanwhile, in central Asia one failed state—Afghanistan—was playing host to a terrorist organization that fed on the anger and frustration of oppressed people who had always lived with failure, knew little else, and had nothing to lose. In the next chapter we look at America's response to these challenges in the second Clinton administration and in the first fateful years of George W. Bush's presidency, when a watershed event suddenly swept away all the ambiguity that had characterized American foreign policy in the 1990s.

---

22. Although a careful analysis of the federal budget is beyond the scope of this book, it should be noted that the claim of budget "surpluses" of the 1990s depended, to a large extent, on the use of smoke and mirrors. Since the early 1950s, the share of federal revenues derived from payroll taxes has grown steadily (from about 7 percent in 1952 to 32 percent in 2001). These taxes in theory go into a "Social Security lockbox" but are in fact regularly used to pay for current programs having nothing to do with retirement benefits. Thus, even during the high-flying nineties, the federal "surplus" was based on an illusion.

8

From Intervention to Preemption
America's New Crusade

OVERVIEW

This chapter covers the second term of the Clinton two-term presidency and the first few years of President George W. Bush's tenure in office. In the first part of the chapter I discuss Clinton's aims in foreign policy, such as cementing close relations with Russia and China, expanding NATO, fostering a healthy world economy, and slowing the nuclear arms race. I go on to examine the circumstances that conspired to make him an embattled president. At home he would fight for his political life; abroad he would order the U.S. military to attack several small countries, including Afghanistan, Sudan, and Serbia. In the remainder of the chapter I focus on the foreign policy of George W. Bush, especially after September 11, 2001. In particular, I look at the "war on terrorism," the ouster of the Taliban regime in Afghanistan, and the invasion and occupation of Iraq. Recent trends in U.S. foreign policy are put in historical perspective and some comparisons are drawn between Bill Clinton and George W. Bush. Finally, I analyze and evaluate the new doctrine of preemption and ask whether it is likely to achieve its intended aims.

Managing the nation was always the president's main job. After World War II, American presidents also set about managing the world. America's archrival in the cold war was also, paradoxically, America's partner in this enterprise—a contradictory relationship that grew out of the nuclear stalemate otherwise known as "mutual deterrence."

Another dimension to the relationship was less obvious but no less important. This aspect of the cold war did not become evident until after the East-West conflict receded into history. For more than four decades, the United States and the Soviet Union actually *shared* the burdens of maintaining stability and managing conflicts. The Soviet Union "subjugated" Eastern Europe after World War II, according to the conventional wisdom in Washington, but seen from a different perspective Moscow maintained order in the eastern "half" of Europe and in central Asia, as well as inside the ethnically diverse perimeter of its own empire—historically, these areas were prone to conflict. Now that the cold war was over, they were once again scenes of toil and trouble.

RUSSIA: NEITHER ENEMY NOR PARTNER

No longer America's adversary or rival, Russia was also no longer America's partner

CHRONOLOGY, 1997–2003

1997   Thailand, Indonesia, and South Korea experience severe economic reversals with worldwide ripple effects

1998   President Clinton implicated in sex scandals, leading to impeachment proceedings in House; Iraq expels United Nations arms inspectors; United States bombards Baghdad for four days

1999   President Clinton survives impeachment trial in Senate; economic crisis in Brazil spreads to other countries in region; NATO launches Operation Allied Forces against Milosevic regime; Asian financial crisis stabilizes

2000   Wall Street suffers historic collapse; United States permanently normalizes trade with People's Republic of China (PRC); in presidential race too close to call, Supreme Court gives election to George W. Bush

2001   Terrorists hijack commercial airliners and fly two into World Trade Center, one into Pentagon (worst terrorist attack in U.S. history); United States attacks Afghanistan's Taliban regime; Congress passes "Patriot Act"; Anthrax scare emanates from unknown source

2002   Violence between Israelis and Palestinians intensifies; President Bush proposes cabinet- level Department of Homeland Security; Bush Administration calls for "regime change" in Iraq, says United States considering attack

2003   Rift opens in NATO alliance, pitting the United States, Great Britain, and Spain against France, Germany, and Belgium over timing of proposed Iraq invasion; U.S. invades Iraq and declares victory while combat fatalities escalate throughout year

in keeping a lid on conflict in the areas previously under its "management." Nonetheless, President Clinton cultivated close personal relations with Boris Yeltsin as the centerpiece of U.S. policy toward Russia.[1]

The United States and Germany offered Yeltsin economic incentives to withdraw from Eastern Europe; to acquiesce in German reunification and NATO expansion; and to allow former republics (including the Baltic states) to move into the Western orbit. These incentives were also aimed at rewarding and reinforcing Yeltsin's commitment to political democracy and a decentralized economy. The theory was that a democratic Russia with a market economy would be interested in trade with the West, not war or military adventures. Such a Russia would be likely to cooperate in conflict management (or stay out of conflicts altogether) and less likely to use its considerable capacity for mischief. Russia was no longer a superpower, but it could easily play a major "spoiler" role if it chose to do so.

Thus, American "foreign aid" to Russia during the 1990s was by no means purely altruistic. It was in America's interest to help the Kremlin revitalize the Russian economy and stabilize the government. It was, for example, vitally important to help Russia gather within its own shrunken borders and under its own control all the nuclear weapons the defunct USSR owned. It was also in America's interest to provide financial and technical assistance for the safe and swift disposal of Russia's decommissioned nuclear weapons. Finally, the Clinton administration wanted to maintain the momentum toward deeper cuts in existing nuclear arsenals that were a reflection of a bygone era.

The United States and Russia were at odds over the ethnic conflicts in the Balkans, however, and the secession movement in Chechnya. In Kosovo, American and Russian forces "nearly came to blows" in 1999, a sign that the end of the cold war did not guarantee a harmony of interests between the two nuclear giants.[2] In Chechnya, the Clinton administration, grateful for Yeltsin's acquiescence in NATO's eastward expansion, looked the other way in 1999–2000 as Moscow conducted a brutal counterinsurgency campaign against rebel forces (and the civilian population) seeking independence.

Relations between the United States and Russia were only part of the foreign policy puzzle in the new Europe. It was in America's interest to encourage the former Communist states to establish liberal democracies and market economies—that much was clear, but how? How could the United States switch from being reactive to being proactive in a part of Europe that had been off-limits to U.S. influence for almost half a century?

---

1. Strobe Talbott, *The Russia Hand: A Memoir of Presidential Diplomacy* (New York: Random House, 2002); see also Sarah E. Mendelson's review essay, "The View from Above: An Insider's Take on Clinton's Russia Policy," *Foreign Affairs,* July/August 2002, pp. 150–156.

2. Mendelson, "View from Above," p. 155.

One possibility was to open NATO's doors to Eastern Europe. There would be some risks associated with such a move. For one, Russia might fight it tooth and nail. For another, NATO's integrity as an institution might be compromised by the admission of states that had yet to prove themselves as stable market democracies. The question for the Clinton administration was whether the risks outweighed the potential gains.

REINVENTING NATO

With the end of the cold war, NATO had accomplished one of its original aims— namely, the containment of Soviet communism. This was, of course, the declared aim; the undeclared aim, no less important, was the containment of Germany. A related objective was to enmesh West Germany in Western Europe, economically and militarily. By providing reinsurance of America's intent to stay in West Germany, thereby quelling any fear of a German military resurgence, NATO set the stage for normalization of relations between West Germany and neighboring states (Belgium, France, the Netherlands, and the Scandinavian countries, above all).[3] The Soviet decision to build the Berlin Wall in 1961 had helped to defuse a time bomb in central Europe, but it had also underscored the need for NATO and the American trip-wire forces in West Germany.

The two Germanys were reunited in the early 1990s, rekindling old fears on the Continent. This was one reason the Clinton administration did not raise doubts about NATO's relevance despite various attempts to do so from several quarters.[4] The other reason was the need to encourage the processes of reform in Eastern Europe's "emerging democracies."

In short, the question quickly became not whether NATO should disband but whether (and how soon) it should expand. President Clinton lost little time in making the important decision to set a high priority on "NATO enlargement" (as it came to be called). Russia's president Yeltsin objected strenuously but in the end backed down when the United States gave him a face-saving way to do so.[5] Negotiations moved at a brisk pace, and at the end of the decade NATO admitted the Czech Republic, Hungary, and Poland with surprisingly little opposition of any kind.

---

3. Robert J. Art, "Why Western Europe Needs the United States and NATO," *Political Science Quarterly* 111, no. 1 (Spring 1996): 12.

4. The Cato Institute, a libertarian policy "think tank," for example, challenged NATO's relevance in the 1990s. See Ted Galen Carpenter, ed., *NATO at 40: Confronting a Changing World* (Washington, D.C.: CATO Institute, with Lexington Books, 1990).

5. Specifically, NATO (the United States) promised not to deploy nuclear weapons in eastern Europe and to keep billions of dollars in economic aid and foreign investment flowing from the West into Russia.

Still unanswered, however, was the more nettlesome question about NATO's purpose. It would remain unanswered. One other question that would remain unanswered was whether NATO should continue to be confined to the territory of its member states in the future or, on the contrary, become involved in "out-of-area" conflicts. This question has far-reaching implications, especially in light of Eastern Europe's history of ethnic rivalries. As noted in the previous chapter, nowhere were these rivalries more numerous or embittered than in the Balkans.

With UN backing, the United States and its NATO allies carried out air strikes and ultimately deployed combat forces, first in Bosnia and later in the Serbian province of Kosovo. An uneasy truce in Bosnia left many questions about future arrangements in that troubled land unanswered.

Military Intervention in Kosovo

The Bosnian crisis also raised serious questions about NATO's viability, if not its relevance. It revealed deep cracks in NATO's façade and even hinted at cracks in its foundations. NATO member states quarreled over whether or not to intervene and precisely why, when, and how. As later events would show, NATO's disarray over Bosnia was a glimpse into the future.

The age-old conflict between Serbs and Albanians in Kosovo came to a head in 1999. It had been smoldering for a decade, but now the Yugoslav dictator Slobodan Milosevic decided to crush the Albanians once and for all. The problem for Milosevic and the Serbs was that 90 percent of the population of Kosovo was Albanian (called Kosovars), but the region was highly prized for historical and cultural reasons by the Serbs. A guerrilla movement calling itself the Kosovo Liberation Army (KLA), organized to defend ethnic Albanians against a feared crackdown after 1989, demanded independence. Milosevic refused and moved against the Kosovars in 1999. Serbian forces began systematically driving Kosovars out of their homes, villages, and, ultimately, out of Kosovo into Macedonia, Albania, and other neighboring states. The United States first sought a peaceful resolution and when that failed led a NATO bombing campaign code-named Operation Allied Force in March 1999.

Once again, the cracks in NATO became highly visible. At home, the Clinton administration was under pressure not to commit ground forces a second time in "the Balkan tinderbox." Abroad, Germany's new chancellor, Gerhard Schroeder, anxious to avoid a showdown in the Bundestag and possibly in the streets, led the campaign against putting troops on the ground in Kosovo. Clinton bowed to these pressures, publicly ruling out such a move. This appears to have been the signal Milosevic was waiting for. He now gave the go-ahead for a wholesale assault on the Kosovars.

The result was a grisly replay of the atrocities in Bosnia. Milosevic's strategy, to the world's horror, appeared to be "ethnic cleansing." The scale of the horrors inflicted on defenseless civilians—women and children, the elderly, no one was spared—demanded a response from the international community. As in Bosnia, all eyes turned to the United States, and, once again, President Clinton came face-to-face with the downside of being Number One—namely, bearing political and moral responsibility for acting or not acting. Earlier, in Rwanda, he had not acted and was severely taken to task by critics. In Kosovo, he acted, but not decisively enough to satisfy his critics or to stop the suffering.

What Clinton did was to order gradually escalating air strikes. What he did not do was to demonstrate his resolve as commander in chief of the world's foremost military power to use as much force as necessary. The effect was to cause Milosevic to accelerate the holocaust against the Kosovars. Milosevic was acting; Clinton was reacting. Now NATO had little choice but to ratchet up the bombing and keep pummeling Serbia—while not sparing Belgrade—until Milosevic agreed to withdraw his forces.

That NATO would prevail in a showdown was never in doubt, but it was a victory without a celebration. By the time NATO's intervention finally brought the Milosevic government to its knees, well over a million Kosovars (roughly three-fifths of the entire ethnic Albanian population) had been driven from their homes. The survivors returned to wrecked homes and villages, and the Kosovars prepared for self-government. But lives and homes were destroyed, and peace depended on the presence of 50,000 NATO and UN troops, including more than 5,000 American soldiers.

NATO and the United States were now committed to two open-ended nation-building projects in the Balkans (Bosnia and Kosovo). The European contribution to the effort had been minimal. U.S. air and naval forces accounted for most of the 6,000 bombing missions carried out under NATO auspices. In the words of German foreign minister Joschka Fischer, "The Kosovo war was mainly an experience of Europe's own insufficiency and weakness. We as Europeans never could have coped with the Balkan wars that were caused by Milosevic without the help of the United States. The sad truth is that Kosovo showed Europe is still not able to solve its own problems."[6]

The Kosovo crisis also demonstrated anew that America's European allies do not speak with one voice in NATO, recent efforts at a common foreign and defense policy within the EU notwithstanding. But Europe's military and political disarray means the United States continues to bear most of the burdens, whereas America's allies reap many of the benefits—and escape the blame when things go wrong.

Finally, if NATO was of limited help to the United States in the Balkan wars, the United Nations was even less. The ever-present possibility of a Russian veto

---

6. Quoted in Ivo H. Daalder and Michael E. O'Hanlon, "Unlearning the Lessons of Kosovo," *Foreign Policy,* fall 1999, p. 137.

made the Security Council a risky bet: in the Kosovo crisis, the Clinton adminis-tration, despite its preference for multilateral action, circumvented the UN alto-gether.

Disillusionment with the United Nations and multilateralism would soon harden into steely antagonism. Idealism and diplomacy would then give way to the harsh realities of power politics. The war hawks were about to make a major comeback. But it would take a bitterly disputed election and a daring strike at the heart of America's power and wealth for that to happen.

Kosovo Aftermath: Peacekeeping and the Demise of a Dictator

The joyless end of the fighting in Kosovo was accompanied by an imposed "peace." The United Nations put its own "interim administration" in charge, with NATO troops on the ground as a kind of police force. The declared aim of "substantial autonomy and self-government" for the province was ambiguous to say the least. The UN-NATO regime disarmed the KLA and promised to protect the tiny (5 percent) Serbian minority in Kosovo against recriminations by angry ethnic Albanians. It was a promise not perfectly kept; many Serbians in Kosovo were attacked or threatened.

In sum, nothing was settled. There was no end in sight for the UN protec-torate so long as Milosevic was in power. For all its good intentions, the United Nations once again proved itself ill-equipped to govern. UN administrators were unfamiliar with local customs and struggled with a baffling language barrier. NATO forces now in the odd role of protecting Serbians met with hostility from the outraged Kosovars. Meanwhile, there was an institutional and legal vacuum, with neither laws, nor courts, nor local police to fight ordinary (and not-so-ordinary) crime.

The economic impact of the war on Serbia was devastating. After years of enduring economic sanctions imposed by the United Nations and the European Union, the effects of NATO bombing raids against infrastructure and strategic industries were severe. Serbs had grown accustomed to a relatively high standard of living during the previous decades of the cold war but were now facing hard-ships and shortages. Nonetheless, the Serbian people were divided politically. Because Milosevic blamed the West all along for interfering in Serbia's domestic affairs, the NATO air raids against Serbia and the imposed "peace" in Kosovo that followed fed the government's propaganda machine. Still, many Serbs wanted the kind of democratic reforms that had been realized elsewhere in Eastern Europe and opposed Milosevic's dictatorial rule. That Milosevic was a ruthless dictator could not be denied: he controlled the press, rigged elections, and dealt harshly with all manifestations of opposition. The upshot was a divided and ambivalent populace, with fear and anger mixing to create a highly volatile situation.

Public demonstrations against Milosevic mounted in 2000. In September, with nationalists angered by the dictator's failure to hold the country together and democrats emboldened by his capitulation in the face of American military might, Serbian voters finally turned Milosevic out of office. When at first he refused to accept the result, mass demonstrations soon forced him to step down. Charged with corruption and abuse of power, he surrendered to the very authorities he had previously controlled and directed. Shortly thereafter, the new democratically elected government of President Vojislav Kostunica extradited Milosevic to The Hague to be tried before a UN tribunal for war crimes.

Although the continued presence of U.S. ground forces in the Balkans troubled many observers, the fact remains that the demise of Milosevic would almost certainly not have come when it did, if at all, without U.S./NATO intervention. The question was not whether the situations in Bosnia and Kosovo cried out for external intervention. They clearly did. The question was why it should have fallen to the United States to do it when many of the richest and most technologically advanced countries in the world were located right next door to Yugoslavia.

TERRORISM: MISCHIEF OR MORTAL THREAT?

In 1993, for the first time in its history, the United States came face-to-face with the problem of international terrorists operating inside the country. In retrospect, the attack on the World Trade Center in that year was a wake-up call, but the country did not wake up. The attack killed six people, injured many more, and left millions of New Yorkers traumatized. The boldness of the act and the specific target—a gleaming symbol of American wealth in the heart of Manhattan's commercial district—signaled the opening of a new chapter in the story of America's struggle against the enemies of democracy. But it would take another eight years and a staggering blow from out of the blue before America's policymakers would get it.

Whether these "enemies" constituted a full-blown national security threat or simply a nuisance was unclear in 1993. The American public soon learned that Islamic militants had carried out the attack, but the precise motive, why they had targeted the United States, was not clear. Over time, that mystery would be solved, but the answer would itself puzzle American policymakers. The planners and perpetrators of this conspiracy, as well as the financier and mastermind behind the scenes whose bearded image would in time become the very face of terrorism, hailed from America's closest allies in the Arab world, Egypt and Saudi Arabia, not from America's avowed enemies, Iraq and Iran.

Hence the puzzle: How could it be that our own strategic allies, repressive police states at that, would countenance terrorist plots against the United States? And if they denied any complicity (which they did), what could the United States do about it? We could not threaten, much less invade or bomb, our own allies. Nor could we stand by and do nothing—especially when a series of escalating terrorist incidents involving American "targets" in the Philippines, Saudi Arabia, Kenya, and Tanzania removed all doubt that the 1993 bombing of the World Trade Center was not an isolated event (see box). The first of these follow-on events (an Islamist plot in the Philippines to blow up American passenger planes over the Pacific) occurred in 1995, the worst prior to 2001 (the U.S. embassy bombings in East Africa) happened in 1998.

President Clinton, facing his own life-or-death political struggle at home, ordered air strikes against targets in two Islamic states in August 1998—Sudan (Egypt's next-door neighbor) and Afghanistan (host to a network of terrorist training camps operated by a fanatical Saudi expatriate named Osama bin Laden, heir to a $300 million fortune).[7] In both instances, the targets were destroyed without achieving the intended objective. In Sudan, a facility thought to be manufacturing poison gas turned out to be a pharmaceutical plant. In Afghanistan, a guided missile intended to kill bin Laden arrived too late.

The failure of these two missions caused a loss of face President Clinton could ill afford at this time and deepened the frustration of White House policymakers who had puzzled over problems posed by the rise of Islamist extremism since the first days of the Clinton presidency.[8] Controversy over how to deal with "political Islam" (or "Islamism") had, in point of fact, been rife in Washington at least since the Carter administration. It pitted advocates of accommodation against those who believed there was no dealing with the devil—idealists versus realists. For the latter, the only answer was confrontation.[9]

President Clinton was inclined to seek accommodation with Islamic militants because he sympathized with the plight of the Palestinians (idealism) and because Arabs and Muslims are obviously a major force in the Middle East and Asia (realism). This policy irked Egypt's President Hosni Mubarak, who did not hesitate to say, "I told you so," when the terrorists launched a spate of bloody attacks between 1995 and 1998. After the attack at Luxor in 1997, for example, in which fifty-eight foreign tourists and four Egyptians were killed, Mubarak was blunt and biting: "I believe that if the world had cooperated against terrorism, the Luxor strike would not have happened." He added, "The terrorists have protection in Britain and other European countries, while they commit their crimes, collect money, and plan with the Afghani elements, who are all killers."[10]

Mubarak was careful not to criticize the United States, because Washington had been Egypt's paymaster since 1979 (the Israeli-Egyptian peace

---

7. Judith Miller, "Bin Laden: Child of Privilege Who Champions Holy War," *New York Times,* Sept. 14, 2001 (online at www.nytimes.com/2001/09/14/international/14BINL.html).

8. The debate within the Clinton administration is detailed in Fawaz A. Gerges, *America and Political Islam: Clash of Cultures or Clash of Interests?* (Cambridge: Cambridge University Press, 1999).

9. Ibid., pp. 20–36.

10. Ibid., p. 175.

The Terrorist Threat to America, 1993–2003

President George W. Bush officially launched America's war on terrorism after September 11, 2001, but the first skirmishes in this "war" occurred much earlier.

February 1993: Bomb in van explodes beneath World Trade Center in New York City, killing 6 and injuring 1,042.

June 1993: Federal investigators foil plot by Islamic radicals to bomb the United Nations and two Hudson River tunnels.

January 1995: Police in Manila, Philippines, arrest members of Islamic terrorist group testing bombs, allegedly to bomb several U.S. airliners in mid-flight over Pacific; accused leader Ramzi Yousef later arrested in Pakistan and also charged with planning 1993 World Trade Center bombing.

April 1995: Truck bomb destroys federal building in Oklahoma City, Oklahoma, killing 168 and wounding more than 600. Two Americans are charged (and later convicted).

November 1995: Car bomb explodes outside U.S. Army training center in Riyadh, Saudi Arabia, killing 5 Americans, wounding 30.

April 1996: FBI arrests Theodore J. Kaczynski, a Montana hermit, and charges him with "Unabomber" letter bomb attacks over eighteen-year period.

June 1996: Truck bomb explodes outside an apartment complex in Dhahran, Saudi Arabia, killing 19 Americans and wounding 280.

July 1, 1996: Federal agents arrest 12 members of "Viper Militia," a Phoenix, Arizona, group accused of plotting to blow up government buildings.

July 1996: TWA Flight 800 crashes and explodes shortly after take-off from New York, killing all 230 passengers; cause unknown.

July 27, 1996: Pipe bomb explodes at concert during Summer Olympics in Atlanta, Georgia, killing 1 and injuring 111.

August 1998: U.S. embassies in Kenya and Tanzania are bombed, killing 224 people in Nairobi, mostly Kenyan passers-by.

October 2000: Speedboat-bomb attack on *USS Cole* in Aden, Yemen, killing 17.

September 11, 2001: Hijackers crash two commercial jet airliners into World Trade Center towers, one into Pentagon; fourth hijacked plane crashes in Pennsylvania field; estimated 3,000 killed.

October 12, 2002: Bomb blast in Bali resort kills estimated 180 people; blamed on militant Islamic group linked to Osama bin Laden and al Qaeda.

August 8, 2003: Car bomb at Jordanian embassy in Baghdad kills 11.

August 17, 2003: Terrorist bomb attack destroys UN headquarters in Iraqi capital Baghdad, killing 17, including Sergio Vieira de Mello, top UN envoy in Iraq.

November 15 and 20, 2003: Suicide bombers in Istanbul attack two synagogues, a British-based bank, and the British consulate, killing as many as 50 people and injuring more than 600.

treaty), and also because by this time the Clinton administration had come round to his way of thinking. Especially after the embassy attacks in Africa, there would be no more pussyfooting with Islamic militants. The hawks and confrontationists were being vindicated. Radical Islamists were setting the stage for a future American president to declare war on terrorism, but in 1998 no one knew what was coming and no one could have imagined that the struggle in store would have no boundaries.

The war in Kosovo, the old unsettled dispute between India and Pakistan, a bloody independence fight in East Timor, and the intensification of the fighting in Russia's breakaway republic of Chechnya dominated the agenda in 1999. The abatement of the Asian financial crisis and a buoyant stock market that made millions of Americans feel rich and secure offset these sources of instability to some extent, but a darkening shadow was falling across the globe. Terrorism had been a fact of life in many parts of the world for decades, but it had not yet struck directly at the heart of the world's foremost Great Power—at least not in a way that caught a president's undivided attention. That, of course, was about to change.

WILL THE REAL GEORGE W. BUSH PLEASE STAND?

In stark contrast to his father, George W. Bush had had no prior experience in foreign affairs when he took office as the forty-third president at the start of the new millennium. His only qualification for the high office was serving as a two-term governor of Texas. He had been a mediocre student at Yale, an amateur baseball player, and a problem drinker. During the campaign his embarrassing ignorance of international politics and the outside world in general would likely have cost him the election had he not been running against a candidate (Vice President Al Gore) who seemed incapable of attracting voter sentiment. As it is, he came in second in the popular vote and had to be anointed by a handful of conservative Supreme Court justices.

Americans knew little about where or how George W. Bush would lead the country. What little he had said about foreign policy suggested that he believed the United States was overextended in the world. There was no way of knowing whether this criticism was based on conviction or was a campaign tactic designed to put his opponent, Gore, on the defensive.

Egged on by neoconservatives, he charged that the Clinton administration had allowed the United States to lose its edge. On the one hand, he suggested that if he were elected president the defense budget would get a big boost; on the other, he criticized the Clinton administration for committing troops to UN peacekeeping operations in Bosnia and Kosovo. In general, he had a low opinion of the United Nations and was disinclined to pay back dues unless the UN reduced America's share and "reformed" its bureaucracy.

President George W. Bush appeared to concur with the former secretary of state Madeleine Albright's dictum that the United States would "act multilaterally if we can, unilaterally if we must." Nonetheless, Bush leaned toward unilateralism, causing one observer to predict, "A new Bush administration, therefore, would likely find itself more at odds with traditional American allies during times of crisis than the Clinton administration."[11] This prediction, of course, turned out to be dead on the mark.

George W. Bush also appeared to support stepped-up nuclear disarmament efforts but simultaneously advocated restarting research and development on a limited antimissile defense system, although it was anathema to the Kremlin. He opposed the Comprehensive Test Ban Treaty and expressed doubts about the possibility of close cooperation with Russia.

In office, however, President Bush mellowed—or perhaps the world looked different to him from the windows of the Oval Office. True, he had brought hard-line veterans of the Reagan era into the government. They were well ensconced in the Pentagon and the White House. But he had counterbalanced these hawks by naming Colin Powell, the moderate and well-respected former chairman of the Joint Chiefs of Staff, as his secretary of state. And he chose Condoleezza Rice, a "cautious realist" who was skeptical about the wisdom of "nation building" and U.S. participation in UN peacekeeping efforts, to be his national security adviser. As the prominent neoconservative William Kristol later told *Frontline,* "On September 10, 2001, it's not clear that George W. Bush was, in any fundamental way, going in our direction."[12]

Thus, within the new Bush administration there were two distinct and competing foreign policy tendencies. On the one side were the pragmatists and realists, who thought that foreign policy was all about managing conflict rather than fixing all problems. In this view, many problems cannot be fixed. The national interest called for a military strong enough to maintain order and stability in the world, but American power should be used sparingly. War was a last resort, to be used only to protect vital interests and only after diplomacy failed.

On the other side were the intellectual heirs of Ronald Reagan's "evil empire" speech, or "neo-Reaganites," who took an ideological or "evangelical" view of the world and believed that problems like tyranny and terrorism could be

---

11. Stephen Zunes, "Little Shift in Foreign Policy under (President) George W. Bush," *Foreign Policy in Focus* [no date], accessed Mar. 20, 2003, at www.foreignpolicy-infocus. org/index.html.

12. Readers can access the *Frontline* series online at www.pbs.org. This interview has aired repeatedly on PBS, including on Mar. 20, 2003, at the beginning of the second Gulf War. The Kristol interview was conducted on Jan. 14, 2003. Entitled "The War behind Closed Doors," it can be accessed in its entirety online at www.pbs.org/wgbh/pages/frontline/ shows/Iraq.html.

fixed.[13] They were impatient with solutions that did not solve anything and were prone to moral crusades. They welcomed multilateral action if others saw the world as they did, but they had no qualms about acting unilaterally where America's vital interests were at stake. They trusted hard power, which can be calculated and controlled, over soft power, which can only be cultivated. In sum, they combined a penchant for power politics and military force—a kind of ultra-realism—with a moral agenda reminiscent of Wilsonian idealism.[14] The contra-dictory tendencies so often found in American foreign policy were present in the Bush administration from day one.

AN ACT OF WAR: SEPTEMBER 11, 2001

The second bombing of the World Trade Center was a turning point. It shifted the plates beneath the nation's body politic and forced a neophyte president to take national security strategy out of its holding pattern. For the hawks in the admin-istration, it was an opportunity made to order, but first they would have to co-opt Secretary of State Colin Powell or persuade the president to ignore his advice.

When President Bush addressed a joint session of Congress some nine days after the September 11 attacks, he expressed a grim resolve to bring those behind the mass murder of innocent Americans (and others) to justice. (All the actual perpetrators were dead.) Calling the kamikaze bombings "an attack on civiliza-tion," he made three crucial points:[15] first, America was at war; second, the United States would make no distinction between terrorists and states that harbor ter-rorists; third, there would be no neutral ground to stand on—in his words, "Either you are with the U.S. or you are with the terrorists." All three points had far-reaching implications, but only time would tell just how far the president would go in waging his self-declared "war on terrorism."

The president identified "a collection of loosely affiliated terrorist organi-zations known as al-Qaeda" as the invisible hand behind the September 11 attacks (and many others). He said Osama bin Laden was the group's leader and that Afghanistan's fanatical Taliban regime was playing host to al Qaeda and bin Laden. He then demanded that the Taliban hand over all al Qaeda authorities harbored in Afghanistan, release foreign nationals, close terrorist training camps

13. Prominent neo-Reaganites in the new Bush administration included Vice President Dick Cheney, Secretary of Defense Donald Rumsfeld, Vice President Cheney's chief of staff "Scooter" Libby, and Under Secretary of Defense Paul Wolfowitz.

14. Recall how Wilson justified U.S. entry into World War I: "to make the world safe for democracy."

15. Keith Windschuttle believes this phrase contains the key to understanding what motivated President Bush to respond so ferociously and, he argues, appropriately. See his arti-cle "The Cultural War on Western Civilization," *New Criterion*, Jan. 2002, pp. 4–16, esp. the last page.

operating in the country and hand the terrorists over to the United States, and give the United States full access to the camps to ensure that they stopped operating. These demands were "not open to negotiation" and the Taliban had no choice but to "hand over the terrorists" or face extinction—a classic ultimatum.

The Taliban proved to be no match for the United States and its allies (mainly the United Kingdom and the indigenous Northern Alliance). There were relatively few American and allied casualties.[16] The invasion accomplished "regime change" and wiped out the terrorist camps, two key objectives. It failed to accomplish one other objective—killing or capturing Osama bin Laden. The fact that bin Laden and his top lieutenants managed to escape meant that the victory was incomplete. And having the world's "Number One International Terrorist" remain at large was the kind of unfinished business that could in time come back to haunt the administration.

In the first phase of the war on terrorism, President Bush apparently looked mainly to his trusted secretary of state, Colin Powell, not Pentagon hawks, for guidance. In late November 2001, when military operations were already in full swing, the *New York Times* columnist Bill Keller wrote: "[T]he Bush administration has been sounding more like Colin Powell than like anyone else. . . . The way Powell puts it is that the attack on America 'hit the reset button' on foreign policy. . . . He contends that America has not only moved, at long last, beyond the cold war but has also vaulted past the 'post-cold-war period,' that confusing interim search for purpose in a world without a center of gravity."[17]

Keller put his finger on an important point. The September 11 attacks gave clear focus to American foreign policy for the first time in over a decade. They also gave pragmatists like Powell a real problem to solve and, perhaps, a new opportunity to solve it.[18] By prompting governments around the world to rally to America's cause, the attacks created a golden opportunity to put "soft power"— far cheaper and less risky than unilateral military action—to work. Here was a world tailor-made to suit the talents and temperament of America's top soldier-statesman. But diplomacy was about to be jammed into reverse.

---

16. By the end of 2001, the heavy fighting was largely over. At that point, the invading forces had suffered a total of 35 fatalities, including 30 Americans. Available evidence suggested the number of Afghan civilians killed owing to collateral damage was 1,000, but this figure is impossible to verify (the actual number is probably higher). When the first phase of the war ended, about 50 Americans had died. A conservative estimate would thus put the ratio of Afghans to Americans killed at about 20 to 1.

17. Bill Keller, "The World According to Colin Powell," *New York Times,* Nov. 24, 2001 (online edition).

18. Ibid. In Keller's words: "Tense American relationships with Russia and China and even in the intractable Middle East, he [Powell] says, now seem more amenable to breakthroughs." As it turned out, this was wishful thinking—no "breakthroughs" occurred, although there were some signs of movement in the war between Israel and the Palestinians.

In the aftermath of September 11, the United States would invade a sovereign state, oust its leaders, and change its regime—not once, but twice. The first time, in Afghanistan, effective diplomacy preceded and legitimized military action. The second time, in Iraq, diplomacy failed, and world opinion saw the American-led invasion as illegitimate. In the United States, critics of administration policy who had looked to Secretary of State Powell as "the lone grown-up in an administration with a teenager's twitchy metabolism" were bitterly disappointed and disillusioned.[19]

Diplomacy failed in the run-up to the second Gulf War—that much is clear. But why it failed is endlessly debatable. Perhaps Colin Powell was to blame for his failure to persuade President Bush to give the UN arms inspectors more time; or Pentagon "hawks" for beating the war drums too long and hard; or President Bush for being too impatient; or the French for being too impertinent. Surely, any full and fair explanation must take into account Saddam Hussein's record of aggression, deception, and brutality, to say nothing of his intransigence in the face of UN demands that he disarm.

No civilized onlooker familiar with the Iraqi dictator's rule could have any sympathy for him or the regime he headed. Twice he had attacked neighboring states without provocation. He had used poison gas against enemy forces (Iranians) and against his own people (Kurds). He had imprisoned or killed his political opponents and used torture, rape, and murder as tools of political control. His two sons were apparently cut from the same bloodstained cloth.

Thus, when President Bush spoke of Iraq as being part of an "axis of evil" in his State of the Union address some four months after the September 11 attacks he was justified in using the word "evil." It was the "axis" in that now-famous phrase that raised a lot of eyebrows—that, plus the crusading tone of the speech. Iran and North Korea were the other two countries included in this axis—both had nuclear ambitions and represented a potentially greater threat to U.S. interests than Iraq (see Chapter 9). In the charged atmosphere of flag-waving patriotism, few Americans dared to question whether any one of three countries—dwarfed by the United States in both latent and actual power—posed a serious threat to America.

The full extent of the transformation in America's worldview after September 11, 2001, can be put into better perspective by recalling that in 1796 President George Washington advised a young America to pursue a policy of strict neutrality in its foreign relations, and that in 2001 President George W. Bush ruled out such a policy, not only for the American people but also for the whole world. If the purpose was to rally Americans behind the flag, it was unnecessary; if the purpose was to rally the world around America, it was counterproductive. People in

---

19. Bill Keller, "Why Colin Powell Should Go," *New York Times*, Mar. 22, 2003 (online edition).

other lands would ask, What gives the United States the right to declare unilaterally that another state cannot choose to stay on the sidelines? That is, after all, what the United States did 200 years ago.

Making the Case for Invading Iraq: The Bush Doctrine

President Bush's State of the Union address in January 2002 laid down a marker on Iraq. The president vowed to "prevent regimes that sponsor terror from threatening America or our friends and allies with weapons of mass destruction." In this connection, he mentioned North Korea and Iran, but it was Iraq he had uppermost in mind. "Iraq continues to flaunt its hostility toward America and to support terror," he told Congress and the American people. "The Iraqi regime has plotted to develop anthrax, and nerve gas, and nuclear weapons for over a decade." Here he was disingenuous; in fact, Iraq had been working on WMD since the 1980s (when George H. W. Bush was vice president), secretly aided and abetted by the United States.

Warming to the topic, President Bush declared, "States like these . . . constitute an axis of evil, arming to threaten the peace of the world." Then these words: "By seeking weapons of mass destruction, these regimes pose a grave and growing danger. They could provide these arms to terrorists, giving them the means to match their hatred. They could attack our allies or attempt to blackmail the United States. In any of these cases, the price of indifference would be catastrophic." The true meaning of this passage would not be revealed until September of that year, when Bush spoke to the General Assembly of the United Nations. The purpose of this speech, full of fighting words, was to notify the member states that the world after September 11, 2001, was not big enough for both Saddam Hussein's Iraq and the United States. With the Taliban routed and al Qaeda on the run, the United States and its allies had supposedly cut off the head of that snake. Now it was Iraq's turn to remove its own fangs or suffer the same fate.

As commander in chief of the most powerful fighting force in world history Bush threw down the gauntlet: "Iraq has answered a decade of U.N. demands with a decade of defiance. All the world now faces a test, and the United Nations a difficult and defining moment. Are Security Council resolutions to be honored and enforced, or cast aside without consequence? Will the United Nations serve the purpose of its founding, or will it be irrelevant?"[20] He told the General Assembly that the United States wanted the United Nations to be "effective, and respectful, and successful." Therefore, "We want the resolutions of the world's most important multilateral body to be enforced." That, he said, was not

---

20. This speech can be accessed verbatim online at http://www.whitehouse.gov/news/releases/2002/09/20020912–1.html.

happening. In fact, the president was "making clear" what the United States expected of the United Nations: "We must choose between a world of fear and a world of progress. We cannot stand by and do nothing while dangers gather. We must stand up for our security, and for the permanent rights and the hopes of mankind. By heritage and by choice, the United States of America will make that stand. And, delegates to the United Nations, you have the power to make that stand, as well." Here was a clear warning of America's intent to act (1) unilaterally, if necessary, and (2) with or without UN authorization. As an exercise in diplomacy, this speech is an enduring example of how not to do it.

In September 2002, the White House released a document entitled "The National Security Strategy," which declared, "America is now less threatened by conquering states than we are by failing ones. We are menaced less by fleets and armies than by catastrophic technologies in the hands of the embittered few. We must defeat these threats. . . ."[21] Several months earlier, however, President Bush, speaking at West Point, told graduating cadets that America would "defend the peace against the threats from terrorists and tyrants" and "preserve the peace by building good relations among the great powers."[22] On this point, he either changed his mind or did not really mean what he said.

Less than one year later, in March 2003, any intention of "building good relations" lay in tatters as the United States waged a controversial war against Iraq to "defend the peace against terrorists and tyrants." What had gone wrong?

In a word, diplomacy was placed on the back burner in 2002. The president's evangelizing and at times apocalyptic language and his crusading zeal had alienated many governments, including key NATO allies such as Belgium, France, and Germany, even apart from the substance of U.S. policy. When the president spoke at West Point he talked about this "time of opportunity for America" and how "We will work to translate this moment of influence into decades of peace, prosperity, and liberty." Our national security strategy, he said, arises from "a distinctly American internationalism that reflects the union of our values and our national interests." And then these ringing words: "The aim of this strategy is to help make the world not just safer but better."

What kind of a world did the president have in mind? "In pursuit of our goals," he said, "our first imperative is to clarify what we stand for: the United States must defend liberty and justice because these principles are right and true for all people everywhere." There are certain "nonnegotiable demands of human dignity," he told his West Point audience, to include: "the rule of law; limits on the absolute power of the state; free speech; freedom of worship; equal

---

21. "The National Security Strategy," released by the White House, September 2002 (online at http://www.whitehouse.gov/nsc/nss.html).

22. President Bush's West Point address, June 1, 2002 (online at http://www. whitehouse.gov/ news/releases/2002/06/20020601-3.html).

justice; respect for women; religious and ethnic tolerance; and respect for private property."

The president's rhetoric was suffused with idealism and bluster. Whatever the intent, the effect was to make the rest of the world nervous. In 2002 the United States was more powerful (and therefore more dangerous) than it had been during World War I, when President Wilson set out to "to make the world safe for democracy." When the world's preeminent Great Power announces its intention to make the world "not just safer but better," and arrogates to itself the exclusive right to make and enforce the rules, allies and adversaries alike feel threatened.

But the president's crusading idealism was not the only reason the United States was becoming increasingly isolated in the world. The other was the replacement of "traditional concepts of deterrence" with "preemption." "Legal scholars and international jurists," the president intoned, "often conditioned the legitimacy of preemption on the existence of an imminent threat." To meet the new threats posed by rogue states and terrorists, it was necessary to "adapt the concept of imminent threat." The new strategy Bush unveiled at West Point would provide the legal and political rationale for the invasion of Iraq: "The United States has long maintained the option of preemptive actions to counter a sufficient threat to our national security. The greater the threat, the greater is the risk of inaction—and the more compelling the case for taking anticipatory action to defend ourselves, even if uncertainty remains as to the time and place of the enemy's attack. *To forestall or prevent such hostile acts by our adversaries, the United States will, if necessary, act preemptively*" (emphasis added). The president acknowledged the possibility that *others* might try to exploit this new made-in-America rule of international conduct, warning the rest of the world not to "use preemption as a pretext for aggression."

None of this bravado—neither its substance nor its tone—would play well in national capitals around the world. London would be one notable exception, but there would be few others.[23] Ironically, as American military ascendancy was climbing to a new high, American diplomacy had fallen to a new low, lower even than during the darkest days of the Vietnam War.

Occupying Iraq: How Long and at What Cost?

The massive U.S. invasion of Iraq met little resistance. In a matter of days, the American forces, backed by the British, rolled into Baghdad. As the Americans

---

23. For the record, the governments of Australia, Poland, and Spain also backed the United States throughout the crisis over Iraq. The UK and Australia committed troops, and Poland made a token contribution to the military effort. The Bush administration called it a "coalition," but it was basically a bilateral U.S.-UK undertaking.

seized control of the country and the capital, the Iraqi government did a remarkable vanishing act. Saddam Hussein himself was nowhere to be found.

The country America had now taken over had a ruined economy made worse by the intensive bombing that accompanied the invasion and the extensive looting that followed the disappearance of Iraqi police authority. It was a fragmented society encompassing antagonistic communities that pitted Sunni Muslims against Shia Muslims, Iraqis against Kurds, and Saddam loyalists against Saddam haters. Finally, it was an Islamic society with bitter memories of colonial subjugation (under the British and French) and a decidedly anti-Western worldview.

The United States quickly moved to set up a Coalition Provisional Authority (CPA) under an American proconsul, Paul Bremer. At the same time, the United States created the so-called Iraqi Governing Council (IGC), choosing the wealthy Iraqi expatriate (and Saddam nemesis) Ahmed Chalabi to head it. Things went badly from the start. First, Saddam Hussein remained at large, no doubt plotting his return to power, organizing an underground resistance movement, and doing everything possible to sabotage occupation efforts aimed at reviving the Iraqi economy. Second, daily guerrilla-style attacks, accompanied by occasional terrorist bombings, took a steady toll on American forces and caused Secretary General Kofi Annan to pull most UN personnel out of Baghdad. By the fall of 2003, more U.S. soldiers had been killed *after* President Bush had declared victory in Iraq than before. Third, the general breakdown in law and order was so severe that Iraqi women were reportedly reluctant to venture out for fear of being robbed or raped. Fourth, months after the main fighting had ceased, reconstruction was still dragging. Public utilities (electricity, gas, and water supplies) and other basic services (telephones, for example) were being slowly restored but at a pace that only fed the growing frustration of the Iraqi people.

At home, the war's aftermath was not playing well either. Vietnam had proved that building public support of any war was necessary for retaining political power. President Bush built popular support by basing the decision to launch a preemptive strike on intelligence reports that supposedly proved Iraq was building weapons of mass destruction. However, six months after the invasion no such weapons could be found despite a massive and costly effort to do so. The failure to find these weapons was not only embarrassing to the White House, but it also called into question the justification for a war that was dragging on, costing tens of billions of dollars, causing a huge budget deficit, and becoming increasingly unpopular.[24] Even worse for the administration, the failure to find a "smoking gun" in Iraq called into question the whole concept of preemption.

---

24. The best estimates set the cost of the occupation at about $1 billion per week, or roughly $60 billion a year. The Bush administration asked Congress for $87 billion for 2004, mainly to cover the cost of the continuing war and reconstruction efforts in Iraq. About $20 billion was earmarked for reconstruction and recovery. The bill also included funding for ongoing operations in Afghanistan.

After World War II the United States occupied Germany and Japan. More than half a century later, American military forces are still there. Would the same thing happen in Iraq? Germany and Japan became close allies. The majority of Germans and Japanese accepted the American military presence.[25] Would Iraqis *ever* accept an American presence?

AMERICA'S NEW CRUSADE IN HISTORICAL PERSPECTIVE

It is too soon to pass final judgment on the Bush administration's foreign policy. In politics nothing succeeds like success. If the United States emerges safer and more secure from the turmoil at the start of the twenty-first century, if the Middle East is a more peaceful place, and if the world is, indeed, safer and better a decade after America's "war on terrorism," then the critics will fall silent and historians will bow (as they did after World War II) to the president who led the nation in perilous times.

But the "downside" potential and risks are formidable. Many defense and foreign policy experts predict dire consequences if the United States persists in its unilateral approach to problem solving.[26] And many view the doctrine of preemption as an ominous step for a country that pretends to respect the rule of law and the rights of others.

Having no crystal ball, perhaps the best scholars can do is to put the new national security strategy into perspective. Historically, we have seen how the United States shed its isolationist habits of mind and policy after World War II. Internationalism became a "bipartisan" stance. The foreign policy debate shifted from isolationism versus internationalism to a contest pitting one "school" of internationalists against another. Furthermore, liberals themselves were divided over foreign policy and, interestingly enough, could be found on both sides of the line.

Thus, both liberal Democrats and conservative Republicans could often agree on the need for a tough "containment" policy vis-à-vis the Soviet Union and a strong military. At the same time, there were those liberals who continued to believe that international organizations—especially the United Nations—were the answer to the problem of conflict in international politics.

One the one side was realism, represented by Dean Acheson in the Truman administration, John Foster Dulles in the Eisenhower administration, Robert McNamara, the Bundy brothers (William and McGeorge) and Walt Rostow in the Johnson administration, and Henry Kissinger in the Nixon administration (as well as Nixon himself). Eleanor Roosevelt, Henry Wallace, and Chester Bowles were

25. The island of Okinawa, where most U.S. forces in Japan are based, is an important exception, although even there anti-American protests have generally been muted.
26. Leading critics of unilateralism include Joseph Nye, John Mearsheimer, Gen. Wesley Clark, former secretary of state Madeleine Albright, and others too numerous to mention.

among the prominent champions of the neo-Wilsonian school of thought after World War II. Also belonging to this faction of the Democratic Party was Adlai Stevenson, who twice ran for president against Dwight Eisenhower (in 1952 and 1956) and served as John F. Kennedy's ambassador to the United Nations. In the 1960s Sen. Eugene McCarthy, George Ball, Gen. Matthew Ridgeway, Sen. George McGovern, and Paul Warnke were associated with liberal (Wilsonian) interna-tionalism. A whole school of "revisionist" historians in the 1950s and 1960s attacked basic premises, as well as the policies, of the realists, although not neces-sarily on grounds that admirers of Woodrow Wilson would accept.[27]

These two schools of thought competed for the hearts and minds of the "attentive public" during the cold war, but the anti-Communist realists had the upper hand in the government most of the time.[28] Oddly enough, the postwar president who expressed the greatest reservations about giving the Pentagon a blank check was the Republican president Dwight Eisenhower, the most deco-rated professional military officer to serve in the White House since Ulysses S. Grant. As we will see in Chapter 9, Eisenhower believed the United States could protect itself on the cheap by relying on its nuclear arsenal instead of a massive army. And it was Eisenhower who left office warning the nation to beware of the "military-industrial complex."

Within the broader foreign policy community, the idealists (and antiwar liberals) represented a formidable "opposition" ready to challenge policies (Vietnam is the classic example) that did not measure up to America's principles. By discrediting the Washington establishment, which was in the thrall of realists who believed in the efficacy of hard power and appeared to ignore moral princi-ples, Vietnam gave new impetus to idealism. At the same time, Vietnam trans-formed many former realists into "new liberals" who looked suspiciously like born-again Wilsonian idealists. It is no accident that Americans elected the most idealistic president in U.S. history, Jimmy Carter, in the wake of Vietnam.[29]

After the cold war, the paradigm changed, but liberals and realists alike con-tinued to be haunted by memories of Vietnam. David Halberstam, author of *The Best and the Brightest,* a book detailing the failure of America's foreign policy establishment in the Vietnam War, was among the many erstwhile realists who jumped ship after Vietnam and drifted into the calming waters of idealism.

---

27. Among the many revisionists, some of the most notable are William Appleman Williams, Noam Chomsky, D. F. Fleming, Gabriel Kolko, Gar Alperovitz, and Ronald Steel.

28. The Carter administration (1977–1981) is the one notable exception, but even in that case realism won out in the end.

29. See, for example, James E. Dougherty and Robert L. Pfaltzgraff Jr., *American Foreign Policy: FDR to Reagan* (New York: Harper and Row, 1986), pp. 284–287. The authors write, "In calling for 'world order politics,' which he contrasted with the geopolitical, balance-of-power preoccupations of the recent past, Carter sought to appeal to the American idealistic tradition as a means of building public support" (p. 286).

Many of the "villains" of Vietnam were among the converts to the new anti-interventionist internationalism, including Robert McNamara, William Bundy, and Anthony Lake. "Many Americans," Lake noted in 1976, "still want to hear that we are 'Number One' in the world," but he added hopefully that perhaps there had been "a welcome shift toward recognition of the limits to American power and responsibility." The idea of limits to American power—and goodness—became the guiding principle for these new liberals who had come to doubt the efficacy (and ethics) of political realism.

Enter Ronald Reagan, the darling of the neoconservatives. The 1980s ushered in a new chapter. The themes were optimism, self-confidence, and the goodness of America. What a welcome contrast for "average Americans" fed up with feelings of guilt and remorse! Ronald Reagan was the face of this new spirit, but the chapter was actually ghostwritten by old liberal realists who were now called "neoconservatives."[30] But times change, and so do the terms of public debate.

"A neo-conservative," wrote Kristol, "is a liberal who has been mugged by reality."[31] In the 1980s many Vietnam-era antiwar liberals felt "mugged by reality"—in particular, by the Soviet invasion of Afghanistan and other signs that communism was again on the march. Intellectuals and policy elites who had clambered aboard the détente bandwagon in the 1970s, showered the SALT process with praise, and scoffed at the old-fashioned idea of American exceptionalism now felt betrayed or foolish or both.

President Reagan denounced the Soviet Union as an "empire of evil," promptly scrapped the SALT process, and spoke of America in glowing terms ("the shining city on a hill") reminiscent of nothing so much as the rhetoric of the American Founders. Where Wilsonian idealists and liberals talked of limitations, often (but by no means always) opposed interventionism, and shrank from the use of force for selfish ends, the Reagan administration infused money and energy into the Pentagon, intervened (directly or by proxy) in various regional conflicts, and launched "Star Wars"—the ambitious Strategic Defense Initiative designed to render the United States invulnerable to nuclear blackmail or attack.

To his credit, President Reagan led America out of a period of pessimism and self-loathing back into the sunlight of optimism and self-respect. Ironically, it was the "dawn of victory" in 1989—the breakup of the old Soviet satellite empire in Eastern Europe—that posed the greatest threat to the Reagan Revolution.

---

30. Among others, this group includes Jeanne Kirkpatrick and William Bennett, who were in turn indebted to even older ones like William Buckley and Irving Kristol, who were in turn indebted to still older ones like Friedrich Hayek (*The Road to Serfdom*), Henry Hazlitt, Robert Nisbet, and Russell Kirk. The intellectual pedigree of classical liberalism (modern conservativism) stretches far back in time and contains many illustrious names.

31. Quoted in George Nash, "American Conservatives and the Reagan Revolution," available online at www.libertyhaven.com. Originally published in *Imprimis* 15, no. 5 (May 1986).

With the Soviet implosion, the fear of communism so useful to advocates of an open-spigot approach to military spending lost its relevance. Fatigue was certainly a factor. Perhaps now Uncle Sam could sit down to rest.

Even hard-headed pragmatists like President George H. W. Bush; his secretary of state, James Baker; and Chairman of the Joint Chiefs of Staff Colin Powell were ambivalent about the use of American military might.[32] In his 1999 bestseller, *War in a Time of Peace*, David Halberstam writes that they were "by and large the most careful of men, internationalists, anti-Communists, but not ideologues or moralists."[33] Halberstam recalls the 1980s as a time when the pragmatic Kissinger wing of the Republican Party was engaged in a great struggle with the rabid anti-Communist Reagan wing, which had gained the upper hand. But with the election of the pragmatic, some would even say boring, George Bush in 1988, and the receding Soviet threat, the ideologically charged atmosphere in Washington gave way to a calmer, steadier climate in which to formulate foreign policy. "Bush and his team seemed to have perfect pitch . . . knew how far to go at each moment, how much to push for change, when to back off and let events take their own course, and when to nudge them forward."[34]

Robert Kagan, a neo-Reaganite scholar, takes Halberstam to task for confusing timidity with wisdom. Kagan writes:

> Gorbachev's fall and the breakup of the Soviet Union were an accident, and for the Bush people an unwelcome one. When Gorbachev lost control, they lost control, too. Yet it was precisely the Bush administration's refusal to bring American power to bear on the situation that Halberstam appreciates. The "victor," as he sees it, was the product of a splendid humility and a sterling caution, and of a proper distaste for American power and a sense of global American responsibility. It was a triumph, in short, of the post-Vietnam establishment's worldview.[35]

In Kagan's view, the Clinton White House consolidated this "triumph" of the Washington establishment's anti-interventionist liberal wing. Nonetheless, critics like Halberstam attacked Clinton from the left. Like his predecessor, President Clinton was reluctant to intervene in crises abroad or to commit U.S. forces in regional conflicts. When he did so, it was strictly in the context of (1) multilateral action; (2) with United Nations backing; (3) on humanitarian grounds; and (4) only after he had been bombarded by moral and political

---

32. See Robert Kagan, "When America Blinked," *New Republic*, Dec. 3, 2001, pp. 29–42. This observation and the analysis in the following paragraphs owe much to the Kagan thesis that the old school of liberals and realists (the postwar "establishments") lost self-confidence (and its nerve) after Vietnam.

33. Quoted in Kagan, "When America Blinked," pp. 36–37.

34. Ibid., p. 37.

35. Ibid.

demands to do something. In the eyes of Halberstam and other "new interventionists," Clinton's handling of the war in Bosnia was a shameful story of foot-dragging and half-hearted engagement.[36]

Kagan points out that these humanitarian interventionists were yesterday's anti-interventionists and "détenters" who talked endlessly about the limits of American power. They were having second thoughts, Kagan argues, but never quite figured out why. The reason, he says, is that they had become convinced that "the whole idea of 'American goodness and generosity,' the whole notion that the United States could use its power to make the world safer 'for everyone,' was an absurd myth, the very essence of American 'hubris.' "

> The end of the cold war did not change everything. America was still the same America. It was selfish, but also at times remarkably selfless. It was self-absorbed, but also frequently concerned about horrors and crises overseas. A majority of Americans could be persuaded, if anyone troubled to make the case, that intervening in the Balkans, in Somalia, in Haiti, was the right thing to do, just as they could be persuaded, until their government could no longer persuade itself, that intervening to "save" Vietnam was the right thing to do. Americans still believed in the "myth." They still believed in America the great and America the good.[37]

In neoconservative Kagan's view the United States stands for something worth defending, believing in, and bestowing on others. Armed with the high moral purpose ("liberty and justice for all") and in possession of unmatched military capabilities, America was the world's preeminent power, a country without obvious limits.[38] What limits did exist would be self-imposed. Here in a nutshell is the rationale for the proactive foreign policy that gained ascendancy in the aftermath of the September 11 tragedy.

The invasion of Afghanistan and especially that of Iraq must both be seen in this light. So must concepts like preemption and "imminent threats." The use of military force to make the world better, in this view, is certainly justified. Fighting terrorism and tyranny is the flip side of loving liberty. Caring about right and wrong, good and evil, is what America is all about.

---

36. Clinton was more decisive in the Kosovo crisis, but critics questioned whether the bombing of Belgrade and other Serbian targets was justified; pointed out that Kosovo, unlike Bosnia, was part of Serbia; and doubted the wisdom of putting American troops on the ground in yet another ethnic battle zone in the Balkans.

37. Kagan, "When America Blinked," p. 39.

38. See, for example, Michael Ignatieff, "American Empire (Get Used to It)," *New York Times Magazine*, Jan. 5, 2003, p. 22. America "is the only nation that polices the world through five global military commands; maintains more than a million men and women at arms on four continents; deploys carrier battle groups on watch in every ocean; guarantees the survival of countries from Israel to South Korea; drives the wells of global trade and commerce; and fills the hearts and minds of an entire planet with its dreams and desires" (p. 22).

We saw in the preceding chapters that episodes of crusading zeal are nothing new in American history. But in the past, America's crusades have always been undertaken in the context of countervailing forces in the world, a balance-of-power system functioning to constrain *all* the actors on the international stage, including the United States. In the 1990s, after the collapse of Soviet power, America became the world's hegemon—a nation with imperial might and global reach but lacking a will to world empire or imperial self-awareness. We explore the meaning of this unprecedented situation, and whether it changed after September 11, 2001, in the next (and final) chapter.

FROM CLINTON TO BUSH: A STUDY IN CONTRASTS

Having failed to win the majority of popular votes, Bush lacked a popular mandate. But his standing in the polls climbed rapidly in early 2001, and all talk of the "mandate" issue soon disappeared.

September 11 was a defining moment for the country and for the new president. The Bush administration declared a war on terror and put all other policy priorities on the back burner. Instead of an untested president, the country suddenly had a "take charge" commander in chief. George W. Bush appeared to thrive on the new sense of danger and exuded self-confidence in his own ability to lead the nation. In contrast to his predecessor, he displayed a steely resolve. Gone was the moral uncertainty that had characterized the Clinton White House. There would be no compromise with "evil." The answer to terrorism was power—hard power. America would fight fire with fire, and nobody in the world had more firepower at his disposal than the president of the United States. "Bring 'em on," he would say. The new president's response to the terrorists of September 11 was realism with a vengeance—realism that drew heavily on the patriotic reflexes of an idealistic nation aroused to anger by a wicked enemy.

On matters of principle, President Bush's public declarations after the attacks displayed uncommon moral clarity. There would be no neutral ground in the war on terrorism—every nation would be called upon to choose sides and to pitch in. America would not simply react to the actions of "evil-doers"—it would preempt evil acts at the source. Finally, the United States would demand "regime change" in states that perpetrated terrorism or harbored terrorists. America would seek allies and partners in this struggle but would act unilaterally if necessary. The Bush Doctrine was born and would now take its place among the other postwar foreign policy doctrines. However, it was the first such doctrine to be enunciated since the Reagan administration and, more significant, since the Berlin Wall fell and the cold war slipped into history.

Rarely in the annals of American foreign policy has the contrast between a sitting president and his immediate predecessor been more striking. In personality, temperament, and decision-making style, Clinton and the second Bush were diametric opposites. Clinton's inconsistency in matters of principle contributed to several serious foreign policy failures. The question is whether the opposite extreme—manifested in a moral arrogance impervious to criticism—is any better or more likely to succeed.

No one can say for certain whether Bill Clinton or George W. Bush was (is) the more motivated by principle. However, the record is clear on the question of power: Clinton was not fundamentally opposed to the use of force, but it was outside of his comfort zone. George W. Bush had no such problem.

CONCLUSION

The Clinton administration's foreign policy did not depart in any fundamental way from that of the first Bush administration. Presidents George H. W. Bush and Clinton both preferred multilateral diplomacy and respected the role of the United Nations in conflict management and peacekeeping operations. Both presidents resisted committing ground forces in the Balkans, although humanitarian intervention there enjoyed broad support in Europe and the international community.

Clinton was forced to deal with "failed states" and "ethnic cleansing" whether he liked it or not. His handling of these nettlesome issues vividly illustrates the perennial foreign policy tug-of-war between power and principles and the disarray it so often causes. In President Clinton's second term he ordered missile strikes against suspected terrorist targets in Afghanistan and Sudan, and the bombing of Serbia and Iraq. Clinton also deployed ground forces in Bosnia and Kosovo, where sizeable troop contingents remain as of this writing. In Chechnya, however, where the scale of civilian casualties and the justification for humanitarian intervention was even greater, the Clinton administration looked the other way, as it did earlier in Rwanda.

Clinton cultivated close ties and pursued nuclear arms reduction agreements with the Kremlin, believing that Russia continued to be a key to international peace and stability in the post–cold war era. This cold war carryover was viewed by critics on the Right (neo-Reaganites) as evidence that he was too cautious, that opportunities to enhance America's status and power were being squandered, that America was not assertive enough in using its power to make the world a better place, and finally, that terrorists and rogue states—America's natural enemies—would take America's timidity as a sign of weakness.

Ironically, President Clinton also strongly backed NATO enlargement despite dire warnings from some critics that Russia might be pushed in the very directions the West least desired. Other critics argued that NATO had become irrelevant and ought to be disbanded; that enlarging NATO was premature and would complicate decision making within the alliance; and that it would bring few strategic assets and many political risks. But Clinton prevailed and in the late

1990s NATO opened its ranks to three east European states (the Czech Republic, Hungary, and Poland).

President Clinton's second term was marred by personal disgrace brought on by a sex scandal and subsequent impeachment proceedings, but his stature abroad remained high. When he left office, the world was hardly less troubled than when he had entered: Israelis and Palestinians were killing each other, Russia was pursuing a brutal counterinsurgency in Chechnya, India and Pakistan were teetering on the brink of another war, and Iraq was defying the United Nations in its efforts to find evidence of banned biological and chemical weapons. Worse still, there was a growing terrorist threat to the United States emanating from a network of radical Islamists based in Afghanistan and financed by Osama bin Laden.

When the second President Bush moved into the White House in 2001 the American people did not know much about him. He had not articulated clear foreign policy positions in the campaign, except on the question of a discontinued missile defense program, which he promised to resuscitate. He had brought many neo-Reaganites into the government in high-level positions, but the choice of Colin Powell to be his secretary of state reassured mainstream, moderate internationalists in both political parties.

Before the fateful events of September 11, 2001, George W. Bush's foreign policy was uninspired and unsurprising. The day after the attacks, however, the world looked different, and so did the president. He was suddenly transformed into a resolute figure, America's commander in chief in a time of grave national crisis. When the fundamentalist Taliban leaders in Afghanistan ignored his ultimatum to hand over the alleged culprits (above all, bin Laden), he ordered military action to oust the regime, destroy al Qaeda's training camps, and hunt down as many terrorists as possible. That mission achieved its stated objectives, but it did not result in the capture of Osama bin Laden and it left the political future of the country hanging in the balance while age-old ethnic and tribal rivalries prevented the newly installed government in Kabul from asserting its authority outside of the capital city.

After September 11 the Bush administration tilted toward a neo-Reaganite foreign policy. What this "tilt" meant in practice was a willingness to "go it alone," to use military force preemptively, and to act without United Nations approval if necessary. It also meant a new emphasis on regime change and nation building, aimed at creating democracies in the Middle East and (presumably) elsewhere.

With Afghanistan moved to the back burner, President Bush turned his attention to the Iraqi dictator Saddam Hussein, who, he said, posed an "imminent threat" to the peace of the world. Embracing a new doctrine of preemption, he told the United Nations that if the Security Council did not act to remove the Iraqi threat the United States would. In November 2002 the UN Security Council

passed Resolution 1441 demanding that Saddam Hussein disarm or ⟨...⟩
sequences. When Saddam refused full cooperation with the UN inspe⟨...⟩
crisis came to a head. In March 2003, amid protests at home and abroad⟨...⟩
ordered the invasion of Iraq with the aim of removing Saddam Hussein fr⟨...⟩
power. Skeptics questioned the validity of the White House's claim that th⟨...⟩
United States had secret intelligence proving that Saddam was building weapons
of mass destruction and wondered why the United States chose to invade Iraq
rather than North Korea, which presumably posed a bigger threat. This issue was
only partially laid to rest by Saddam's capture in December 2003.

Whether taking the deposed dictator alive and putting him on trial for mass
murder would help or hinder efforts to stabilize Iraq remained uncertain at the
end of 2003. Several troubling questions begged answers. Why had Saddam surrendered so peacefully? He had to have known he would be publicly humiliated,
put on trial, and quite possibly sentenced to death. Would the spectacle of an
emotionally charged trial suppress the insurgency that threatened the U.S.
timetable for re-establishing sovereign self-rule in Iraq? Also, if the United States
handed Saddam over to the Iraqi people and they put him to death, might he not
become a martyr in the eyes of millions of anti-American Arabs, Palestinians, and
radical Islamists? In sum, capturing Saddam appeared to boost President Bush's
re-election chances; however, considering his risky commitment to nation building in Iraq, this event also had the potential to create new problems without solving pre-existing ones.

At the beginning of the twenty-first century, the foreign policy pendulum
completed a historic swing—from passive and isolationist to active and hegemonic. The Founders' idea of promoting democracy by the power of example gave
way to imposing democracy by force of arms. Behind these very different foreign
policy faces was a certain fundamental consistency. Idealism and realism have
always co-existed in a kind of creative tension and still do. When the United States
was weak and vulnerable, moral superiority was America's only readily available
source of power. In the present era of American ascendancy, morality takes a back
seat to military and technological superiority as a source of power. Morality also
takes a back seat to the use of economic power as both carrot and stick.

There is a risk, however, in touting America's moral superiority while relying on military power rather than reason and moral suasion in the pursuit of foreign policy aims. The risk is that America will be transformed in the eyes of the
world from a symbol of hope to a synonym for hypocrisy. In the lexicon of political realism, the intemperate application of America's hard power threatens to
destroy the sources of its soft power.

iples, and War:

The Limits of Foreign Policy

OVERVIEW

In this final chapter I tie the basic strands of analysis in the previous chapters together. Taking one last look at the role of principles, I suggest that, where foreign policy is concerned, it makes more sense to talk about principles of statecraft than moral principles, because state behavior cannot be judged by the same standards as individual behavior. I then take a closer look at the role of war (or hard power) as an instrument of foreign policy. I also consider the cost of war and draw appropriate conclusions.

As self-preservation is the most basic of all human needs, foreign policy is the most important function of government—"the shield of the republic," in Walter Lippmann's memorable phrase. In 1943, as World War II was raging in Europe and Asia, Lippmann wrote a book with these very words as its subtitle. He asserted that "the foreign policy which had served the United States, on the whole so well, during most of the nineteenth century became dangerously inadequate after 1900." The United States had "expanded its commitments into Asia" after the Spanish-American War at the same time as Germany, which, "by deciding to build a great navy, emerged from continental Europe as a challenger for world power."[1]

Lippmann's incisive little book was, in his own words, "a severe criticism of American policy during this period." Were Lippmann to write a similar book about the second half of the twentieth century, his criticism would very likely be no less severe but would rest on different grounds. In the decades leading up to World War II, the United States failed to readjust to the "revolutionary change" in the balance of power. As a consequence,

---

1. Walter Lippmann, *U.S. Foreign Policy: Shield of the Republic* (Boston: Little, Brown, 1943), p. vii.

America was "unprepared to wage war or make peace" and "remained divided within itself on the conduct of American foreign relations." In the period after World War II, the United States has at times over-adjusted, shelving isolationism and replacing it with a crusading brand of internationalism. The result has been U.S. involvement in local and regional conflicts all over the world and a predisposition toward unilateral military solutions. In the process, the role of diplomacy has declined, presidents have relied heavily on the National Security Council (NSC) rather than the State Department for foreign policy expertise, and professional diplomats have often been marginalized.[2]

THE MEANING OF SEPTEMBER 11, 2001

What sort of book would an astute observer like Walter Lippmann write at the beginning of the twenty-first century? Unfortunately, we will never know, but asking the question can open our eyes to possibilities we might never consider without the inspiration of scholars and commentators who are no longer with us. They interpreted the "bipolar" world of the cold war for us; like them, we must now interpret the "unipolar" world of the post–cold war era for a nation struggling to redefine its role within the newly emerging international system.

The present book reflects not only a post–cold war perspective but also a post–September 11 perspective. The past looks somewhat different to each generation, reflecting recent developments, changing attitudes, and sometimes even new information unearthed by historians and political scientists. The United States is at the center of this brave, new unipolar world. No state or alliance rivaled American military and economic power at the beginning of the twenty-first century. This lopsided distribution of power resulted from the collapse of the Soviet Union a decade earlier, but its significance was never so glaringly apparent as after the terrorist attacks on American soil in September 2001.

The significance of September 11 for American foreign policy is difficult to exaggerate. It has often been compared to the Japanese attack on Pearl Harbor, but the analogy is misleading for several reasons. First, the organization responsible for the attacks on September 11 was not a state or a government and therefore was not a member of any international organization (the United Nations, the International Court of Justice, the International Atomic Energy Agency, the World Trade Organization, and so forth). Second, the attacks did not occur against the backdrop of a "world war" already raging in Europe and Asia, where military aggressors (Germany and Japan) were carving out vast empires. Third, the attacks came after a decade of economic growth and prosperity, in stark contrast to Pearl Harbor, which came in the wake of the Great Depression.

---

2. See, for example, Monteagle Stearns, *Talking to Strangers: Improving American Diplomacy at Home and Abroad* (Princeton: Princeton University Press, 1996), pp. 4 and 124–125.

These differences are only a few of the more conspicuous ones. When FDR addressed the U.S. Congress the day after Pearl Harbor he asked for a declaration of war against Japan. When George W. Bush addressed the American people after September 11 he declared a "war on terrorism"—not on any specific country. America was about to embark on a new kind of war, one that was at once both "hot" and "cold."

Critics charged that this new war was too broad, too ambitious, and too evangelical. It sounded more like a religious crusade, they suggested, than a political strategy for dealing with a specific problem. The Bush Doctrine did nothing to allay these concerns. We turn now to a look at the revolutionary Bush Doctrine in light of other foreign policy doctrines in American diplomatic history.

DOCTRINES VERSUS PRINCIPLES

"Americans resist indoctrination but cherish doctrines."[3] Reducing foreign policy to one-size-fits-all "doctrines" that can be distilled into single sentences is both difficult and dangerous. Nonetheless, starting with Harry Truman, virtually every president since World War I has enunciated a doctrine. When a new "doctrine" is unveiled, old doctrines are rarely put on the shelf. Trying to fit various doctrines together yields something more akin to a jigsaw puzzle with several missing pieces than a coherent policy.

There are rare moments of decision in the history of nations when new dangers or opportunities arise and a new departure in foreign policy is necessary or desirable. In U.S. history, such a moment occurred in 1823 and again in 1947 (see box).

Both the Monroe Doctrine and the Truman Doctrine helped shape the nation's destiny. They had a lasting effect, which is why we still talk about them today. But they are among the very few "doctrines" that have stood up at all well for more than a few years. Most Americans—including university students and faculty—would be hard-pressed to name any other examples, despite the many fleeting presidential initiatives that have been enshrined as doctrines over the past fifty years.

Both doctrines are of dubious and diminished relevance today. The Monroe Doctrine applied to a world dominated by Europe at a time when the United States was relatively weak and vulnerable. The Truman Doctrine applied to a world dominated by the United States when Europe was weak and vulnerable. The Monroe Doctrine ceased to define the limits of America's sphere of influence after 1898 (the Spanish-American War), and the Truman Doctrine quickly became passé after 1989 (the demise of communism in Eastern Europe).

---

3. Ibid., p. 38.

From 1787 to 1947: Two Enduring Doctrines

Monroe Doctrine, 1823—European powers were warned not to seek colonies in the Western Hemisphere or engage in military aggression: "The political system of the allied [European] powers is essentially different . . . from that of America. . . . We owe it, therefore, to candor and to the amicable relations existing between the United States and those powers to declare that we should consider any attempt on their part to extend their system to any portion of this hemisphere as dangerous to our peace and safety"; in return, the United States promised not "to interfere in the internal concerns" of Europe.

Truman Doctrine, 1947—Prompted by a Communist insurgency in Greece, President Harry S. Truman asserted, "it must be the policy of the United States to support free peoples who are resisting attempted subjugation by armed minorities or by outside pressures." Truman conceded this was a "serious course" but told Congress that the alternative was "much more serious."

The problem with "the diplomacy of doctrine" is that a one-size-fits-all approach is unlikely to work over time. The odds are against any foreign policy formula working over the long haul—all the more reason not to get locked in and for presidents not to lock themselves in. Indeed, Murphy's Law applies with particular force in the realm of international politics.[4] Therefore, foreign policy is most effective—or least likely to end in disaster—when it is pragmatic and flexible.

It can be argued that doctrines serve several useful purposes. For example, reference to the Monroe Doctrine or the Truman Doctrine is a kind of shorthand that can greatly facilitate discourse among experts and other knowledgeable observers. A doctrine can also help those less knowledgeable understand what the United States is doing in a given time and place, and why; in other words, it can bring foreign policy into better focus for the masses. Furthermore, the enunciation of a doctrine also puts foreign governments on notice that the United States means business and lets the world know what Washington expects of it and what it, in turn, can expect of Washington. Finally, doctrines are flexible enough to allow a president plenty of decision-making latitude in a specific situation or crisis much (if not most) of the time.

However, skeptics are justified in asking why, in a world of so many sovereign states and therefore so many foreign policies, is the United States virtually alone in its habit of formulating and justifying its foreign policy in terms of a "doctrine" bearing the name of a sitting president? Is it any wonder that

---

4. Murphy's Law holds that in any given situation if anything can go wrong, it will.

America's foreign policy appears arrogant and overbearing when, to cite but one contemporary example, a president who did not receive a majority of the votes cast in his own country claims that the United States has a right to invade another country and install a new goverment there whenever it decides (or asserts) that an imminent threat exists? The international community is acutely aware of the fact that in deciding to invade Iraq when and how it did, the Bush administration was in effect making a new set of rules with which, given America's military primacy, everyone else would have to live or die. No other country dares to make up the rules as it goes along, and in a "unipolar" world when the United States enunciates a doctrine that is exactly what it is doing.

Policy is not to be confused with ideology or theology. Ideology deals with utopia; theology with the hereafter. Policy deals with the here and now.

The Soviet Union, for example, had a utopian ideology, but Soviet foreign policy had little to do with that ideology and a great deal to do with Soviet interests. Thus, in the 1960s the Soviet Union was on far better terms with various regimes that persecuted local Communists (for example, Egypt and Iraq) than with Communist China. By the same token, the United States cultivated close relations with notorious dictators, including Ferdinand Marcos of the Philippines and the shah of Iran, and encouraged the overthrow of some elected leaders (Mohammed Mossadegh in Iran in 1953; Jacob Arbenz Guzman in Guatemala in 1954; Salvador Allende Gossens in Chile in 1972). In 1992 President George H. W. Bush looked the other way when the Algerian military canceled the results of democratic elections that would have brought a militant Islamist party to power.

Policy is by definition operational. It is tailored to meet a current problem or set of problems and ought to make sense to any rational observer familiar with the facts. But in a different situation, in another time and place, the very same policy can tie a president's hands if it has been elevated to a higher moral plane—that is, if it has been transmuted from a matter of policy to one of theology or ideology.

Two recent examples of the dangers inherent in conducting foreign policy according to moral precepts will perhaps suffice. In 1999 President Clinton ordered the bombing of Serbia in retaliation for the latter's brutal attempt to suppress the Albanian majority's desire for autonomy. The press proclaimed Clinton's justification of this policy to be a new doctrine. The so-called Clinton Doctrine reiterated "in every possible variation the imperative for the U.S. to oppose 'ethnic cleansing and the slaughter of innocent people' " (see box).[5]

---

5. Charles Krauthammer, "The Clinton Doctrine," Mar. 29, 1999 (online at www.cnn.com/ALLPOLITICS/time/1999/03/29/doctrine/html).

From 1957 to 2002: Six Doctrines

Eisenhower Doctrine, 1957—President Eisenhower asserted that the United States would use force "to safeguard the independence of any country or group of countries in the Middle East requesting aid against aggression" from a Communist country. Unlike other presidential edicts of its kind, it was adopted as a joint resolution of Congress.

Nixon Doctrine, 1969—President Nixon declared, "America cannot—and will not—conceive all the plans, design all the programs, execute all the decisions and undertake all the defense of the free nations of the world. We will help where it makes a real difference and is considered in our interest."

Carter Doctrine, 1980—President Carter declared, "Any attempt by any outside forces to gain control of the Persian Gulf region will be regarded as an assault on the vital interests of the United States of America, and such an assault will be repelled by any means necessary, including military force."

Reagan Doctrine, 1986—This doctrine refers to the Reagan administration's policy of providing economic and military aid to guerrilla insurgencies against Communist governments, including Afghanistan, Angola, Cambodia, and Nicaragua.

Clinton Doctrine, 1999—President Clinton declared, "I want us to live in a world where we get along with each other, with all of our differences, and where we don't have to worry about seeing scenes every night for the next 40 years of ethnic cleansing in some part of the world."

Bush Doctrine, 2002—The Bush doctrine establishes a strategy for pre-emptive military action against "hostile states" and terrorists groups believed to be developing weapons of mass destruction, insists that the United States will never again allow its military supremacy to be challenged as it was in the cold war, and pledges to use its military and economic power to encourage "free and open societies" via a "distinctly American internationalism."

Critics from many different quarters attacked the president. The policy, said one, was "impossibly moralistic and universal." This critic flatly stated, "It cannot be the policy of the U.S." Why? Because, he pointed out, the Clinton administration had done nothing in August 1995 when Croatia "launched a savage attack" on Serbs in Krajina (part of Croatia). Serbs whose ancestors had been living there for 500 years were driven out in four days—150,000 men, women, and children. It was, in his words, "the largest ethnic cleansing of the entire Balkan wars."[6] He and others pointed out that the Clinton administration had done nothing to stop

---

6. Ibid.

so-called "teacup civil wars, far more deadly, brutal and enduring" in places like Chechnya, Congo, Rwanda, Sierra Leone, Sri Lanka, and Sudan, not to mention Beijing's brutal repression of the Tibetan people.[7]

Similarly, the Bush Doctrine took aim at another "evil," namely, terrorism. In effect, terrorism and weapons of mass destruction are to the Bush administration what ethnic cleansing and regional conflict were to the Clinton administration—a problem the United States would seek to solve by military means if necessary. As we saw in the previous chapter, President George W. Bush proclaimed the intent to act preemptively against terrorists and states who harbor terrorists, to bring about regime change in these states, and to do so with or without the cooperation or approval of the international community. The United States would henceforth use its military and economic power to encourage "free and open societies" via a "distinctly American internationalism."[8]

One critic has described the American idea of internationalism as "a very partial and contradictory world view." He wrote, "The Bush Doctrine will inevitably be coloured by the prejudices of those who have contributed to Republican foreign policy thinking. In this world view, the security interests of Israel and the US are indivisible."[9] Many critics have suggested that the indiscriminate application of the Bush Doctrine could easily backfire. In Iraq, it could lead to even greater regional instability and would help terrorist organizations recruit a whole new generation of suicide bombers.[10]

Even observers sympathetic with the decision to invade Iraq question the wisdom of applying the logic of confrontation in the future: "The moment of an America-led military assault to strip Iraq of all nuclear, chemical or biological weapons . . . is as good a moment as any to ponder whether there might in future be less costly ways of checking the spread of such weapons."[11] As this observer pointed out, "Force has its risks."[12] Implicit in all such critiques of foreign policy

---

7. Ibid. Krauthammer wrote scathingly, "The Clinton Doctrine aspires to morality and universality. But foreign policy must be calculating and particular. Clinton proclaims that he is going into battle for the principle that ethnic cleansing and the slaughter of innocents can never be tolerated by a civilized world. Yet on his watch, half a million innocents were massacred in Rwanda in the only true genocide since the Holocaust, and he lifted not a finger to stop it."

8. See Peter Beaumont, "Now for the Bush Doctrine," *Observer*, Sept. 22, 2002 (online at www.observer.co.uk).

9. Ibid.

10. See, for example, Toby Dodge, "Iraq and the Bush Doctrine," *Observer*, Mar. 24, 2002, also online at www.theworldtoday.org.

11. "After Iraq," *Economist*, Mar. 22, 2003, p. 12.

12. Ibid. Using force without the full blessing of the UN, wrote the *Economist*, "will make future efforts to counter proliferation harder still." Indeed, the "strong-arming of Iraq" and President Bush's "hostile 'axis of evil' rhetoric" may drive countries with "nuclear ambitions" like Iran and North Korea to accelerate "bomb-building" plans.

is a conviction that idealism expressed in a doctrinaire approach to the making of foreign policy, in moral arrogance, in polemical language, in a tendency toward religious or ideological crusading, or in the absence of military self-restraint is ill-advised.

Doctrines are typically couched in moral language and thus highlight America's moral and altruistic aims. But foreign policy in threatening times is rarely if ever motivated by altruism. When the nation's survival is deemed to be at risk, or its vital interests at stake, altruism gives way to pragmatism, and morality gives way to moralism. The latter is a transparent and self-serving substitute for the former and therefore best avoided. Avoidance of moralism is a principle of diplomacy too many American presidents have too often failed to honor.

Does an avoidance of moralism imply that policymakers ought to ignore morality altogether? Definitely not, but making a distinction between moralism and morality is critical to clear thinking about foreign policy. Nations operate in an anarchic world. Rules exist, but there is no effective enforcement authority, no world government. In the final analysis, success (liberty, prosperity, and the like) excites envy, envy easily turns into enmity, and self-defense is the only guarantee of survival. It is therefore always necessary to temper moral and humanitarian concerns with caution and pragmatism—that is, with a strong dose of realism. The most difficult challenge for the leaders of rich and powerful nations has always been and will always be to balance these two competing claims—the desire to do "the right thing" against the necessity of self-preservation—in the formulation of foreign policy.

Perhaps the best that can be done is to identify principles that can stand the test of time and try to be faithful to them insofar as possible while recognizing the limits of moral conduct in international politics. Principles are not to be confused with policies (or doctrines). Big foreign policy decisions are almost always rationalized in terms of principles, but the actual policy may or may not stand the test of time. Most "doctrines" do not. The Truman Doctrine, for example, which made sense at the time, is irrelevant without the Soviet Union.

Foreign policy at its best is flexible, pragmatic, and unencumbered by dogma. Guidelines and principles, however, can be very useful. For example, one of the maxims (or guidelines) that has helped princes and policymakers avoid disastrous mistakes in the past—or been ignored at great cost—is "Talk rather than fight." Below is a sampler of foreign policy principles that might prove useful so long as they are not treated as moral imperatives. They are guidelines, at best, not commandments. American presidents have observed these maxims selectively:

1. Talk rather than fight.
2. Fight rather than give up something worth fighting for.
3. Stay out of other people's fights unless vital national interests are clearly at stake.

4. Encourage democracy and freedom, but respect the right of other nations to decide for themselves whether to revolt or submit to tyranny.
5. Avoid hypocrisy (practice what you preach).
6. Lead by example rather than exhortation, intimidation, or coercion.
7. Use carrots rather than sticks whenever possible, and where force is necessary show due respect for the Constitution, the United Nations Charter, existing treaty obligations, and international law.

This list of principles does not purport to be complete. One principle of statecraft not found on the list is anathema to Americans: Surrender without a fight. Surrendering without a fight may be suicide for Great Powers, but it made sense in 1938 to Czechs facing the prospect of war with Hitler's Germany, or to the hapless Melians facing certain annihilation by Athens, one of the superpowers of Greek antiquity (Sparta was the other).[13]

The Vietnam War would probably have ended much sooner and turned out somewhat better had American policymakers recognized earlier that it is better to concede at the negotiating table than to stay in a fight you cannot win. Since World War II, the United States has paid scant heed to maxim number three ("Stay out of other people's fights"), although some have been more predisposed to use military force overseas than others. President George W. Bush, for example, is less cautious in the use of military force than his father was.

Once in power, individual decision makers can put principles into practice or put them on the shelf. Donald Rumsfeld enjoyed a reputation as a tough and effective corporate CEO who was said to be fond of management maxims. As secretary of defense in the current Bush administration, one of "Rumsfeld's rules" is "Don't divide the world into 'them' and 'us.' " Another is "Visit with your predecessors from previous administrations. Try to make original mistakes rather than needlessly repeating theirs."[14] Readers can judge for themselves whether President George W. Bush (or Mr. Rumsfeld personally) has followed these two maxims. This type of exercise serves to illustrate another maxim: Maxims are no better than the people who create them.

In international politics, principles cannot always be put into practice but must not be deliberately flouted or disdained, because to do so is to run the risk of "blowback," (adverse effects of current policies felt in the future but rooted in the past). This maxim applies with special force to a superpower without any serious rivals because of the natural tendency for a hegemon to fall victim to hubris.

---

13. Cited in Thomas M. Magstadt, *Understanding Politics: Ideas, Institutions, and Issues*, 6th ed. (Belmont, Calif.: Wadsworth, 2003), pp. 505–506. See also Thucydides, "The Melian Conference," in *Readings in World Politics*, 2nd ed., ed. Robert Goldwin and Tony Pearce (New York: Oxford University Press, 1970), pp. 472–478.

14. Lexington, "The Not-So-Quiet American," *Economist*, Mar. 20, 2003, p. 34.

Are there maxims that a Great Power ought to be especially careful to observe in the twenty-first century? Here are four worth considering:

1. First, do no harm.
2. When harm is unavoidable, do less harm than good.
3. The more power you have relative to your adversaries, the more you can afford to exercise restraint.
4. If you do get into a fight be prepared to do whatever it takes to win.

EMPIRES AND BLOWBACK

Only a few Great Powers have ever had the wherewithal to maintain a military presence on foreign soil. Throughout history, this practice has been associated almost exclusively with great empires and imperialism. From the seventeenth century to the early twentieth century (World War I) the Great Powers of Europe competed in establishing colonial empires but generally fought only limited wars for limited objectives on the Continent. Wars with neighbors often involved disputed or coveted territories, but the aim was rarely if ever the overthrow of existing governments or military occupation. (Napoleon Bonaparte was the major exception to this rule.)

The empires of the modern age have thus been of the kind that did not threaten the existence of Europe's political regimes (mostly monarchies prior to the twentieth century), opened new territories for conquest outside of Europe, turned the gaze of Europe's sovereigns away from territorial conquest on the Continent, and provided arenas of competition for Europe's rivals. Europe's imperialist powers did, of course, conquer, subjugate, occupy, and administer the territories over which they held sway. These territories encompassed every region of the world, including the Americas, or the Western Hemisphere.

The Spanish and Portuguese were the first to arrive on the scene in the "West Indies" (mainly the Caribbean islands) but were soon followed by the British and French in North America. The race for overseas real estate intensified in the nineteenth century, by which time most of the European states were participants (notable exceptions were the Scandinavian countries and Switzerland). By the end of the nineteenth century, the roster of European imperialist states included the Dutch, Belgians, Germans, and Italians, as well as Tsarist Russia with its vast holdings in the European steppe (the plains of southern and eastern Europe), the Far East, and central Asia.

The blowback from these imperial ventures was earthshaking. World War I itself can be interpreted as a consequence of blowback, a result of intrusion into the Balkans of two great empires—the Ottoman Empire (Turkey) and the Hapsburg Empire (Austria). Similarly, the turmoil that engulfed the former colonial territories (the so-called third world) after 1945—including civil wars, "national liberation" struggles, and violent revolutions—is a glaring example of blowback. For the political scientist in search of evidence, the postwar history of Africa, Asia, and Latin America provides near-absolute proof that foreign rule almost always brings a delayed reaction of some sort, usually violent, at some time, often years or even decades after the offense to which it can be traced.

As we saw in Chapter 2, the Americas were themselves still an arena of European competition in the early nineteenth century. The Monroe Doctrine declared the Western Hemisphere off-limits to this kind of "competition" in the future. For the British, the American Revolution with its famous rallying cry, "no taxation without representation," was a form of blowback. For the Spanish, the revolutions in Latin America inspired by Simón Bolívar of Venezuela were dramatic evidence of blowback.

Blowback did not hit France, Great Britain, and Portugal with full force until after World War II, but then it hit hard enough to cause a complete breakup of all three empires and, in the process, destabilize these regions so severely that the aftershocks continue to reverberate down to the present day.

What does Europe's imperialist past have to do with America's present? The answer lies in the lessons history can teach us if only we treat it respectfully. The United States stands at a crossroads where the temptation is great to go down a road well traveled by Europe's imperialist powers in the eighteenth and nineteenth centuries. The United States conquered Germany and Japan in 1945 and more than half a century later continued to maintain military forces in these two countries. The United States also left a large military force in South Korea after 1953, where it remains to this day.[15]

In the 1990s, following "humanitarian interventions" in Bosnia and Serbia, U.S. forces remained in those two countries as well. In 2001 the United States conquered Afghanistan, where American forces continue to guarantee a modicum of law and order. Finally, in the spring of 2003 the United States invaded Iraq and encircled Baghdad, ousting Saddam Hussein from power. Although the war continues as of this writing (November 2003), American officials are looking ahead to a post-Saddam era, when, they say, a democratic (and pro-Western) government will be installed. All signs point to a long-term American military presence in Iraq.

There appears to be nothing to stand in the way of a Pax Americana in the Middle East or central Asia or on the Korean Peninsula. The United States entered the twentieth century as an emerging Great Power; it exited the century

---

15. In 2000 the United States maintained nearly 70,000 armed forces personnel in Germany, about 40,000 in Japan, some 36,500 in Korea, and about 10,000 troops in the former Yugoslavia, divided between Bosnia and Serbia (Kosovo). See *Military World 2000 Almanac* (online at www.militaryworld.com).

as the only superpower. One view holds that America ought to use its military and economic supremacy to make the world safe for democracy and free enterprise (and thus for the United States). Perhaps. But in so doing America also needs to take the problem of blowback into account.

It has been said that the Middle East is the graveyard of great expectations. Any policymaker who is unaware of this fact needs a refresher course in history. In the former colonial regions, invasion and occupation by white-skinned Westerners is forever associated with the specter of "imperialism." Of course, this does not mean that the United States cannot defeat other "rogue states" just as it defeated Afghanistan and is now defeating Iraq. But winning a war is one thing; ruling a defeated country from afar is quite another, and sooner or later blowback is inevitable.

The public only dimly understands the economic and political cost of maintaining military forces in a hostile environment. In Germany, Japan, and South Korea, the indigenous populations have generally accepted the American military presence. Whether this same level of acceptance can be expected in Muslim countries is extremely doubtful.

In any event, heavy reliance on military power is always very costly in both economic and human terms. As we have seen, the Bush Doctrine contemplates the use of military force in order to prevent situations of "imminent danger" from becoming future calamities like the September 11 attacks or worse. In the spring of 2003, opinion polls showed that Americans overwhelmingly approved of the decision to attack Iraq. This support, however, began to soften as the death toll in Iraq crept up day after day during the summer despite the administration's earlier premature announcement that "major combat" was over.

Public enthusiasm for the war in Iraq ought not to obscure the heavy cost of war in general. The next section is designed to put the "war option" into historical and statistical perspective.

THE DEADLY "GAME" OF WAR

A famous American general once said, "War is hell, boys." Casualty figures are revealing and often contain surprises. For example, the ratio of enrolled soldiers to citizens was exactly the same in the War of 1812 and the Korean War (3.8 percent). The participation rate for the Vietnam War was almost as high as for World War I.[16] However, the figures for post-1945 contain a large number of forces not directly engaged in war—in other words, they reflect the enormous expansion of

---

16. "Statistical Summary: America's Major Wars," United States Civil War Center (online at www.cwc.lsu.edu/cwc.other/stats/warcost.htm).

American military commitments around the world expressed in the form of "literally thousands of overseas military installations."[17]

There are many ways to look at casualty figures for America's major wars, but few that are more poignant than comparisons between pre– and post–World War I (see Table 9-1). Prior to the wars of the twentieth century, the total number of Americans killed in combat on foreign soil was 8,813 according to official records at the Department of Veterans Affairs in Washington, D.C. In the twentieth century that figure jumped to 426,812, or roughly 97 times more than the previous century. This nearly hundredfold increase in combat deaths cannot be explained by mere demographics either: between 1812 and 1990, despite the massive influx of immigrants in the late nineteenth century and a doubling of the population between World War II and the Gulf War, America's population increased "only" thirty-four times.

In addition, there are always many noncombat deaths in the armed services during war. In the Mexican War, for example, 1,733 soldiers fell on the battlefield and another 11,550 died of other causes. In World War I, nearly 10,000 more American soldiers died off the battlefield than on it. And in the 1990–1991 Gulf War the ratio of "combat" to "other" deaths was nearly one-to-one.

If we look at total casualties, the picture is no less dramatic. Prior to the twentieth century, American casualties in foreign wars totaled 28,308; the corresponding number for the last century was roughly 1.75 million, or about sixty-one times more.

All told, America's major wars (including the Civil War) have resulted in 650,954 battlefield deaths. This figure, however, does not include the 13,853 other service-related combat deaths, nor does it include 229,661 out-of-combat deaths.

Roughly 1.5 million Americans have been wounded in battle, many severely wounded. The latter include thousands of amputees and otherwise physically or mentally impaired veterans. The total number of armed-service casualties is over 2,750,000. Left out of these statistics entirely, of course, are the enemy's war casualties and, most tragically of all, the civilian victims of war—including children—the so-called collateral damage.

Soldiers are asked to pay the ultimate price, but civilians—whether as innocent bystanders, family members, or taxpayers—pay a heavy price, as well. Living

---

17. See, for example, Chalmers Johnson, *Blowback: The Costs and Consequences of American Empire* (New York: Holt, 2000), p. 36. Johnson provides a glimpse of the magnitude of America's commitments around the world: "At the height of the cold war, the United States built a chain of military bases stretching from Korea and Japan through Taiwan, the Philippines, Thailand, and Australia to Saudi Arabia, Turkey, Greece, Italy, Spain, Portugal, Germany, England, and Iceland—in effect ringing the Soviet Union and China with literally thousands of overseas military installations. In Japan alone, immediately following the end of the Korean War, there were six hundred U.S. installations and approximately two hundred thousand troops. There still are today, ten years after the end of the cold war, some hundred Department of Defense facilities located outside the United States ranging from radio relay stations to major air bases."

Table 9-1 The Human Cost of America's Wars

Conflict	Enrolled	Combat	Other	Wounded	Total
		Combat	Other	Wounded	Total
Revolutionary War	200,000	4,435	—	6,188	10,623
War of 1812	286,000	2,260	—	4,505	6,765
Mexican War	78,700	1,733	11,550	4,152	17,435
Civil War					
Union	2,803,300	110,070	249,458	275,175	634,703
Confederate	1,064,200	74,524	124,000	137,000	335,524
Combined	3,867,500	184,594	373,458	412,175	970,227
Spanish-American War	306,800	385	2,061	1,662	4,108
World War I	4,743,800	53,513	63,195	204,002	320,710
World War II	16,353,700	292,131	115,185	670,846	1,078,162
Korean War	5,764,100	33,651	—	103,284	136,935
Vietnam War	8,744,000	47,369	10,799	153,303	211,471
Gulf War I	2,750,000	148	145	467	760

(Header: Casualties → Deaths (Combat, Other), Wounded, Total)

Source: United States Civil War Center. "Statistical Summary: America's Major Wars." http://www.cwc.lso.edu/cwe.

veterans are entitled to medical and other benefits for life. As of May 2001, there were more than 19.4 million living war veterans in the United States (this figure does not include another 6 million or so veterans who did not serve during a time of war). The total number of war veterans and dependents on the compensation and pension rolls was 2,635,702, including over 50,000 children, some 9,300 parents, and 483,288 spouses. There can be no question that veterans deserve whatever benefits they receive. But the cost of these benefits to society—some $51 billion in 2002—is substantial.

The war in Iraq and its costly aftermath inadvertently drew attention to the role of social class in America's new professional military. The George W. Bush administration—a government by and for a privileged elite in the eyes of many Americans—showed no hesitation about ordering others who are less privileged into battle and asking the middle class to pay for it. President Bush's farcical military record is a well-known fact; what often goes unnoticed is that few of the foot soldiers in Iraq or Afghanistan come from the ranks of America's rich.

When critics of President Bush's tax cuts pointed out that the biggest winners are the very wealthy, defenders of the administration charged them with trying to incite "class warfare." The wars America fights *are* "class wars" in a sense that is quite new in American history. Now that the military draft is history, the sons and daughters of the rich are rarely counted among the nation's warriors. The soldiering class is drawn largely from lower-income groups, including the two largest minorities (blacks and Hispanics). Not surprisingly, the armed services recruit heavily in the inner cities of America, where the rate of success is much higher than in the suburbs. Paradoxically, this situation, which is so convenient for those in the top income brackets, is in jeopardy, because a growing number of army reservists sent to Iraq are disaffected.

WAR AND THE ECONOMY

Certainly, no president would ever admit to fighting a war for economic reasons. Unfortunately, a preemptive war in an oil-rich region like the Middle East is bound to raise eyebrows and suspicions. Was the second Gulf War not all about ensuring Western access to Persian Gulf oil? This view of the motivation behind the Bush administration's current policies is grossly oversimplified, but it does point to a persistent belief that war can be—and in this view often is—good for the economy.

One school of thought in America views war as a way to resuscitate a flagging economy. This view stems largely from the experience of World War II. That war, of course, occurred at a time when the nation was struggling to overcome by far the worst economic depression in its history. Leaving aside the fact that the U.S. economy was starting to revive before Pearl Harbor, there is no doubt that wartime production accelerated the recovery. According to several economic historians, the U.S. economy grew by 50 percent or more between 1939 and 1945.[18]

But World War II was atypical in many ways. First, it was a global war that disrupted trade and brought nearly all the advanced economies to a standstill; second, the United States was one of the few countries (along with Canada and Australia) that did not suffer the destruction of its economy; third, with its economy intact, the United States became the major producer and supplier of the guns, machines, food, fuel, clothing, tents, medicines, and all other things needed to keep itself and its allies (primarily Britain and Russia) in the war.[19] Defense spending associated with the wars in Korea and Vietnam also fueled economic expansions, although on a smaller scale.

The first Persian Gulf War, however, was quite a different story: the aftermath witnessed a drop in stock prices, consumer spending, and business investment—in a word, a sharp recession starting the month after Saddam Hussein's army invaded Kuwait. Thus, the same train of events responsible for President

---

18. Paul Kennedy, *The Rise and Fall of the Great Powers* (New York: Vintage Books, 1989), p. 357. In using this estimate, Kennedy cites two other sources.

19. Ibid., pp. 347–372.

George H. W. Bush's high popularity ratings in 1990 also triggered the economic downturn that led to his defeat at the polls in 1992.

In any event, war is a costly and high-risk way to stimulate a national economy, and it is potentially very disruptive for the world economy, upon which the prosperity of nations large and small is increasingly dependent. It is axiomatic that economies in general, and market systems in particular, thrive in peaceful, stable environments. This same holds true, of course, for free societies.

Wars always carry a hefty price tag for taxpayers, but perhaps because it seems unpatriotic to talk about it there is rarely any real public debate or even information on the actual cost of a given war. The cost of World War II, the most expensive war in American history excluding the cold war, was $15,655 *per person*. It would have cost more than $2 trillion to fight the same war in the 1990s.[20] In times past, America's wars lasted for years rather than months. The Gulf War of 1990–1991, by contrast, lasted only days but cost $61 billion nonetheless. As stated earlier, the members of the allied coalition reimbursed the United States for the lion's share of this amount (almost 90 percent), so the actual cost to the American taxpayers was about $7 billion (about the same as for the Spanish-American War), or $235 per person. Because of the multilateral financing of the first Gulf War, the United States could fight forty-nine wars just like it for about the same amount of money as the losing effort in Vietnam. The second Gulf War, however, is proving to be far less affordable than the first one.

The Chilling Cost of Cold Wars

Wars consume resources of every kind at a rate unmatched by any other human endeavor. Prior to the twentieth century, war was mainly the "sport of kings." It was a very expensive sport that only the richest monarchs could afford to play. Even then, they did not maintain large standing armies but instead mobilized for each individual war. This basic approach did not change fundamentally until the twentieth century.

As we saw in Chapter 5, after World War II the Soviet Union did not demobilize. With the onset of the cold war, the Truman administration decided to put the United States on a kind of permanent wartime footing called "military readiness" or "preparedness." When the policy of "containment" turned into a call for military solutions (Cuba, Dominican Republic, Grenada, Korea, Lebanon, Libya, Panama, and Vietnam), the impact on the American economy was enormous. President Eisenhower darkly warned of the dangers associated with the rise of the "military-industrial complex" in the United States. That was one of the hidden

---

20. The figures cited here can be found online at www.cwc.lsu.edu/cwc/other/stats/warcost.htm, the homepage of the United States Civil War Center.

costs of the cold war, a cost reflected not only in a distorted economy but also in a distorted political decision-making process, as well as a democracy in which constitutional guarantees are too easily compromised in the name of national security.

What were the direct costs of the cold war? The question is difficult to answer because it is not self-evident how to define direct costs. According to one estimate, the total cost of nuclear and other weapons worldwide between 1945 and 1996 was $8 trillion.[21] Americans paid unprecedented defense bills during this period, prompting this admonition from President Eisenhower: "The problem in defense spending is to figure how far you should go without destroying from within what you are trying to defend from without."[22] The Pentagon's spending climbed steeply after September 11, 2001, from about $256 billion in 1998 to a figure approaching $400 billion near the end of 2003.

We can get some sense of the opportunity costs of the cold war when we consider that between 1940 and 1996 the United States alone stockpiled more than 70,000 nuclear weapons at an estimated cost of $5.5 trillion, according to a Brookings Institution study published in 1998.[23] To put this sum of money into perspective, it is more than the monies disbursed for Medicare and veterans' benefits combined during that same period.[24] The cost of maintaining an ongoing U.S. nuclear weapons program nearly a decade after the Soviet collapse was still roughly $35 billion a year. The Brookings study estimated the future cost of managing nuclear waste and disposing of obsolete nuclear weapons at some $400 billion.[25]

Whether the enormous outlay of public funds in the four decades between 1947 and 1989 was money well spent is debatable. The federal government has debated with itself as to how much defense spending is enough. In 1964, for example, President Lyndon Johnson's top economists at the old Bureau of the Budget, eager to promote Great Society domestic spending programs, estimated that a force of 450 Minuteman missiles would be quite adequate. Military planners at the Pentagon put the figure at 10,000! Defense Secretary Robert McNamara liked a different number—exactly 1,000.[26]

21. Jeremy Isaacs and Taylor Downing, *The Cold War: An Illustrated History* (New York: Little, Brown, 1998). Originally made public as a CNN documentary series of the same name (online at www.cnn.com/SPECIAL/cold.war/episodes/24/epilogue/). The figures cited in the present study can be found at this Web address.

22. Ibid.

23. Stephen I. Schwartz, ed., *Atomic Audit: The Costs and Consequences of U.S. Nuclear Weapons Since 1940* (Washington, D.C.: Brookings Institution Press, 1998).

24. Peter Passell, "Flimsy Accounting on Nuclear Weapons," *New York Times,* July 9, 1998 (online at www.mtholyoke.edu/acad/intrel/costnuke.htm).

25. Schwartz, *Atomic Audit.*

26. Ibid.

Clearly, the numbers were intrinsically meaningless. Considerations and pressures other than national security were driving these wildly varying estimates. The Brookings study demonstrates in fine-grained detail that huge sums of taxpayer money were lavished on a cold war concept of nuclear deterrence that far exceeded what many civilian and military experts deemed necessary. There were many reasons for these excesses, including the faulty belief that nuclear weapons provided a "bigger bang for a buck" (in other words, that they were highly cost-effective). Pork barrel politics, lack of transparency, exaggeration of the Soviet threat, inter-service rivalries, and bureaucratic inefficiencies all share in the blame. The Brookings group concluded, modestly enough, that stricter accountability and greater public understanding were (are) needed.

Fortunately, nuclear war has thus far remained potential. Ironically, one of the opportunity costs of an overemphasis on nuclear deterrence during the cold war was too little attention paid to nuclear nonproliferation and counter-proliferation and too little effective leadership in this area. Will the onset of another cold-war crusade now lock the United States into the same predicament?

The High Cost of Hypocrisy

It is difficult morally and politically to lead a campaign for nuclear restraint while exemplifying the opposite behavior in the eyes of the world. Leadership by reverse example looks like hypocrisy, not diplomacy. In these circumstances, it was little wonder that the Bush administration's attempts to rivet world attention on the problem of "weapons of mass destruction" (including chemical and biological weapons) failed. The fact that the United States has had large stores of biological and chemical weapons, and retains the capacity to produce more at any time, is not lost on other nations.

After the attacks on September 11 the United States had a rare opportunity to lead a multilateral effort aimed at reducing the WMD danger. That lost opportunity must be counted as one of the hidden costs of the second Gulf War, ironically justified in terms of the urgent need to eliminate the elusive WMD Saddam Hussein allegedly hid from UN inspectors. The political fallout from the war in Iraq; the lurch toward unilateralism; and the general alarm in Europe and beyond over the U.S. penchant for preemptive military action all combine to make it less likely than ever that Washington can get the cooperation it needs to reduce the threat posed by WMD in the hands of terrorists and tyrants.

In sum, the care and feeding of America's nuclear gorilla as well as the enormous "military-industrial complex" President Eisenhower cautioned against is one of the lingering costs of the first cold war, or cold war I. The advent of the second cold war (cold war II) after September 11, 2001, will perpetuate and even accelerate these costs in the coming decades, imposing a heavy burden on future generations of taxpayers (including today's college students). Students of foreign policy must consider (1) whether the United States has the power and resources (including the willpower) to see another cold war through to the end; (2) whether the exercise of military and police powers associated with this new struggle is compatible with America's principles (including liberty, justice, and democracy); and (3) whether diplomatic means in specific situations might achieve satisfactory results at less cost than war or direct military intervention.

BACK TO THE FUTURE

Can America avoid a second cold war? Is the United States destined to fight an endless series of "little" wars? Is another world war inevitable?[27] The answers to these questions hinge on leadership, above all. The diplomatic and political skill that our elected leaders and the people they appoint to key posts bring to bear on foreign policy problems can make all the difference. Americans have always been skeptical of deterministic theories (Marxism, for example). A belief in "free will" is one of the most fundamental principles of American political life. Wars, in this view, are not inevitable. Nations choose war.

Perhaps the United States ought to quit NATO, quit the UN, and close its military bases abroad. Doing so would take the United States back to a time in its history when most Americans agreed with the isolationist stance of George Washington, John Adams, and Thomas Jefferson. But the world has changed a great deal since the time of the Founders. The United States has also changed a great deal. As we saw in Chapter 2, the fate of the new Republic hung in the balance for several decades after the American Revolution. The Great Powers of Europe (including France and Spain, as well as Great Britain) were still major stakeholders in the Western Hemisphere. There was always the chance that they would continue to view the Americas as an arena of competition.

Of course, all that has changed. The United States is no longer a fledgling nation comprised of thirteen former colonies still wary of federalism. Today, America is the undisputed hegemon of the Western Hemisphere (see Table 9-2). As such, it has no land-power rivals on its borders. Not only is the United States the only regional hegemon in existence, but it is also, arguably, the only all-round Great Power left in the world, and certainly the only one with the requisite power-projection capabilities to give it global reach. Indeed, it has no serious rivals at sea or in the air.

---

27. See, for example, Maureen Dowd, "Dances with Wolfowitz," *New York Times,* Apr. 9, 2003 (online version). Dowd comments darkly, "the end of Operation Iraqi Freedom should not mark the beginning of Operation Eternal War." Dowd also noted in this article that "[t]he former C.I.A. director James Woolsey . . . bluntly told U.C.L.A. students last week that to reshape the Middle East, the U.S. would have to spend years and maybe decades waging World War IV. (He counted the cold war as World War III.)"

Table 9-2 Balances of Power: The Dawn of the Twenty-first Century				
	Potential power		**Actual power**	
	GNP	**Population**	**Army**	**Nuclear warheads**
North America				
Canada	$793 billion	31.6 million	60,000	0
Mexico	641 billion	103.3 million	183,000	0
United States	10.88 trillion	289.5 million	655,541[a]	10,729[b]
Northeast Asia				
China	1.39 trillion	1.3 billion	2,200,000	410
Japan	3.94 trillion	127.2 million	151,800	0
Russia	392 billion	143.5 million	348,000	10,000
Europe				
France	1.67 trillion	60.2 million	411,800	470
Germany	2.39 trillion	81.9 million	516,000	0
Italy	1.42 trillion	57.6 million	164,000	0
United Kingdom	1.77 trillion	60.3 million	301,150	185

Sources: Figures for armies are from IISS, *Military Balance 2000/2001;* figures on nuclear arsenals are from Robert S. Norris and William M. Arkin, *Bulletin of Atomic Scientists* 56, No. 5 (September-October 2000); figures for GNP and population are from *Economist,* "The World in 2003."

a. This number includes only active-duty personnel in the army and Marine Corps in 2000; there were also 373,193 active-duty navy personnel and 355,654 air force personnel. The total for all the armed forces was 1,184,338.

b. The source of this figure is the National Resource Defense Council. It includes a small number of nuclear weapons scheduled for disposal in 2002.

As we saw again in the second Gulf War, the "Stars and Stripes" has become a powerful symbol of American patriotism and national unity. American military might is truly awesome (recalling the Pentagon's use of the phrase "shock and awe" to describe the strategy and tactics in Iraq).

Along with wealth and power goes commensurate responsibility. The world now looks to the United States for leadership. Clearly, America cannot turn its back on the world or close its eyes to danger and suffering. The U.S. economy is inextricably enmeshed in the global economy. Instability in one region often spreads to other regions and can easily have worldwide ramifications. In the Middle East, instability can also disrupt the flow of petroleum products needed to power the oil-dependent economies of America and its allies.

If both isolationism and interventionism have serious drawbacks in today's world, where does that leave us? Is there a Golden Mean, an intermediate stance between isolationism and interventionism that might be more promising than either extreme? Perhaps it would be possible for the United States to maintain a strong presence on the open seas and in the sky (outer space) but to get off other peoples' property. Such a policy would require a good deal of debate and refinement in order to gain the approval of Congress and the public. But given the stakes, it is irresponsible *not* to consider alternatives to a new foreign policy that looks strikingly similar in many respects to the old policy (containment).

CONCLUSION

It is only fitting to conclude with some reflections on power and principle—the main theme of the book. The United States does not fight wars for the sake of democracy as a principle, only to defend the practice of democracy at home. Defending American democracy has at times required the United States to fight wars abroad (for example, in the two world wars). Americans have been told by presidents, politicians, and clergy (among others) to believe that our purpose is to make the world safe for democracy (Wilson), to fight totalitarianism (FDR), or to make the world safer and better (George W. Bush)—anything but the real reason. So if Americans are naive about power, if Americans act as though principle really matters in world politics, a major reason is that America's leaders have always said so.

In truth, realism competes with, and tempers, idealism in American foreign policy, and has since the nation's founding. The problem with idealism is twofold: first, it is not always associated with a sense of limits, and second, it can too easily be attached to *any* argument or policy. A policy driven by power motives can be as readily justified on idealistic grounds as one driven by lofty principles. Hence, to critics, the Bush Doctrine of preemption looks like an example of realism carried to extremes, but to sympathizers it is proof of the administration's commitment to fighting terrorism (an evil) and promoting democracy (a good). Realism properly applied, however, takes account of both power and principle and recognizes that principles can be a potent source of power in world politics. If the demise of the Soviet Union proves anything, it is this: military might by itself is a poor measure of a nation's power.

Building a sound foreign policy is all about striking balances—between honesty and secrecy, self-confidence and humility, independence and interdependence, ideals and self-interest, and the like. Above all, policymakers have an obligation to balance power goals and principles, which from a practical standpoint are not goals so much as guidelines. Applied to policy, this balancing is a process rather than an act. There is never a time when all things important are in perfect balance, never a time when all things are equal in the realm of politics. The task is thus inherently frustrating and fraught with danger. In international politics, an error in judgment on the part of the president can be fatal for countless young men and women serving in the armed forces and costly for an estimated 230 million American taxpayers (and, indirectly, millions of non-taxpayers, as well), who often feel helpless in the face of rising federal deficits and dwindling federal benefits.

As I have shown throughout this book, America rarely if ever bases its actions in foreign affairs on moral principle alone. Like other Great Powers, America nearly always acts—or intends to act—on its interests. But unlike the others, America always *pretends* to act on principle, and Americans with rare exceptions actually believe it when presidents justify, and apologists memorialize, America's self-interested actions in glittering moral terms.

Thus, the U.S. government did not take western lands from Native Americans by force, but rather, America was merely following its divinely ordained "destiny," displacing benighted "savages" with God-fearing settlers, and spreading "civilization" in the process. Similarly, during the cold war America did not back brutal dictators and absolute monarchs in the oil-rich Persian Gulf (and elsewhere), but rather, it aided pro-Western governments in the fight against "godless communism." America's conquest and military occupation of Iraq in 2003 was not about oil or power, either, but instead was part of a "war against terrorism" and the "axis of evil" (Iraq, Iran, and North Korea). In general, judged by its rhetoric, America's use of military force in the world is always about moral principles (justice, liberty, democracy) and never about power (land, oil, access to overseas markets).

Given the fact that all states seek the security that power alone provides, none of the above is particularly unique or even surprising except for one thing—when a popular president tells the American people a fairy tale about American history or why the United States has to fight yet another war in yet another obscure place in order to spread the benefits of democracy in the world, Americans—rich and poor alike—believe it. It is this popular *belief* in American "exceptionalism," not the reality of a nation morally better than the rest, that helps explain how the United States rose from the status of a pariah state struggling to survive in the late eighteenth century to become the hegemon of the Western Hemisphere a century later. It also helps explain how America grew from being the richest country and a rising Great Power in the late nineteenth century to becoming the only *global* Great Power (or "superpower") a century after that. In other words, principle is the key to understanding America's power, but in a very different sense from that perpetuated by those who would have us believe the myth of American moral superiority.

Parents sometimes tell small children "little white lies" to spare them the harsh realities of life until they are "old enough." If government treats adults—voters and taxpayers all—like children, telling the nation less than the truth about the real reasons that America goes to war, it is no wonder the American public is susceptible to moralistic appeals and emotional manipulation. There is, of course, an equal and opposite danger in the other direction, one best understood by recalling that in the 1930s the United States did not steel itself or face off against Germany soon enough to nip the malignant phenomenon of Nazism in the bud. Pretending that a very real threat did not exist was a form of self-deception to which both the general public and the politicians were particularly prone during the Great Depression.

People always have choices, and choices always have consequences. Public opinion is a powerful force in liberal democracies, a fact often overlooked or underestimated by the public but one well understood by the politicians who face reelection.

Americans do have principles they try to live by—so do Europeans, Asians, Arabs, and Africans. But these principles apply to themselves first and foremost. We are pleased when other nations turn to democracy, when other governments respect the rule of law, and so on. However, we are not moved to fight for other people's rights, only our own. The evidence is ample and irrefutable.

Does this realism rule out the possibility that presidents are at times motivated by principles? Definitely not. The argument here allows for this possibility and, indeed, views it as a potential liability. One who tells a big lie (or fails to tell the whole truth) sometimes gets trapped by it ("oh what a tangled web we weave . . .") or starts to believe it. Moreover, when presidents decide to send young men and women to fight on foreign soil knowing some of them will die, they have a psychological need to believe that what they are doing is right. So they tell themselves as well as the nation that we are fighting for principle not for power. And they believe it. LBJ is the example everybody of the Vietnam War generation will remember as the ex-president who could no longer believe the lie and consequently died with a guilt-ridden conscience.

When neither the president nor the public understands the real reasons for going to war, the danger of going to war for the wrong reasons—or of not staying out of war for the right ones—rises. In sum, people do care about principles, and Americans are products of a political order defined by its principles. But the salient characteristic of international politics is anarchy, not order. Where there is no effective order there are no effective principles, and power decides who will decide.

So the tension between the pursuit of power and a commitment to democratic principles is deeply rooted in American politics. There is no easy solution to the problem, except to recognize it and await the reward. The reward will be great or small in proportion to the ability of America's leaders—present and future—to distinguish between the nation's true interests and all the rest. We will know when and if that happens because then the country will have achieved the optimal mix of hard and soft power needed to defend its interests abroad while it seeks to practice its principles more perfectly at home.

Index

About the Author

THOMAS MAGSTADT earned his Ph.D. at Johns Hopkins School of Advanced International Studies. He has taught at the Graduate School of International Management, the Air War College, Augustana College, University of Nebraska at Kearney, and University of Missouri–Kansas City; worked for the federal government as an intelligence analyst; and was a Fulbright lecturer in the Czech Republic. He chaired the Department of Government and International Affairs at Augustana College and the Department of Political Science at University of Nebraska at Kearney, where he was also the director of the Midwest Conference on World Affairs. He is the author of two political science textbooks, *Understanding Politics: Ideas, Institutions, and Issues,* 6th ed. (2003) and *Nations and Governments: Comparative Politics in Regional Perspective,* 5th ed. (2004). His articles have appeared in such publications as *Worldview, Reason, National Review,* the *Political Science Reviewer,* and many major newspapers. He is currently researching and writing a book on contemporary Europe.